370.1   3316
                      9 00
      Welch
        The Romance of
              Education.

DATE DUE			
MAR 8 '82			
AP 5 '84			

Imperial Public Library
Imperial, Texas

THE ROMANCE OF EDUCATION

The Romance Of Education

by Robert Welch

WESTERN ISLANDS

PUBLISHERS

BOSTON   LOS ANGELES

THE AMERICANIST CLASSICS

All Rights Reserved

The text of this publication or any part thereof may not be reproduced in any manner whatsoever without permission in writing from the publisher.

Copyright © 1973 by Western Islands

Published by
WESTERN ISLANDS
Belmont, Massachusetts 02178

Manufactured In The United States Of America

Imperial Public Library
Imperial, Texas

3316

For

Marian Probert Welch

In happy memory of the days, now gone forever, when we used to talk about the plan.

Table Of Contents

	Prologue	ix
	Preface	xv
Chapter I	Why Bother?	1
Chapter II	What Is Education	19
Chapter III	The Romance Of Languages	29
Chapter IV	Fun For The Dabbler	43
Chapter V	The Romance Of History	55
Chapter VI	The Romance Of History (Continued)	75
Chapter VII	The Romance Of Mathematics	103
Chapter VIII	More Mathematics	117
Chapter IX	More Mathematics — Towards The Deep End	149
Chapter X	Invitation To Poetry	161
Chapter XI	Old Books And New Reviews	197
Chapter XII	The Last Word	263
	Epilogue	271
	Index	281

Prologue

The book you are about to read is not important enough to have a history. But it does have a somewhat unusual past.

As will be indicated by the original preface, which follows this misplaced postscript, the composition was finished in September, 1946. But it was not submitted to any publisher and, to this day, it never has been. Nor do we know why, even now. (That "we" is editorial camouflage for the author of the book.) At our present age we can remember what happened fifty or sixty years ago without much trouble. But the details of what took place in the middle of a busy life are more difficult to recall.

The combination of reasons why this manuscript sat on a shelf for twenty-six years, however, undoubtedly includes the following: (1) The author wanted to consider his opus as a first draft, to be improved and made more professional before it was offered for publication. (2) In the spring of 1946 he had made his first trip to England, to study the socialistic measures being imposed on that country by its Labor Government. So he was already being swept into a fight, against the same advance of socialism in the United States, which was to dominate the rest of his life. (3) Then, under the increasing pressures of his struggle to understand, and eventually to expose, the Communist Conspiracy behind the socialist front, an academic diver-

sion entitled The Romance Of Education *was actually and completely forgotten for about twenty years.*

"So," you are expected to ask at this point, "what finally brought this sleeper to life?" And we do not even know positively the answer to that question. But about six or seven years ago somebody, among our associates in the management of The John Birch Society, *must have discovered this neglected brain child hiding among some published volumes of Will Durant. Or maybe it was pointed out to him by a remorseful parent, who had just come across the poor thing again. So the discoverer decided to explore its pages. Eventually he not only persuaded somebody else to read the manuscript, but urged the author to publish it. From that point on this telepathic impulse grew and spread like wildfire. To the extent that today, seven years later, there must be all of five people (adults, at that) who have politely recommended that we put this dissertation in print. And naturally we have yielded to such heavy and widespread pressure. Especially since the author's present control over one small publishing house neatly circumvented the possibility that some smart editor would turn it down.*

In all seriousness, however, let us assure you that we ourselves have not read the manuscript since it was completed twenty-six years ago. It is the next thing that we intend to do after writing this foreword to a preface. Perhaps we shall then decide to put it back on the shelf. (In which case you will never read the sentence that you have just read!) Or possibly, having acquired during the last quarter of a century some slightly increased awareness of our own ingorance, we shall find many things in these pages which we feel must be changed before they are offered to the public. It is far more likely, though, that we shall merely add a footnote here and there to show how

Prologue

much greater knowledge and wisdom we have amassed since writing some particular item!

And that brings us to the purpose of this clear and present warning — a warning to ourselves as well as to our audience. We must remember, and we want to remind you, emphatically enough to keep you reminded, that every sentence in the body of this book was written before some of our younger readers were even born. These pedantic excursions, therefore, will reflect an attitude towards education and its purposes which may seem strangely foreign to a world where college degrees are mass produced on an assembly line. We live today in an intellectual and moral environment — especially for those captive young victims who inhabit our college campuses — where enough knowledge to turn on a television set has become the main distinguishing feature between contemporary man and the lower animals.

Or at least this superior faculty has now made most other knowledge seem (for untold millions) to be totally unnecessary. So naturally we expect our book to be ridiculed in many quarters. Most justified among these critics will be a few real scholars who are disturbed by our dilettantism in a conducted tour amid the realms of gold. To them we bow with humility, and murmur "mea culpa." But the most vociferous of our detractors will be the professional destroyers of our civilization who, for conspiratorial purposes, have been trying so hard to convince the rising generation — and all of their elders who are stupid enough to listen — that a dirty mind in a dirty body is the acme of sophistication and the goal of all our culture.

With that breed we refuse, in this small volume or about it, to become embroiled. If Walter Savage Landor will forgive our paraphrase, here we quarrel with none, for none is worth our strife. Instead we simply "carry on," with all the innocence and unpretentiousness and delight of a confessed amateur. We presume to introduce you, in a nostalgic vein, to the mood of a long gone age — of three whole decades ago! It was the tail end of an era, when a respect for experience, a regard for tradition, a basically sound sense of values, and a reasonable level of over-all sanity, still prevailed. Above everything else, for our present interest, it was an age in which the concept and ideal of becoming "a gentleman and a scholar" was still comprehensible to anybody who could tell a hawk from a handsaw.

Actually there are a few such starry-eyed characters yet extant today, even among the young. At our speeches to dozens of college audiences during the last few years, we have still found many wonderful boys and girls who felt deep gratitude for the civilization, the opportunity, and the freedom which they had inherited. And who, in the midst of all the nihilistic indoctrination to which they were being subjected, still maintained their determination to become spiritually solid and intellectually elite men and women. What is more, almost all of these gallant youngsters had relatives back home who encouraged their aspirations and supported their point of view. Even though these kindred spirits, young and old alike, may scorn our shallow diggings as too elementary for their attention, we salute them, one and all. And we cherish the belief that, because of many forces presently at work, this "remnant" of the past may become a forerunner of the future, which will arise phoenix-like from the ashes of a crumbling culture.

So now, after this small bit of self-introduction, we say to those who do accept our invitation, let's move on, and read the original preface together. If it turns out that your tour guide has been repeating here some of the same

Prologue xiii

thoughts, and even the same phrases, that he put on paper when the world was only middle-aged, just smile at this sign and privilege of advancing years, and keep on reading. For the author will now don his somewhat more youthful cloak again, as we then explore with you a few surface areas, of man's laboriously won knowledge, that have been well dug up and carefully cultivated by countless inquiring minds before us. We hope that many young readers, from eighteen years to eighty, will share with us some pleasure in these unsophisticated rambles, and occasionally even stare with us and at us in a wild surmise, as we stand together silent upon a peak in Darien.

Preface

Fortunately, to preach on the desirability of education it is not necessary to be an educated man. For the theme of this book is not the advantages of education, after it has been acquired, but the pleasure of working to acquire it. In a book of such nature the most desirable characteristic, and one of the most difficult to achieve, is a convincing sincerity. For that reason I wish it were possible for me to sit down and talk a few minutes with each reader before he opens these pages. As that is not possible, I am doing the next best thing, and trying to get your attention for these few remarks, before you wade into the first chapter.

If we could sit down together, the normal procedure would be for me to introduce myself. So, first of all, I am neither a professor nor a professional writer. I am in the candy business. Twenty-five years ago, after searching diligently for that field in which it seemed least impossible to get a start without either capital or experience, I bought a second-hand coke stove, a copper kettle, a stone slab, and a formula — all on time — and became a candy manufacturer. By the grace of God and many kind creditors I have been in the candy manufacturing business ever since.

Most of that twenty-five years I have not been smart enough to get my work done in a reasonable working day, but have thought that I was required, by either circumstances or ambition, to keep at the job of making or selling candy evenings and week-ends as well as during business hours. The time I could give to books was stolen in odd snatches and rare interludes.

That introduction should automatically relieve me of any expectation, on the reader's part, that I have any sound foundation of scholarship. Certainly it gives me the benefit of an amateurish standing, which enables me to express opinions without risking any academic reputation. I have none to risk.

It is easy for such an author, unskilled but enthusiastic, to slip into a parade of secondhand knowledge in such way that every paragraph might seem to be calling attention to his erudition. This is a pitfall that I have tried hard to avoid. But it is not possible to talk about a love of books for three hundred pages without referring to them; without quoting, paraphrasing, and criticizing poets and scientists, historians and philosophers. When I need an illustration or an analogy I have to reach out and take one. To preface every such individual reference with the explanation that there is no pretense to any stock of similar material in my mental warehouse, beyond the exhibit which I thus put in the show case, would be a tiresome procedure for both the reader and myself. So I wish to make my disclaimer of any such pretense, here in the beginning, once and for all.

In this book I have tried above all else simply to be myself. For this reason even the shield of the "editorial we" is dropped, in favor of the frank first person singular, except when it is obviously a simple grammatical convenience. And my underlying humbleness in the face of all the vast stores of knowledge in any branches, even those which I have explored for so slight a way in my casual rambling, is too genuine for me to need to restate it on every page. Thirty adult years of living with books, always as a pleasure rather than for any financial or professional advancement they might bring me, have served above all else to show how superficial is what I have learned on any subject, or ever can learn. In these chapters I do not strike any monotonous pose of humility, partly because I do not know how; but mainly because the humility is too real to make any such pose necessary. Even my ignorance no longer astounds me, because I live with it every day.

And so it is on this basis, kind reader, of your not charging me with foisting off veneer as real mahogany — because you have a signed confession in advance — that you are invited to go along with me in this discussion of education. I am sorry that it has to be a one-way conversation, for as much as I like to hear myself talk, I can also listen. But it has the advantage that you can put me aside whenever you want to, or skip whole chapters of what I am saying, without being impolite. And the very fact that you have bought (or borrowed) this book shows that you have probably done some thinking on the same subject. If you should care to speak your own piece in a letter, no matter how critical, I shall be an attentive and interested audience.

Belmont, Massachusetts
September 3, 1946

CHAPTER I

Why Bother?

When there is a good movie down the street, several excellent radio programs awaiting the turn of the dial, and an exciting contract-bridge feud to be resumed at your next door neighbor's, why bother with books? Especially, with serious books? It's a fair question. We believe we can give a fair answer, and the whole purpose of this little volume is to make that answer convincing.

But a dozen people would reply to the question in a dozen different ways. Some would simply say: "Don't!" Skipping this advice, from those who honestly admit that they do not think the game is worth the candle, we would still have several different reasons given for pursuing knowledge with industrious patience. Let's try to appraise some of these other answers before beginning the discussion of our own.

The first assertion we would meet is certainly some form of the doctrine that learning is a road to wealth. Some of the strange shapes this doctrine can take may be illustrated by an incident remembered from my childhood on a farm in North Carolina.

In Perquimans County of that state a public spirited lady whom I knew once took it upon herself to promote a bond issue to provide the area with better schools. Except in the county seat of Hertford the average public school at

1

that time was conducted for three months only, in the middle of the winter. It was a one-room affair, with one teacher, who injected the alphabet into the youngest pupils and elementary algebra into the oldest, in such minute doses that the danger of permanent infection was negligible. The supposition of the lady in question that there was room for improvement did not seem entirely unreasonable.

Like the riddle of the egg and the hen is the question of which came first and produced the other, good roads or the Ford. But this was before the days of either, and I was chosen to help out in the matter of transportation. To see a few neighbors within a range of only six or eight miles required a day's battle, in a horse-drawn buggy, with a continuous series of cavernous mudholes which constituted a highway only by being public mudholes instead of private ones. The struggle involved to enable us to accomplish each interview, therefore, was such as to call forth the most sustained efforts of salesmanship whenever a prospect was cornered. If the lady couldn't actually convert the victim to a favorable attitude towards the bond issue, it was her purpose to wear him down until he promised faithfully to vote for it anyway. There was further justification for this policy in the need for letting our horse rest an hour at each stop before we undertook amphibious operations once more.

One farmer was met under the elm tree beside his house, just as he left the kitchen after finishing his midday dinner. He proved to be a particularly easy convert, though the missionary of enlightenment didn't discover this until she had talked for three-quarters of an hour. While the farmer stood patiently beside the buggy, and the horse whipped his tail ineffectively at predatory flies, the inspired lady poured forth in a persuasive torrent the advantages of education. At last, running out of ammunition, she asked the still silent farmer if he would vote for the bond issue. "Yes, mum," he replied. "I'll vote for hit all right. I believe in eddication, myself, especially for my young'uns. I want my boy to be able to take fifty cents and go to town and not let nobody cheat him."

This story gives expression, in its crudest form, to the benefit most frequently extolled on behalf of education. "Statistics prove," runs the argument, "that of all the young men raised in Podunk County in a certain generation, those who graduated from college were, at the age of fifty, averaging two thousand and thirty-seven dollars per year more income than their contemporaries who never had acquired degrees. Only umpteen hundredths of one percent of all adults own college diplomas, but this small fraction furnishes more than half of the names in *Who's Who*. Every thousand dollars spent on a college education is an investment averaging twenty-three percent, compounded fortnightly, for the rest of the graduate's life. A Podunk sheepskin is worth more per square foot than Manhattan real estate. Don't sell education short."

The contentious critic has a reply to this proposition, however, somewhat as follows: "All the statistician has discovered is, of course, that the most ambitious and energetic boys went to college in the first place. They would have been earning more anyway, even if going to school had been made against the law when the whole generation was four years old. Since the harassed publishers of *Who's Who* put all college presidents and deans and most full professors in the book automatically, and scan the complete list of doctors, lawyers, and preachers with expectant attention, the book's pages naturally glisten with A.B.'s, M.A.'s, Ph.D.'s, LL.D.'s, B.Sc.'s, D.D.'s, and a few other pre-New Deal alphabetical combinations. Nobody knows whether the dividends credited to the investment in education were not really due to a tendency of the same investors to put more work and drive into their struggle for pecuniary success than their companions who didn't bother to go beyond grammar school. Certainly a number of Fords and Chryslers and Rockefellers have sold academic education very short indeed without dying in the poorhouse."

And the satirical critic would retell an old and familiar story which I hope to be pardoned for inserting here because of its appropriateness. An Italian immigrant, newly arrived and destitute, got a job as a janitor of the Arlington High School. The job, and his happiness at being securely settled, lasted for one week. For when Mr. Cosimo's first pay envelope was presented to him, and he was asked to sign a receipt, it was discovered that the new janitor did not have sufficient education to write his own name. This illiteracy among employees being contrary to the policy of the school, Tony Cosimo was regretfully discharged.

He felt very bad about it. But during the week he had made a friend of another Italian who owned a banana pushcart, and Tony was offered the job of helping this friend to sell bananas. In a few weeks Tony had a pushcart of his own; in a few months he was selling fruit from a horse-drawn wagon; in a few years he owned a number of trucks selling fruit at wholesale to hundreds of retail stores; and in some two decades from his arrival in this country he was head of a huge wholesale produce business, with many hundreds of employees.

Some profitable investment venture suddenly caused Mr. Cosimo to need half a million dollars which he could not very well afford to take out of his business. For the first time in his life he went to a bank to borrow money.

Why Bother?

The president of the bank knew all about the Cosimo produce company, and was very glad indeed to offer the loan. He prepared a note at once. "Just sign right here, Mr. Cosimo," the banker said, "and the money will be available in your account at once."

Tony looked a little embarrassed, as he explained that the note would have to be signed for him by his attorney, or with an "X" signature. The banker hastily agreed that that would be all right, but was unable to hide his amazement.

"Just think, Mr. Cosimo," he said, "here you are a multimillionaire, and unable even to sign your own name. I wonder what you would be now, if you had had more education."

"That's easy," Tony replied. "I'd be the janitor of the Arlington High School."

But we do not wish to be either contentious or sarcastic on the point, for two or three reasons. One is that the anecdote, at least, makes too strong a case. Clearly the trend in contemporary American business is to make the role of the individual entrepreneur more difficult, and to make administrative jobs in established enterprises the most natural road to some level of financial success. And equally clearly education is an advantage in competition for higher administrative positions. Maybe the salesmen of correspondence school and university extension courses are on solid ground when they stress the pocketbook influence of their wares. If you are thinking about studying algebra as a means of increasing your weekly pay check, or burning so much midnight electricity over philosophy that it will lift you to the presidency of a corporation, then this little book merely stands on the sidelines, and says go to it. You may have a good case, but it's not our case and we do not belong on the witness stand. My opinion on the extent to which the effort is worthwhile doesn't have enough value, or support from thinking about the subject, to justify giving it any elaboration.

Another reason for not entering this dispute is that the two sides soon find themselves talking about two entirely different things. For those who think of a so-called college education, for instance, chiefly as a help towards making money, are naturally the very ones who wish to make it more so. Out with the Latin and Greek, they propose; in with the shorthand, carpentry, and advanced hemstitching. They are quite right that this policy may increase the earning power of its beneficiaries, or the rapidity with which such beneficiaries can become self-supporting. Incidentally, but unfortunately, it also removes the education. And what we are discussing in this book is *academic* study; in this chapter, the attractions which such study can offer. The "earning power" appeal is one of those attractions which the reader would have to evaluate for himself, without my being able to offer help that even I think is worth anything.

Also, we have no encouragement to offer for those who think of scholarship as a means to social success. It's obviously true that a man who became a world-famous authority on Azoic rocks or Latin verse, or the theory of numbers, would be welcomed in a great many exclusive drawing rooms, even if he turned over somebody's teacup every time he got up or sat down. But world-famous authorities are rare. We are not likely to inspire many readers of this book to achieve that distinction. And the collegiate woods are full of garden-variety pedants whom nobody invites to dinner except their sisters, their cousins, and their aunts.

Why Bother? 7

To those ingenuous souls who hope to impress their acquaintances by exhibitions of knowledge, we even offer some free advice: Forget it. The impression is certain to be in the wrong direction. For a display of knowledge, even when genuine, is a sure way to alienate friends and to influence people to like somebody else.

If you really want to be the hit of the party, card tricks are much more effective than repeating something you have just read about early Elizabethan drama. Skill in the latest dance steps will make you welcome with hostesses more readily than quotations from Homer in the original Greek. And the country-club set will invariably take more interest in how far you can drive a golf ball than in hearing the mathematical formula for the path it follows. If fifteen minutes per day with a shelf of classics ever turned anybody into a social lion, just think how much further such a skillful exhibitionist would have gone, in that brand of society, by learning to juggle china plates in the air and to pull live rabbits out of dowagers' low-neck dresses.

The purely negative side of the effect of education on social acceptance and contemporary respect undoubtedly does deserve a bit more consideration. I know a man in Chicago who, highly successful in business, endowed by nature and self-discipline with the considerateness of a gentleman, is extremely sensitive to any slightest lapse from good taste, in others or in himself. Expensive clothes of the quietest quality, immaculate personal cleanliness at all times, scrupulous attention to those courtesies and conventions which constitute good manners, all combine to show a conscious aim for comfortable poise and self-assurance in any social or business gathering. He has a tremendous horror of personal conspicuousness; or of being put in any position, through ignorance or oversight, where he might need to feel abashed.

And yet there are groups in which this man moves where his cultural failings are noticed; and where, to that extent, he makes himself *noticeable* in ways unintended. He would himself be quick to remark that a business associate who says "I ain't going" or "I didn't really do nothing to deserve it" showed insufficient educational background. But he doesn't realize that such insufficiency is measured by various standards; and that there are people who are jarred in the same way by his pronunciation of "saw-turn" for the wine known as Sauterne, or by his distortion of *filet mignon* when it appears on the menu. His business letters are forceful, logical, and persuasive; but there are people who note that in the longer paragraphs his battles with unwieldy syntax are not always victorious.

Our friend is well-informed on current events and recent history. He would be quietly scornful of any conversational companion who couldn't name the American presidents in order since Wilson. But he has been heard to state in serious argument that there never had been any such political entity as Poland until it was given being by the Versailles treaty. There was a time when a king of Poland, John Sobieski, saved all Europe from the invading Turks; the constitution of old Poland has long been famous as a *reductio-ad-absurdum*, which might have been designed to end all constitutions; and the playful carving of that unhappy kingdom by Frederick the Great and his neighboring sovereigns of the "pettycoat régime" formed a chief plank on which the historical prestige of Frederick and Prussia have rested. Obviously, all of these things simply had never occurred, so far as this business man was concerned; and hence his strong opinions on the "Polish problem" of contemporary Europe did not command the respect he thought they were receiving. He would probably give a subscription to *Time* magazine, as a Christmas present, to anybody who showed ignorance of the petroleum sources in the Middle East, but on hearing ancient Mesopotamia mentioned he has been known to ask whether it was in Europe or Asia. And his ignorance of the basic sciences is such that he expresses incredulity as to geologists knowing anything about the age of rocks or astronomers about the distance of stars.

Now it is perfectly clear that not any of the friends this man cares about — or who are worth caring about — think any the less of him because of these little lapses. Too few of his acquaintances are ever conscious of these shortcomings for them to be a serious matter in his scheme of things. They are important only to the extent that their perpetrator is fooling himself about the impeccable appearance he intends to present in all situations. From the social point of view, education, of whatever degree, is not desirable for showing what you do know so much as for not showing what you do not know. And the old adage that it is better to keep your mouth shut and be thought a fool, than to open it and remove all doubt, is no more practicable for active daily intercourse than is avoidance of all society the correct solution for a man who picks his teeth at the table.

Some answers to our master question would fall into an entirely different classification. A couple of years ago we invited a friend of ours, who was also a customer, to have lunch with us. When we picked him up at his office we asked him where he would like to go. "Any place," he replied, "where I can get a drink." So we took him to the Harvard Club.

This was during the dark days of the war when most of

the hotels and restaurants had reduced the alcoholic content of their offerings to the point where it took about three oldfashioneds to make one legitimate cocktail. But the Harvard Club, faithful to something, was still putting a full two ounces of good whiskey in every drink. This friend of ours, who was quite a connoisseur in the field, smacked his lips with delighted surprise as he finished off his first oldfashioned, and ordered a second one. "Well!" he said. "Now at last I see the advantage of a college education!"

This happy comment presents the ludicrous end of a whole gamut of reasons that advocate education as adding flavor to the entertainments of life. When we move from the ridiculous to consideration of certain pastimes and recreations which dignify our leisure, we find that these reasons contain an obvious measure of good sense. The supporters of self-guided study, as a cultural investment which will pay dividends by increasing our enjoyment of the theatre or music or travel, have a much stronger case than the interpreters of income statistics. Their argument deserves a few paragraphs in which to examine it more closely, and the theatre supplies an excellent field for illustration.

In the old Greek legend Pygmalion was a sculptor who carved, out of marble, the statue of a girl whom he named Galatea. And the girl was so beautiful that Pygmalion fell in love with her and prayed to the gods to bring her to life. This legend is the basis and background for the modern play, *Pygmalion*, by George Bernard Shaw. The Pygmalion of the play, a very "uppercrust" Englishman, picks up a street girl with a horrible cockney accent, wagers that in six months he will be able to pass her off as a duchess, does such an excellent job of creation out of this raw material that he wins his bet — and of course falls in love with his Galatea in the process.

Shaw's play is perennially popular, and not long ago we went to see it once again, with a young man to whom it was new. He enjoyed the show very much. But at the end of the evening we discovered, to our regret, that the young man had never heard of the Greek legend, and hence had missed entirely some of the Shavian subtlety and cynical wit. In this case even a very few minutes of previous study, exactly directed in anticipation of the performance, would certainly have repaid the young man in the sauce it would have added to the evening's mental bill of fare.

As playgoers we get out of an evening's attendance not only what the playwright has put into the occasion, but what we ourselves put in as well. To avoid any assumption as to the age of our reader, in choosing our illustrations, let's glance at three very popular plays which reach over the span of a generation in their respective appearances.

Classical drama construction required an observance of the unities of time, place, and story. In plain language this meant that, to avoid straining the imagination of the audience, the action represented on the stage in any one play must be supposed to take place in one day (twenty-four hours), in one spot, and to be entirely concerned with one central story theme. One or all of these three unities have been more generally violated than they have been followed, by Shakespeare, Goethe, and most of the great modern playwrights. But the weight of tradition behind them is so strong and so long, nevertheless, that every true student of the drama inevitably looks with interest to see how they have fared in any particular piece. There was thus an increment of pleasure for many of us, on seeing *The Voice Of The Turtle*, in our appreciation of the author's respect for these unities. His careful observance of all three gave to the play a classical touch which made it seem more completely a work of art.

Our modern English drama arose out of the miracle and morality plays of the late Middle Ages. These miracle plays, outgrowths of church pageants, were presentations of various series of events in the life of Christ. When Marc Connelly wrote *The Green Pastures*, he presented on the stage the activities of God and his angels, as seen through the eyes of a religious, fundamentalist American negro. This was to some extent a reversion, back across four hundred years, to the type of play which moved from one English town to another long before Shakespeare and Marlowe were born. To those of us who were fortunate enough to have studied the early miracle plays, this familiarity with their development certainly added to our interest in Connelly's masterpiece.

For over two thousand years historians and military strategists have been arguing as to why Hannibal did not sack Rome, when it lay helpless before his conquering army. In his play, *The Road To Rome*, Robert Sherwood uses the doubtful but amusing solution that Hannibal was persuaded to exercise conscious charity and nobility towards Rome by the amorous advances of a Roman matron. Clearly anybody steeped in the Punic Wars, and the long bitter rivalry between Rome and Carthage which ended eventually in the complete destruction of the latter city, would enjoy Sherwood's fanciful rendering of history more than somebody to whom Carthage was just a vague name. Or, to choose a practically ageless specimen, for making the same point, a man entirely ignorant concerning the Wars of the Roses can still laugh at the antics of Falstaff in *Henry IV*, but he will miss a great deal of the true drama of the action, as viewed by another man with the necessary historical background.

There is a dramatic device known as *deus ex machina*, or "a god from the machine." Originally it was a player representing a god, actually lowered onto a stage by a machine. This god, or goddess, arriving opportunely near the end of the action, was used by the Greek playwrights to help their mortal characters out of otherwise unsolvable difficulties. In such bald guise, this method of resolving dramatic suspense would be laughed at today. But reminiscences of the device can frequently be recognized in the not too subtle but happy endings of many a movie plot. The heroine's uncle, barely mentioned before, who suddenly shows up to give her a million dollars and prove that she is really the Duchess of Dishwater, so that her pride will now permit her to marry the charming Count Cholmondeley — this uncle is just a modern style *deus ex machina*.

Chaucer defined tragedy as the story of one who falls from great prosperity and high degree into misery and a wretched end. His conception, which permeated early English drama so thoroughly, helped to give shape to Shakespeare's *King Lear*, and Marlowe's *Tamburlaine*. It is a romantic and startling pattern to remember, and to compare with the social theme of contemporary tragedy, when we see *Dead End* or *Mamba's Daughters*. But we still detect Chaucer's thought, living again in the mind of Eugene O'Neill, when we analyze the force of O'Neill's play, *The Emperor Jones*.

The modern theatre is a child of the past, and like any other child is a product of both heredity and environment. The features of this ancestor, the bearing of another, the lineaments of its race and the resemblance to its cousins can all be readily seen. An acquaintance with any part of this ancestry cannot but help to increase our delight in the offspring. But whether it is worth while studying the making a pilgrimage to Plymouth Rock and the "rude bridge" at Concord, where "the embattled farmers stood, And fired the shot heard 'round the world." Geography likewise, mathematics, astronomy, philology, comparative literature, and ethnology; almost all branches of academic learning contribute to the enticements of the open road and the enjoyment of visiting far places.

While travel and the theatre, however, are but two of countless media through which civilized man seeks to amuse himself, our present purpose must let these examples suffice. Otherwise we start an endless catalogue, from the axiom that the study of music enables one to get more out of listening to Bach and Beethoven, to the contention of our youngest son that facility in geometry is of very practical help to his progress in figure skating on ice. N.P. Willis has expatiated in lilting rhyme on the benefits of the culture that goes with carpets over less favorable settings, in the thrill of love making; and even the pleasure of whittling, so well regarded by Calvin Coolidge, is improved by the quality of the meditations of the whittler. But the reader either has already discovered such self-evident truths, in endless array, or can easily do so. We have tried merely to call attention to a few random bits of evidence that our standard of mental living is as important as our standard of physical living, in differentiating our pleasures, in both nature and degree, from those of the lower animals.

But none of these advantages of book learning seem to me to constitute a sufficient answer to the question of why anyone should bother about the effort required for self education. Despite the value of the study of botany, languages, and physics for a greater appreciation of the rhododendron, or the value of the study of history for getting more enjoyment out of the hobby of coin collecting, it is arguable that the difference in appreciation or enjoyment is by no means worth the labor involved. It seems to me at least, as a self appointed attorney for the cause of education, that the addition to our pleasure in other avocations, given by hours of study, must be counted only as *bonuses* or *extra dividends*. We do not plead in this brief that they justify the investment of time in such study. As for the other and more material returns mentioned, I have undoubtedly made my own prejudices clear enough. This prospectus is not addressed to those who believe that a study of Adam Smith — or of all the economists since Adam Smith — is going to put their haberdashery shops in the excess-profits brackets; nor, in turn, to those who feel that the ability to speak French would get them better tables at their favorite night clubs.

There is, it seems to me, one valid reply, and only one, to the question propounded in this chapter. It is simply that self-education is itself a pleasure, and not work, all of the hours or the years or the lifetime that it may be continued. If the program be pursued with the proper attitude, that it is a pastime to be enjoyed, and with a reasonable catering to digressive intellectual curiosity, what may have once looked like work is soon transmuted into the most satisfying of all recreations. The reward is not at the end of the struggle, in the benefits of the *acquisition*, but is continuous, in the satisfaction of *acquiring*, knowledge; not in the gains to be enjoyed *after* becoming a person of some level of education, but in the mental adventure of the *becoming*.

If this point were clear or convincing at this stage, there would be no occasion for writing more. For those to whom the thesis is readily acceptable, there is little promise of profit in reading further. It is because the argument does need to be given strength and weight and clarity, for those who do not accept it on the basis of their own experience, that the following chapters have been diffidently but hopefully prepared. We shall be seeking, in our consciously romanticized but always unpretentious paraphrases of historian, critic, and scientist, to convert a skeptical reader now and then to interest in learning as a pleasure, rather than as a means to an end; and to the thought of excursions in the realm of books and of accumulated knowledge, not as tiresome paths to desirable goals, but as inviting journeys which are delightful in themselves.

CHAPTER II

What Is Education?

Many attempts have been made to establish, directly or indirectly, an acceptable definition of education. Perhaps the most famous of such attempts was by Thomas Henry Huxley, who approached the problem by describing an educated man, as follows: "That man, I think, has had a liberal education who has been so trained in youth that his body is the ready servant of his will, and does with ease and pleasure all the work that, as a mechanism, it is capable of; whose intellect is a clear cold, logic engine, with all its parts of equal strength, and in smooth working order; ready like a steam engine, to be turned to any kind of work, and spin the gossamers as well as forge the anchors of the mind; and whose mind is stored with a knowledge of the great and fundamental truths of nature and of the laws of her operations; one who, no stunted ascetic, is full of life and fire, but whose passions are trained to come to heel by a vigorous will, the servant of a tender conscience, who has learned to love all beauty, whether of nature or of art, to hate all vileness, and to respect others as himself."

This is a brilliant definition of something, and has been quoted here because Huxley spoke as an authority, whenever and on whatever subject he spoke at all. But it does not embody the conception of education which will serve as a text for our present sermon.

The chief difficulty, of course, is that the word education can mean almost anything you want it to, within a wide category of training programs and experiences. It comes from the Latin *e*, meaning *out*, and *ducere*, to lead. To educate, in the original Latin sense, is to lead forth, to prepare those being educated for the problems and encounters outside of their early and narrow horizons. The Romans thought of the term as applying primarily to the training of youth; and, we must admit, skill in running a lathe or operating a stenotype machine would have seemed quite a proper part of "education" to a Roman, if there had been any lathes or stenotype machines on the banks of the Tiber.

But, as we hope to make clearer in another chapter, the more accurate significance of a word of classical etymology, in modern usage, may well be its derived rather than its ancestral meaning. And certainly the minds of all of us, except the most "progressive" educators, leap to the thought of books when the term education is used. The ordinary immediate connotation of the noun is schooling, or the result of schooling, formal or self-imposed, in reading, writing, arithmetic, and the superstructure of arts and sciences built on these foundations.

We find another difficulty in the fact that education is a purely relative word; and there is no quantitative unit by which to measure its level. The word *riches* is also very indeterminate. A man worth a hundred thousand dollars is extremely wealthy to a Mexican peon, but would be thought of as poor by an American multimillionaire or certain Indian rajahs. We can, however, establish our meaning with reasonable exactness, in discussing riches, by saying that a person owns stocks and bonds worth so many million dollars, or has an income of so many thousands per year. The only possible approach to a similar discreteness

What Is Education? 21

of description, in referring to scholarship, is to list our subject's collegiate degrees. And this standard, by which to appraise a man's mental endowments and accomplishments, is about as useful as an open bucket with which to measure high-pressure steam. In fact one of the most ignorant men I have ever known is an A.B., A.M., and LL.B. from Harvard University. And it seems likely that any reader could nominate similarly tagged acquaintances for a similar honor.

Humidity, the meteorologists tell us, is a meaningless word. Only *relative* humidity, being the proportion of moisture in air at a given temperature, has any accurate significance. Education, likewise, acquires no exactness as a term denoting mental qualifications, except as comparative education is projected for an individual in his particular national and social background. And — perhaps fortunately — no scholarship meter has yet been devised.

There is no need, to be sure, for us to try to say *what* education *is*. We need only to say what we mean by education in the title and context of this volume. Having indicated that we are referring to academic learning, and having admitted that there are no absolute and measurable quantities of the commodity, we come to one of those proverbial misconceptions which orators and essayists are always running afoul of in their second breaths — or their second chapters. This is the silly notion that a truly learned man has a head full of facts. He may have; but if so, this cerebral warehousing is purely incidental to his real knowledge and scholarly attainments.

For when there are only facts, real education can be lacking altogether. I know a man who, as a walking encyclopedia of assorted statistics, serves as Exhibit A at his friends' social gatherings; and he does astonish all the neighbors that "one small head could carry all he knew." He can tell you at once how many million acres of cotton land in the southern states are now subject to infestation by the boll weevil, the names of all the satellites of the planet Saturn, and when clothespins were first introduced into Iceland. He may also, and despite this load of memory-rubbish, be an educated man. But if so, most of his friends have never been interested in discovering that characteristic.

How this gentleman came to give a home to such promiscuous information, and why his mind retains it, would be material questions for anyone wishing to find out whether he is a somewhat foolish wise man or just a wise fool. For, obviously, learning by heart all the mathematical formulas in regular use would not make anybody a mathematician, but a real mathematician would nevertheless know such formulas by heart. Memorizing all the important dates in recorded history would not consummate a historian, but any student with sufficiently deep and lasting interest in history would probably acquire all such important dates automatically. Drilling yourself to reel off the names of two thousand species of ants would certainly not make you an entomologist; and yet the late Professor Wheeler, greatest of American myrmecologists, could undoubtedly have named and identified two thousand species of the ant family from memory. If the statistical champion's facts are but incidental acquisitions, in some pattern of wide and purposeful study, then their variety and exactness may indicate that his scholarly mind is blessed with a conducive memory. If they are deliberately accumulated for effect, or even for some honest but misguided purpose of self satisfaction, then our friend should concentrate on learning all the streets of all the cities in America and go on the vaudeville stage. For in

What Is Education? 23

that case he will always find more drudgery than happiness in burning the midnight electricity, and he could learn the whole Encyclopedia Brittanica by heart without becoming an educated man.

For the object of education — to come to the point at last — seems to me to be to find out what you do not know; to get more and more understanding of what there is to learn. The best educated man, either generally or in a particular subject, is the one who is most aware of what he doesn't know. Unfortunately, this sounds like an effort at epigram, built on a paradox for effect. But the aphoristic flavor is unintentional, for this definition seems to me as simple and straightforward a presentation of the actual case as we can make. And if the reader's patience will continue, we hope to prove that the paradox is purely an illusion.

Some light is thrown on this approach by the converse statement that the most ignorant person is the one who doesn't know he is ignorant, who is most unaware of what there is to learn; or, in the gag-writer's phrase, a man who not only doesn't know anything, but doesn't even suspect anything. And clearly, the best understanding of the ignorance of a five-year-old child, on first starting to school, lies in considering the child's total *unconsciousness* and *lack of conception* of the vast field of learning which is ahead of him. The five-year old knows that he is starting out to learn reading and writing and arithmetic. And, if reasonably bright, he already has some slight and vague ideas as to what these faculties of reading and writing and figuring, which he does not yet possess, will enable him to do. To that extent he is already better educated than the savage who doesn't even know that such arts exist.

After two or three years, however, little Tommy

discovers that there are degrees in the ability to read and in the difficulty of the matter to be read; that reading is not just a finite accomplishment you once get through, like the measles, and then no longer have to worry about for the rest of your life. He finds that the step of writing letters and then words just leads you into more work of learning to spell words, and of arranging them in proper grammatical order, and of reaching longer and more complicated words to write. And worst of all, he sees that the more arithmetic he studies, the more skill he attains with the tools of addition, subtraction, multiplication, and division, the more arithmetic there is to learn; the more things like fractions, and percentages, and interest, and square roots, and ratio there are to which these tools are to be applied. By this time the child doesn't know much, but he is beginning to suspect quite a little.

After a while Thomas finishes high school. He has now waded through algebra and geometry, but knows that such subjects as conic sections and calculus and differential equations stretch out ahead. If he is an intelligent youngster he even knows vaguely what some of these studies deal with, and is also conscious of algebraic processes and geometric relationships much more involved than any he has tackled. If the young man has had Latin grammar and Caesar's Gallic Wars, Cicero's Orations, and Vergil's Aeneid, and if he is a good enough student, he now knows that he has only taken the merest glance into the field of Latin literature and language; and he knows that there is a Greek literature and language behind it, forming a huge part of the classical heritage that has shaped our modern world and thought.

In the courses known as "English" Thomas has been introduced to a few scattered samples of a vast storehouse of plays, novels, essays, biographies, and poetry. At least he now knows that the storehouse is there. He may have further gained some inkling, through one-year classes in physics, or botany, or chemistry, of the divisions of knowledge worked in by the scientific specialists. On leaving a good high school, with a good teaching staff, our alert graduate has been educated into realizing how little he knows about any subject to which he turns his attention. He doesn't yet have *enough* education to reach any sound estimate of how much there is to know.

Let's take one more look at this young man a number of years later. And since he has been created entirely by our imaginations, let's make him turn out in whatever way best suits our needs for illustration. Tom has gone through college, getting an A.B. degree, but majoring towards the end in physics. He has then taught physics in some secondary school for three or four years, become more interested in the subject, and gone back to his favorite university for research and post-graduate work. He is now thirty-five, a Doctor of Science, and an Assistant Professor at this same university. To show our humane interest, we should also equip him with a wife, two children, and a lawn to mow and water in the late afternoons. The reader can make him a Republican or a Democrat, and pick out his church affiliations, according to the reader's own preferences in such matters.

This Doctor-Professor has now learned enough physics to realize that he can't ever possibly begin to study thoroughly the whole subject. Of the many subdivisions he has chosen *light* as his particular domain. He is well aware that he will never know anything about sound, or mechanics, or magnetism, or hydrostatics, in the sense that specialists in those subjects would think of knowledge; but he *does know* that there are such provinces in which other able men are spending their lives in steady exploration.

Being busy, the Doctor has opportunity to maintain only a cursory interest in non-scientific literature, of the past or the present. He sees on every side enclosures of learning, where the grass looks very green, which he hasn't time to invade. In most cases he merely knows they are there. But in some few instances, in order to get at and till his own field properly, he has to make use of paths over neighboring acres. To deal with the wave-lengths of light, and the distances and speeds with which light propagation is concerned, our physicist finds that he needs more and more mathematics. Trigonometry, the calculus, differential equations and the other instruments of applied mathematics become familiar to his hands. More or less incidentally, he catches glimpses of that whole vast land of arithmetical research which constitutes the chief range of the pure mathematician. Our Doctor never comes to know any mathematics, except in its most fundamental workaday uses, but he does gain a better view of his own ignorance of the subject than if his studies in physics had not made him a next-door neighbor.

For consideration of the sources of light both chemistry and astronomy become important. For investigations into the break-up of light, into the shades and colors which we distinguish, by absorption and reflection and refraction, botany becomes an adjunct to chemistry and physics. For reading what other scientists are writing and have written on the same matters, in German and French and even Latin, the Professor finds increasing need for a familiarity with other languages. He never becomes a scholarly chemist, or botanist, or astronomer, or linguist; but he does gain a sufficient working "smattering" of the subjects indicated to have some comprehension of his ignorance therein, and of the staggering bodies of knowledge confronting the specialists in each subject. In those few

What Is Education? 27

fields, anyway, he knows the direction in which to start, to find out something he needs to learn for his own immediate purposes. This is the measure of his education, against that of the man who doesn't know where to look for formula, theory, or statistic, because he doesn't even know they exist or that he is ignorant concerning them. "To know what to ask is already to know half" runs the ancient philosophic adage — anticipating these present remarks by some two thousand years.

Not facts, but the ability to find facts when wanted; not the accumulation of particulars, but an awareness of the general to which these particulars belong; not the little knowledge we may have acquired, but the extent of our recognition of the expanses we have only glimpsed; these are the marks by which each of us must appraise his educational advance. In simple truth education is merely a process of finding out, ever more clearly and intelligently, how little we know.

CHAPTER III

The Romance Of Languages

Let's review briefly our argument up to this point. Perhaps it will be easy now to repeat in one paragraph what we needed twenty-eight pages to say the first time.

Unconscious ignorance, we believe all will agree, is a natural animal state. Realization of that ignorance is a first step towards education, on the part of child or savage. Comprehension of the nature and extent of our ignorance is commensurate with, even synonymous with, our education itself. Gaining such comprehension, by delving into the subject until its vastness is more and more clearly revealed, is a fascinating pursuit. It is doubtful when or whether serious study should be self imposed as a duty, by any adult; but serious study can be enjoyed by many adults, as a privilege and a pleasure.

It is my task now to attempt to clothe this skeleton of argument with the flesh of exposition and examples. The reader is invited to take a casual ramble with me over some academic plots which are usually regarded as dry and uninviting, and as tilled only for the sake of a crop to be harvested at the expense of tiring labor. We shall try to see if the labor cannot be metamorphosed into enjoyment by the attitude of the worker and by the increasing understanding which the labor brings about. The plots chosen are those labeled *Languages, History, Mathematics*, and *Poetry*; chiefly because my qualifications as a guide, in these particular acres, are not quite so dismally inadequate as they would be in *Philosophy, Astronomy, Chemistry,* or dozens of other divisions and subdivisions in the fields of knowledge that stretch out on every hand. Most of us first meet the study of languages in the form of English grammar and rhetoric, English composition, and then grammar and translation in Latin or French or German. The introduction is seldom made by an inspired lover of languages, nor under such circumstances as to predispose us in favor of our new acquaintance. Irregular verbs, cognate stems, and unfamiliar syntax are likely, as a result, to remain pet dislikes of many of us for the rest of our lives. Let us select philology, therefore, as a fair and first topic for discussion. The average reader will regard it as a sufficiently forbidding vineyard in which to go toiling for fun rather than for hire. Maybe, in meandering idly over just a small part of this field, we can still point out some rows whose cultivation offers a tempting challenge, or some shady nooks where the happiness of an absorbing interest may be found.

There was an epigram, tossed from hand to hand in English literature, for a hundred years following the Stuart Restoration, to the effect that speech was invented to conceal thought. This epigram, paraphrased by Voltaire, was later ascribed specifically (but erroneously) to Talleyrand. Hence it has come to be considered, by all but the diplomats, as the fundamental policy of diplomatic intercourse. It may well be, for all I know. But for you and me the purpose of language, spoken or written, is to express what we are thinking. And since language is composed of words, the ultimate goal in the study of languages is to learn the substance and shades of thought conveyed by words, in their various forms, genders, declensions, conjugations, and other disguises.

The Romance Of Languages

Let's note, first, in our approach to this understanding of words, that speech was not invented at all, but developed — undoubtedly very slowly at first — out of the grunts and murmurs and gesticulations of primitive man. Starting perhaps a billion years ago, with the early stages obscured or lost in an archeozoic past, man himself has arisen, by variations so gradual as to have been unnoticeable at the time each occurred, from earlier forms of life up through the saurians, the mammals, and then the primates. Starting perhaps a million years ago, man's articulate speech has evolved up through the elementary identifications of things and actions on the part of savages, through combinations and modifications of ever-increasing variety and subtlety, until it embraces our most complex and philosophical terms of today.

Take, for instance, the word *baby*, which our remote ancestors got simply from the ba-ba made by one, and follow it through a few lines of ascent. By repetition over hundreds of generations, on the tongues of later men whose memories carried no trace of where it came from, this word became in one language *buobo*, and eventually our word *boy*. For meaning in a different direction we find that, to early tribes, anyone who was unintelligible or a foreigner was spoken of as going ba-ba. Or, as we now have it, the foreigner *babbled*. Pursuing this same direction further, we find that the ancient literate races classified foreigners and savages alike, describing them as people who ba-ba-ed, or barbarians. After the Latin word *barbarus* had thus evolved and been established, it began to convey as part of its meaning other attributes of "foreigners" besides their stammering speech; and the word itself propagated different variations carrying different parts of these combined meanings, as the Latin tongue broke into the various dialects which became the modern Romance languages. So that, through a natural orthographic change which took place in many similar Latin words by the time they became French, *barbarus* became *brave*, and eventually our English word *brave*. It once meant "fierce and wild," as foreigners were; our present meaning has taken on a somewhat different coloring. During the same centuries another form of the same word *barbarus* became *barren*; once meaning "uncultivated, untamed," as the savages were, and applied to fields in that sense. It, too has acquired additional shades of significance.

Let's now consider just these few outgrowths of one fundamentally onomatopoeic word, and form a sentence: *The* babbling *and* barren *woman* babies *the* brave barbarian boy. Every word in that sentence, except the four we have italicized, comes from the fact that in the earliest grunts with which man began to develop the power and thought of coherent speech, he described a baby as something that goes ba-ba. And it would undoubtedly require many chapters this size just to record the known and traceable linguistic descendants of that far-reaching piece of early mimicry.

This brings us to a helpful discovery. Instead of simply learning what a word means, it is both more instructive and more interesting to learn why it means it. Memory will seldom drop a word whose story has been ferreted out; and its current significance, as used by our own generation, is likely to be more accurately understood. More important, the meaning of words ceases to be something cut and dried to be extracted from a dictionary or the back of a French grammar. The search for such meaning becomes an intellectual magic carpet, transporting us from one revelation to another concerning man's whole progress from barbarism to whatever enlightenment we now possess.

The word *estimate* will serve as an example. Webster's Collegiate Dictionary says that it means "to form an opinion of, to gauge, judge, appraise"; and that it comes from the Latin *aestimare*, which meant approximately the same thing. But why and how did the Latin word *aestimare* come to have any such meaning? In this case it is fairly easy to run down the etymological history of the term.

In the early days of the Roman city-state, sheep and cattle still served as a common denominator in which to express the values of all other property. The computation of 753 B.C. as the date of the founding of Rome is accepted by all authorities as reasonably accurate. At that time metal was already being employed as a medium of exchange in the more civilized areas of the world, such as Asia Minor and the Tigris-Euphrates valley, but was still making its way slowly as a universal currency. Coins of fixed and guaranteed weight were probably first given wide circulation by the Lydian kings of the seventh century before Christ. So that not, probably, until at least two or three centuries later did such metal money begin to creep into usage among the peoples of central Italy. When this occurred, the metal so used was either copper, or a copper alloy, for which the Latin name was *aes*.

The problem then arose of converting values, formerly defined in a count of so many oxen, into units or weights of this new currency, *aes*. The merchants and the money changers and every man who wished to swap anything he owned for anything somebody else owned was under the necessity of "coppering" these possessions; that is, of making a satisfactory appraisal of them in measures of copper. From the fact that this determination of value was the result of bargaining and guessing and the opinion of the appraiser the word *aestimare* derived its connotation which *estimate* still has with us today. Investigation into the ancestry of a word frequently reveals linguistic bedfellows more strangely assorted than those brought together by the exigencies of politics. Or, more accurately, an incongruous and surprisingly varied progeny may be found thriving as contemporary offshoots of one philological tree. The word *supercilious*, for an illustration, meaning an attitude as expressed by the eyebrows, and hence "patronizing contempt," is derived from the Latin *super*, over, and *cilium*, eyelid. The Latin word for eyebrow was *supercilium*. But *cilium*, as something that protects the eye, has a lineage which can be traced back to a very ancient root of the Indo-Germanic tongue. Descended from that root, and still showing phonetic evidence of their kinship, were the Sanskrit word *sarman*, meaning protection, the Anglo-Saxon *helan*, to cover, to conceal, the old Irish *celim*, I conceal, as well as the Greek *kalyptein* and the Latin *celare*. From various ones of these intermediate ancestors we get, among many others, the following English words: Hall, cell, cellar, conceal, clandestine, occult, hell (!) – a place where the dead were hidden away and protected – supercilious, helmet, and hull. They may not look like members of the same clan, but these words are all cousins down under the consonants.

Sometimes there is humor in the chronicle of a word. Note *travel*, or *Jersey*, or *sandwich*. Travel, which is etymologically the same as travail, referring to the labors of childbirth, comes into English from the French *travailler*, meaning to labor, to undergo strenuous pains and duties, and derives ultimately from the Latin *trapelium*, signifying an instrument of torture. To many of us, wartime conditions revealed

The Romance Of Languages

for "traveling" an honest kinship with its linguistic forbears.

The Isle of Jersey, in the English Channel, was named in Roman times Caesarea, or Caesar's Island. Through mutations along the line of Caesarea, Chesry, Jesry, and then Jersey, this word reached its present form. So that not only the state of which Trenton is the capital, but the Jersey sweater which you wear, and the Jersey cow which you milk, all still serve today to perpetuate the fame of Julius Caesar. And of course this is only one of almost countless forms in which his name survives. As a result of the imperial family which he founded, half the rulers of the modern world have been known as Tsars, or Kaisers, or Caesars in one form or another.

As to *sandwich*, there was an eighteenth-century Earl of Sandwich who liked to gamble so well that he could not tear himself away from play at cards long enough to eat. It became his habit to have a servant put a slice of meat between two pieces of bread, and bring the concoction to him at the gaming table. Thus he invented a dish which has grown in popularity ever since, and gave his own name to the English language as one of its most common words.

Of course it is easy to carry our inquiries into the word *sandwich* further back. Wich, or wych, or wick came originally from or through the Scandinavian, and meant an inlet or a creek; specifically, a salt-water inlet or creek, since the idea of salt was also a part of the original connotation. In America we have bestowed many place names such as Cripple Creek, Perth Inlet, and Creekville. In ancient England there similarly arose such names of places as Harwich, and Greenwich, and Warwick, many of which we in turn have inherited. *Sandwich* had once designated some sandy salt-water lagoon; many sandwiches we have eaten at picnics seemed to preserve traces of this origin in their composition and taste. But the real connection lay in the fact that some distant ancestor of the gambling Earl had acquired his family name because he lived near such a lagoon.

The mention of salt recalls that our word salary comes from the Latin *salarium*, the fundamental meaning of which was money given to soldiers with which to buy salt, or salt-money. The unconscious memory of this derivation is still carried, after two thousand years, in our statement that a "man is not worth his salt." Just as pin money still means the kind of small change that was first given by husbands to their wives to enable them to buy a paper of common pins when that useful artifact was first invented. Many a time-hallowed phrase has an original concreteness of expression, now lost in the general or metaphorical interpretation, which can be rediscovered only by looking into the family histories of the proud old nouns and verbs that compose the idiom.

A similar contribution of the study of languages is to enable us to express with precision in one tongue ideas for which there is no easy equivalent in another, or to understand the full idea conveyed by such expressions. When a historian speaks of the prevalence of the *Mutterrecht* conception in Egypt of the Pharaohs, for instance, it's not because he prefers German to English, but because there is no one word or phrase in English to summarize that matriarchal background of a society in which the state is actually ruled by men, but the family largely by women, and in which even the men are inclined to trace their ancestry through the female line. *Drang nach Östen* can be translated as "push towards the East." But *Drang* means a great deal more than "push," as witness the fact that it is usually translated as "stress" when it appears as part of the

The Romance Of Languages

phrase *Sturm und Drang*, used to identify that turbulent upsurge of romanticism in German literature to which Schiller furnished, perhaps, the leading impulse. And aside from the varied shades of meaning of the word *Drang*, there are many other difficulties in the way of interpreting the phrase comprehensively without giving the background of German political thought in which it was born and thrived. The original expression, *Drang nach Östen*, conveys this historical background at once as a very part of its meaning; there is no translation short of several paragraphs which can do the same. Or, when Emerson entitled one of his poems *Waldeinsamkeit*, it was not because Emerson couldn't write both concise and beautifully poetic English. It's because there was no English word or combination of words, within the limits desirable for a title, which would picture for his reader the happy pleasure of being alone in the woods that he intended to talk about.

These illustrations from the German could be multiplied indefinitely in that and other languages. The English word "tomorrow" and the Spanish word *"mañana"* are, superficially, equivalent terms, but a book could be written on the differences in possible connotations of the two. We frequently hear *"au revoir,"* or some humorous corruption of it such as "olive oil," simply because our speech does not supply any way of saying the same thing with equal casualness. *"Caveat emptor"* means considerably more than "let the buyer beware," because the very use of the Latin form implies a reference to the legal principle of which this warning is the base. We boldly defy anybody to translate *laissez faire* adequately in less than a paragraph. And so on, almost *ad infinitum*.

This discussion immediately brings into clear focus the very method by which a living language steadily grows through accretion; through what might be called the immigration of foreign words. The continued use of *persona grata*, for instance, to convey succinctly the belief that a certain person and his ideas are looked on with favor by a given group or at a given place, will eventually result in persona grata becoming a perfectly good English term; just as the original Greek plural *phenomena* is no longer thought of as Greek, but as a commonplace part of our English vocabulary. Sometimes such words undergo slight mutations in the course of their importation, as in the case of the Russian *intelligentsiya* which became intelligentsia, or the French *la cellophane*, which became simply cellophane under the impact of our commercial directness. But they are coming in all of the time. Wherever they fill a need for which there is no ready servitor in English, they remain. And that this process, far from being a one-way proposition, is common to all active tongues, can be illustrated in a minute by such adoptions into perfectly acceptable French as *bifteck* and *milord*. That this tendency, among contemporary languages, has been speeded up by modern developments in transportation and communication, is obvious. As the world decreases in relative size, the languages of the earth are growing closer together just as surely as are its peoples.

So far we have been noting the study of words, their origins, careers, and relationships, only as a guide to better interpretations of their meanings. But such study is often the best, and sometimes the only, medium through which to reach important information in ethnology, archaeology, and many other sciences. There is poetic fitness in this dependence of the "ologies" on the evolution of words. For while the "logy" that makes up the tail feathers in such strutting peacocks of nomenclature as ichthyology, ornithology, and ophiology, has a derived significance of

The Romance Of Languages

"discourse, theory, science," it is fundamentally the Greek *logos*, meaning simply "word." "Words concerning ancient things" is still the basic meaning of archaeology. Sometimes the student of these ancient things is concerned with words, as the only means of making progress.

History, in particular, is almost as dependent on etymology as etymology is on history. For illustration of this dependence let's pay a visit to the pages of Mommsen, the great German annalist who was among the first to use it with real effectiveness. In writing the history of Rome, Mommsen was faced with the difficulty that there were no records whatsoever, nor even trustworthy legends, concerning those early migrations by which the tribes who were later to become the Greeks and the Italians had separated from an older common stock in Central Asia and then had eventually separated from one another. But he was very much interested in determining the levels of culture which had been reached at the time various migrations and settlements took place. Language formed practically his only evidence. And the convincing historical background of the Greek and Roman states which he built up out of comparative philology is still one of the all-time marvels of scholarship, too extensive and too erudite for us to do more than extract a few small samples here, to show his method of operation.

It had already become obvious, from the similarity of Sanskrit to other Aryan dialects, that the Sanskrit-speaking Hindus had belonged to the parent Indo-Germanic stock, before passing across the Himalayas into India. Mommsen deduced that these Asiatic tribes had been still largely pastoral, and had barely reached the beginnings of agriculture, at the time they were scattered by the migrations in question. He did this through showing that the words for "cow" and "bull" and "dog" and other domestic animals were basically the same in Latin, Greek, and Sanskrit; while the terms denoting plow, and tilled land, and cultivated grain were not common to the three languages at all, but had been acquired independently by the different tribes subsequently to these early dispersals.

"On the other hand the building of houses and huts by the Indo-Germans is attested by the Sanskrit *dam(as)*, Latin *domus*, Greek *domos*, (English, *domicile*); Sanskrit *vecas*, Latin *vicus*, Greek *oikos*, (English, *villa, village*); Sanskrit *dvaras*, Latin *fores*, Greek *thura*, (English, *door*); further, the building of oar-boats by the names of the boat, Sanskrit *naus*, Latin *navis*, Greek *naus*, (English, *navy*), and of the oar, Sanskrit *aritram*, Greek *eretmos*, Latin *remus*, (English, *row*), *tri-res-mis*, (English, *trireme*); and the use of wagons and the breaking in of animals for draught and transport by the Sanskrit *akshas*, Latin *axis*, Greek *axon, am-axa*, (English, *axle*); Sanskrit *iugam*, Latin *iugum*, Greek *zugon*, (English, *yoke*)." Thus does Mommsen proceed to demonstrate to what extent, and in what spheres of evolutionary ferment, our common ancestors had made progress in groping towards civilization before the future Hindus, Greeks, and Romans broke away and headed for their respective seats of permanent residence. The elements of their religion, the degree to which they were aware of and measured the passage of time, the organization of family and of clan and the lack of organization into larger social groups; all of these and many similar observations are given trustworthy documentation through the study of languages alone.

By a continuation of this process Mommsen showed that "from the common cradle of people and languages there issued a stock which embraced in common the ancestors of the Greeks and the Italians; that from this, at a subsequent period, the Italians branched off; and that

The Romance Of Languages

these again divided into the western and eastern stocks, while at a still later date the eastern became subdivided into Umbrians and Oscans." But all this was the merest beginning. For throughout the two thousand pages of his painstaking chronicle of the rise of Rome, Mommsen continues to use on almost every page the analysis of words, to discover or elucidate the facts of his history. The whole is a thrilling exhibition of the powerful tool that research into languages can become, in establishing the nature and sequences of contributions by the past to the world culture of which we are now the heirs.

Discoveries concerning languages have occasionally played a highly dramatic part in unveiling for our modern eyes the history of early nations. Unfortunately, the excavations which have now led us to so extensive a knowledge of the Assyrian and Babylonian empires had hardly been started in the time of Mommsen. And there has been nobody among the Assyriologists with the ability and willingness to attack the problems of their annals and culture so persistently through the revelations of philology. But in 1837 Sir Henry Rawlinson came across, disclosed to the world — and later translated — the tri-lingual inscriptions carved on the Behistun rock in the Zagros mountains. On this cliff, overhanging the main route from King Darius' newly-conquered Babylonian domains to his Persian homeland, the Great King had caused to be inscribed the story of his conquests, twenty-five hundred years ago, in three contemporary tongues, one of which was Babylonian cuneiform. Our knowledge of cuneiform really dates from the work on this Behistun inscription, by Rawlinson and his successors. And without a steadily increasing familiarity with the language of the neo-Babylonian empire, much of the modern digging into the ancient mounds along the Tigris and Euphrates rivers would have been almost fruitless of historical result.

The story of the Rosetta stone, found by Napoleon's soldiers in 1799, is better known. This piece of black basalt contained a short message in three languages. One language was Greek. One was Demotic. The third was Egyptian hieroglyphics, which had previously resisted all attempts at decipherment. The French scholar Champollion, using clues supplied by the easily read Greek, was able to make a beginning towards the transliteration and translation of hieroglyphics, which eventually opened up to nineteenth-century research the whole field of Egyptian inscriptions and literary remains.

If an inhabitant of some planet circling Alpha Centauri were to write a Wellsian romance about the race of beings on a fictitious planet Earth, and allow two such conveniently fortuitous discoveries as those of the Behistun rock and the Rosetta stone to aid his groping race towards a better knowledge of their past, he would undoubtedly be accused by the Centaurian critics of letting his romantic imagination run away, beyond the barriers of realism and probability. There must have been occasions when the work of Rawlinson and Champollion seemed mostly patient drudgery, even to themselves. But in the better perspective given us by time, and undoubtedly given them by inspiration, their endeavors stand out as exciting examples of mental adventure. It is difficult to conceive of more gratifying uses by any man of his mind and will than this opening of the gates to vast new realms of knowledge which were formerly closed off by an inpassable barricade.

CHAPTER IV

Fun For The Dabbler

For those of us who must take our education as a hobby, knowing that one must eat before he can study Esperanto, there is little chance of acquiring the thoroughness of erudition required to make any worthwhile contribution to philological knowledge. There is little sense in aspiring to be Champollions or Rawlinsons. We are well aware that these chapters, so far as they are intended to encourage any skeptic to get out First Year Latin instead of the *Saturday Evening Post* for an evening's entertainment, will make no headway by implying that you or I can become Mommsens in short order — or ever. Our purpose, instead, is to turn our searchlight momentarily into the entering valleys, along the level plateaus, and onto some of the highest peaks, in our cursory inspection of this mountain range of language study, so as to show the prospective traveler what he may expect, however far or however short a distance his ambition might carry him.

Only a moron will pay serious attention to an advertisement expounding the thought: "How do you know you can't play the piano if you have never tried?" But such appeals to men's ignorance of their own ignorance do nothing to disprove the fact that the study of music can be a pleasure at all stages of such study; from the first time middle C is pointed out on a piano keyboard and the first scale is learned, through all the stages of increasing skill and deeper interpretation until the pianist becomes a Paderewski if he has the makings of a Paderewski in him. One can study the piano two hours a day for two years, perhaps, and play satisfactorily the melodies of Stephen Foster or the favorite hymns of his church. He can practice the piano three hours a day for five years, and be able to rattle off Humoresque, or Melody in F, or the Barcarolle from the Tales of Hoffman, so as to delight his relatives — and himself. He can practice four hours a day for ten years, and be able to play Schubert's Impromptus, or Chopin's Minute Waltz, or Rachmaninoff's Prelude in C Sharp — if his teacher will let him drop Czerny's Exercises long enough. Or he can study and practice the piano six or eight hours a day for twenty years, and play Beethoven's Moonlight Sonata so the virtuosos will all beam with pleasure, or Liszt's Second Hungarian Rhapsody so that they will all condemn him as a facile exhibitionist. And, no matter how far he goes, if he puts his head and heart into the time he does give to the study of music, he will find pleasure in every step of the way.

The same pattern applies to the study of languages. We have to put a certain amount of hard work into playing scales and arpeggios before acquiring the technique to interpret simple tunes satisfactorily. But there is some melody and charm even in the scales and arpeggios themselves. We have to devote some honest toil to the grammar and elementary vocabularies of any language we invade, before we can form or understand sentences. But an alert curiosity will make even this task revealing and interesting.

Nothing could seem more dry, in anticipation, perhaps, than the early chapters of a Greek Grammar. And yet, in the very first lesson of a First Greek Book, we find that

Fun For The Dabbler

the word for "general" is *strategos*, giving us an immediate and possibly new conception of "strategy" as simply something worked out by generals. The word *skene*, meaning a "tent," as used by soldiers, leads us to the fact that, in the earliest days of the Greek drama, the actors made their entrances onto the stage from a tent (*skene*) at the back; and our word "scene," whether now denoting a change of actors on the stage, the view of a city, or the background of a century, is the result of this long-forgotten custom. *Angelos*, signifying messenger, reveals beyond doubt that the original meaning of "angels" was "messengers of God." This prompts an aside concerning The City of the Queen of the Angels (La Ciudad de la Reina de *Los Angeles* was the original Spanish name). There might be an argument as to any plethora of true angels existing in that metropolis today, but self-appointed "messengers of God" certainly swarm there in great abundance.

Even in the supposedly dismal introduction to conjugations, declensions, and such horrors, we discover that the Greeks made a sharp distinction between the *dual* number and the plural number consisting of more than two units. They had different endings to distinguish these forms from each other as well as from the singular. This starts a puzzling and interesting reflection as to whether the distinction is indicative of the greater nearness of the early Greeks and Greek language to the tribal beginnings of us all; and whether it is an outgrowth of that use of the binary system of numbers, in which savages have counted to two and by twos for ages, before reaching the ability to count by tens or twelves as in the decimal or duodecimal systems with which we are familiar.

Obviously, the asides and digressions set off by this first lesson and first vocabulary alone would carry us far beyond a reasonable space allotment for this chapter. So let's go on to that stage of language study roughly parallel to the level of the piano student who can play *Old Kentucky Home* and *Abide With Me* for his own enjoyment. Among the delightful applications of even an elementary acquaintance with language is the simple translation of the names of people and places. Satisfaction of a normal curiosity in this respect will frequently furnish much food for thought, and lead us far afield.

It's true that many music teachers will frown on a pupil's attempting to play anything, except the proper exercises, until a technique has been acquired far superior to that indicated in the paragraph above. And I am afraid that many an orthodox language-teacher would insist that a student should stick to his grammars until he acquired reasonable mastery of a language or two or three, before getting lost, disguised as a linguist, in a lot of encyclopedias and etymological dictionaries. But I am just dumb enough to disagree with both of them. The drudgery of finger exercises can certainly be made to seem more worth the effort by occasional application of the skill thus acquired, however small that skill may still be; and I suspect that many a boy, started hopefully on music lessons by his parents, would not have fought so persistently (and usually successfully) to abandon the program if he had been allowed to horrify the teacher's ears once in a while by amusing himself with *Little Brown Jug, The Old Gray Mare*, or whatever his young fancy thought piano lessons ought to be good for at a given age. And it is no perversely unworthy instinct on the part of a bright college boy that makes him want to study anything and everything except the actual assignments of his teachers. The tediousness of learning can always be relieved by a rambling investigation into the uses and corollary disclo-

Fun For The Dabbler 47

sures of what one has already learned. In the case of language study, as we are talking about it here, *you* are engaged in such study, if at all, purely for fun and your own interest, by the very hypothesis of this book. My humble advice is that you do not hesitate to go looking for that fun, and a maintenance of that interest, by any kind of delving into the ramifications of language which may appeal to you.

By way of illustration, let's practice what we preach. It so happens that I live on Fletcher Road, Belmont. Anybody with the slightest knowledge of Romance Languages will immediately recognize Belmont as signifying "pretty hill." A moment's further reflection will identify Fletcher as an anglicized form of the French *flêcheur*, meaning arrow-maker. We can wonder what ancient artisan, turning out *flêches*, or arrows, and given the surname *Flêcheur* as a result, is now dimly honored by having the street on which I live named for one of his distant descendents. And there is also a historical question prompted as to whence came this French influence, in a suburb of Boston, which resulted in Gallic nomenclature for both our city and our street. The answer to that inquiry involves, of course, the whole aftermath of the Norman Conquest of England.

Sticking to the personal, simply because our own names would interest most of us first, the name Robert — by some trick of an ironic fate with its tongue in its cheek — means "bright in fame." The "Ro" part is kin to the Old Norse word *hroth*, and the Anglo-Saxon *hreth*, both meaning "fame" or "glory." And the "bert," from Old High German *beraght*, Anglo-Saxon *beort*, has reached another form in the English word "bright." Not that anybody cares, except us Roberts, some of whom may never have taken the trouble to run the word down before.

But the Welch part of this writer's particular cognomen has a history of more general concern. For all the inhabitants of Wales and the residents of other lands who boast of Welsh descent, as well as those who bear the family names of Welch or Welsh or Walsh, owe their identification by this set of letters to one of those interesting and accidental developments which frequently enliven the work of a word-detective.

In Roman times there was a Celtic people known as the Volcae, who lived in that part of Southern France of which Narbonne was the capital. These Celts must have had a propensity for migration, as one tribe is reputed to have settled in Germany, and another is known to have been among the *Gauls* who invaded and settled in Asia Minor, in the province afterwards known therefrom as Galatia. In fact, probably due to the German colony, their very name Volcae, ultimately metamorphosed into Old High German *Walh*, came to signify not just these Celts, who were strangers, but any strangers or foreigners. In Anglo-Saxon this designation of *weal*, or "foreign," was applied to the inhabitants of what is now Wales; hence that land and all our cousins get their respective names.

It is of passing interest that the same history is preserved in the word "walnut," which (originally *wealh knutu*) meant the Celtic or foreign nut. (We speak similarly of the *Brazil* nut today.) And the Swedish *valnöt* or Danish *valnöd* for the same product of the grove retains an even closer or more obvious resemblance to the Volcae, from which the first half of these words was derived, than does the "walnut" of our English speech.

Even to an egocentric linguist, however, there is fun in exploring the historical and etymological background of other peoples' names. It is well known, of course, that the prefix Mac, in all of its various forms, means "son of." The first MacArthur, and undoubtedly many other MacArthurs, were thus identified by neighbors who knew them best as the sons of an Arthur whom they knew even better. So that General MacArthur, in bestowing the first name Arthur on his son, may have been only following the same instinct which causes so many of us to make a "junior" out of one of our progeny. Arthur MacArthur, or Arthur, the son of Arthur, may denote genuine and justifiable pride in an old family name and tradition, instead of being the merely questionable trick of alliteration which some critics have suggested.

Other illustrations of this same tendency to incorporate "son of" eventually into a new family name are not so generally recognized. The Old Welsh prefix *ap*, for instance, was once widely used; Thomas ap Richard, or Thomas ap Robert being a way of specifying a given Thomas by telling who his father was. In time the *ap* was written (and spoken), between the names it separated, with more and more tendency to elision, until finally the *a* disappeared altogether, and the *p* became attached to the final name. So that we have Pritchard and Probert and many similar results in our telephone books today. And the French word *fils*, especially in its old French form, *filz*, was employed in the same way, particularly by English court circles in the centuries following the Norman Conquest, to denote the *illegitimate* sons of kings and nobles. Thus Fils-Roi, which ultimately became Fitzroy, was originally applied to the son of a King who undoubtedly had legitimate offspring known as Prince This and the Duke of That; and the name Fitz-Clarence borne by a family today indicates that some far-back ancestor was the son of a Duke of Clarence who had not confined his amorous attentions to his lawfully-wedded spouse.

A sufficient smattering of language-kinships merely to enable one to follow and understand the explanations of such etymological records can, of course, be used to indulge a stimulating curiosity in many inquiries besides that prompted by all the queer name-concoctions in a city directory. We have already pointed out the advantage for vocabulary building in such discoveries as that *proletariat* once meant, literally, the "children-bearers," or that *cotillion* once meant "petticoat," or why Sheridan named his famous blunderer Mrs. Malaprop. We'd like to add here merely that this search and *re*search can at times become as much fun as trying to deduce the "who-dun-it" in a topnotch mystery story. And without conscientious caution, it's just as easy to make the wrong guesses in one field as in the other.

One such wrong guess is quite famous. In *Heroes And Hero Worship* Thomas Carlyle said: "King is Kön-ning, Kan-ning, Man that knows or can." This has been paraphrased as "He is king who can." Carlyle was assuming that our English word king, being cognate with the German *könig*, was derived from the same teutonic stem as the German word *können*, meaning "to be able," and its cognate English word "can." It was a brilliantly poetic thought that originally he became king who was able to do things and to make his title of "the able one, the one who can," respected. Unfortunately, philology proves conclusively that "king" and its German equivalent *könig* derived their original significance from the fact that they referred to a group or clan or nation of people of one race, or who were *kin* to each other. Hence these words signified in time the acknowledged head or ruler, as representing this consanguineous assemblage. English *king* and *kin* and

Fun For The Dabbler 51

German *kind* (meaning a child) not only all stem from the same root, but somewhere in the lower branches of that philological tree appear the Latin words *genus*, meaning "race," and *gignere*, "to beget," and the Greek *genea*, meaning "birth." So that a gathering of the "king" family of words extant and thriving today would include such diverse specimens as kindred, knight, nation, germ, genealogy, kind, genus, genius, gender, genial, benign, congener, and eugenics. But the group does not include *can*. Nor does a parallel group in German include the cognate word *können*. These products of linguistic evolution hang on an entirely different bush. "I can," now denoting the ability — frequently the physical ability — to do something, originally meant "I have learned how, I have the knowledge," and is connected with the Scotch *ken* and the German *kennen*. A trace of this fundamental meaning is preserved in the adjective "canny," as still applied today to a smart person with a lot of "know how." Carlyle's epigram fell flat, so far as its etymological support was involved. Shakespeare, for all of his "little Latin and less Greek," had a much surer instinct for word-relationships when he let Hamlet say that the king was "A little more than kin and less than kind."

Such ramblings in the byways of elementary language study have one characteristic in common with the eating of peanuts. You are always going to stop after looking up just one more word, or after eating one more nut. But let's desist right here, and move on to the third stage of our analogy with the study of music. Our student could now play Paderewski's Minuet in G or a good piano version of Verdi's Anvil Chorus for his own enjoyment. Our parallel linguist can now read one foreign language reasonably well, even if he can't speak it. And this brings him to the most obvious of the many satisfactions obtainable through such increasing familiarity with foreign tongues, which is the pleasure of reading, in the original, literary productions that suffer from translation.

This is difficult to illustrate, of course. But maybe a reader now and then will be kind enough to take my word for the truth of this observation, as supported by even my own limited experience. And perhaps, if we choose examples from a language so widely known as French, there will be other readers who will nod their heads in ready agreement. A couple of easy and unpretentious specimens would be the famous poem, *Carcassonne*, by Gustave Nadaud, and Aesop's fable of *The Fox And The Crow*, as told by LaFontaine. A superlative attempt at liberal translation of the first was made by John R. Thompson, and Guy Wetmore Carryl produced an excellent English paraphrase of the second. But they both fall short of the originals. And an actual conversion of either French piece into English, without loss of flavor, is almost inconceivable.

For a heavier sample, we might take Edmond Rostand's play, *Cyrano de Bergerac*. Certainly any translation which fully duplicated the impressions and effectiveness of the original would be a miracle. Or let's reverse the direction, and consider a French translation of Shakespeare's *Macbeth*. Clearly the stirring suggestiveness of "All hail, Macbeth," with which the witches greet the man who "shall be king hereafter," is painfully missing in the French version, which converts this greeting to "*Bonjour*, Macbeth." Translation sifts *out* — not in — the innuendoes and subtleties of artistic accomplishment.

A recommendation I should like to make here is that anyone interested in any foreign language begin to read books in that language, *without translating*, at the earliest possible moment. It is permissible to keep a dictionary at your elbow, of course, and look up words whose meaning you cannot surmise from the context. You would do the same thing in reading English that contained words beyond your vocabulary. And in both cases, without looking up every unknown word, you might occasionally miss part of the sense. But you will be surprised and pleased, nevertheless, at how your ability to grasp the meaning and think in the language will grow with each book you plow through, until presently you will be reading the French, or Spanish, or German almost as readily and with as much pleasure as English itself. There is nothing at all original about this suggestion. But since it is something I have practiced for a long time, perhaps I may be forgiven for preaching it now.

To return to our pianist once more, we believe the reader will grant that somewhere in this period of progress we have roughly indicated the music-lover will cease to need encouragement from the outside. Given the opportunity, he will increasingly seek happiness at his piano by the prompting of his own desires. For any of countless reasons he may go no further with music, or may actually give it up. But the reason will not be lack of interest, once he has reached a certain level of immersion in the art. For then more and more he finds that music can interpret and express all the ranges of feeling and depths of knowledge that can be materialized, for transmission from one mind to another, through any other medium. Only his own shortcomings as an interpreter limit the ever greater returns from the time he can devote to his avocation.

Similarly, the student of languages who has a comparable amount of progress behind him no longer needs these lectures to tell him how stimulating the subject is. He too may abandon his delving into genitive endings and aorist moods, because he can make more money coaching basketball or because he becomes even more fascinated by amateur photography. But again the reason will not be any lack of appeal in philological study, nor will he drop its pursuit without reluctance. For at some stage he, too, discovers, what every true student in every field wakes up at last to see, that universal experience is contained within the reaches of his own special subject. He realizes, with each day of work beckoning on still more invitingly to other days, that language is the great connecting link between all forms and all branches of human knowledge, and that semantic research opens numberless doors to other chambers and corridors of our spiritual inheritance.

CHAPTER V

The Romance Of History

Unfortunately, historians occurred rather late in history. Of the papyri, parchments, clay tablets, and stone inscriptions which constitute the earliest written records there are no known fragments more than about six thousand years old. A scientific friend of mine says that the age of the earth is about two billion years. If you press him hard enough in an argument he might give in five hundred million years, either way. But for comparison with six thousand years, even the minimum of a billion and a half is quite a stretch.

So there are two divisions of history. Let us suppose that the era of the earth's existence had been covered by the combined work of a dozen scientific and historical societies, in one hundred huge volumes of one thousand pages each. And that the same amount of space in these chronicles had been devoted uniformly to each century from the beginning to the end. In the first ninety-nine volumes of this work there would be no mention of man at all. Not until somewhere about Page 950 of the very last volume would he appear, and then as a brute savage recognizable only to the anthropologists. And when we finally came to men who were reading and writing and recording the happenings around them, *we would be on the last half of the very last page of the whole collection.*

Nevertheless, we are concerned in this section only with

that last half page of the hundred thousand pages. Unraveling the tale of what has gone before is the work of the astronomer, the geologist, the paleontologist, and their associates in the physical and zoological sciences. It's great work, if you can do it. Our job, however, is to take a look at "the accepted legend" which is history; the distillation of man's own records of those events in which he has taken part. It may sometimes seem true that "history teaches us nothing except that we learn nothing from history." But there is much pleasure for the individual in trying to learn what has gone on before and what results in the future we can guess by extrapolation on these movements and forces of the past.

For most of us the best introduction to the pleasure of reading history is through biography. Just as fact is, in very truth, stranger than fiction usually dares to be, so are the lives of the real Alexanders, Caesars, and Napoleons more dramatic than those of their counterparts in the poetic tragedies and glamorous romances of the most imaginative writers. Courtesans more seductive, true lovers more faithful, barefoot boys more ambitious, haughty aristocrats more proud, whining agitators more self-seeking, true martyrs more self-sacrificing, heroes more gallant and villains more cunning than appear in any movie thriller; these stalk the pages of history and make it as they go. For illustration let's isolate a few exhibits in the almost infinite parade.

Iknaton

Here is a couple who would be unbelievable in fiction, except possibly in some tragic fairy tale. For the man is an oriental prince, young, handsome, brilliant, and kind, who peacefully ascends the throne of the greatest empire then in existence. With a vast harem at his disposal, and with promiscuity such an established national custom that the very priests of the state religion have hordes of temple concubines, he is monogamously faithful to his one chief wife, and lavishes on her all the romantic ardor of a love-struck poet in our western world. Even when she bears him seven daughters and no sons, the king remains devoted to her alone. The Queen, also young, beautiful, and wise, both deserves and returns such unusual devotion. Here is romance in an ivory tower as might be dreamed of in the imagination of Coleridge, or might satisfy the passionate purity of Lanier.

But this king is not to be known to history chiefly as a lover. He is the first great monotheist in all philosophy. Conceiving of the life-giving sun as the one and only God, he will have no other gods before himself or his people. With iconoclastic fervor he uproots priests and temples alike, builds an entirely new capitol city to escape the tentacles of tradition, decrees his new religion as the exclusive worship of his subjects, and seeks truth so earnestly that even the artists break centuries-old conventions and, for a decade, picture animals and men as they really are.

It is only one decade, however, that the great drama lasts. For this ruler of a war-created empire seeks peace, so assiduously that the conquests of his fathers fall away in revolt, and finally his own kingdom crushes him in the surge of its returning superstition. He dies, broken hearted and a tragic failure when barely thirty years old, with the glorious empire he inherited now a shattered wreck.

This was in 1362 B.C. The young man was Amenhotep IV, Pharaoh of Egypt. But he is better known by the name, which he chose for himself, of Iknaton, meaning "The Sun-god is satisfied." His queen was Nofretete. Their likenesses, among the finest portraits in any art form of any country, have come down to us in exquisitely sculptured stone. And we also can still read, over three thousand years later, that long poem to the sun which Iknaton himself wrote, and which Will Durant calls "the fairest surviving remnant of Egyptian literature." Surely here are hero and heroine to catch our fancy; to reward us for wading through a thousand dreary pages of monotonous wars.

Archimedes

But it is not just among kings or warriors that we find individual actors, in our long human play, who make us stop and rub our eyes. Those scenes which take place in a Hellenistic setting, especially, are thronged with half-gods of the intellect. There was Thales of Miletus, who was able to foretell an eclipse of the sun in 585 B.C. And Anaximander, also of the sixth century B.C., who built an accurate planetarium, drew the first known map of the inhabited world, and stated that men as well as the other animals all arose from fishes through a gradual process of organic evolution. Just to list such outstanding Greeks in the field of philosophical science alone would fill half a page. But let us center our transient attention on one named Archimedes, who was born in or about 287 B.C.

He did not live in one of the Ionian cities, nor on the mainland of Greece, but in the Greek settlement of Syracuse on the island of Sicily. Fate was very kind to Archimedes in many ways. He was fortunate enough not only to be the favored relative of a king, but to have that king, Hieron II of Syracuse, one of the most enlightened of rulers. Possessed of one of the best brains that recorded history presents for our admiring appraisal, Archimedes was also blessed with both the leisure and the disposition to use his mind in the pursuit of knowledge. The result was a happy life, and "a sum of mathematical achievement unsurpassed by any one man in the world's history."

Archimedes left his native Sicily as a young man, to study mathematics at Alexandria. When he had learned all that the successors of Euclid could teach him he returned to Syracuse to continue his researches. The profound results of his work he conveyed to other scholars in the most beautifully concise explanations in the whole field of scientific thought. Ten of his works have survived, and are a part of the foundations of today's geometry, conic sections, hydrostatics, and mechanical physics.

Our hero was the original prototype of the absent-minded professor. He forgot his meals to continue working on some theorem which intrigued him; he forgot his bath to puzzle over the displacement of water by some object in his bathtub. The best-known incident of his life hinges on his preoccupation with the latter problem. King Hieron had given him the task of finding out whether a certain crown, supposed to be pure gold, was not really alloyed with silver. Its weight was the same as that of the gold supplied to the artisan who made it, but had some of the gold been saved by substitution? When the idea suddenly dawned on Archimedes that the amount of water displaced by the crown would give him its exact volume, for comparison with the weight, he is supposed to have rushed naked out into the streets shouting "Eureka! Eureka!" — or "I have found it." What he had found, far more important than the amount of gold which had been filched, was a simple method for determining the specific gravity of any object, and the basic law for bodies floating in a liquid.

And yet Archimedes could turn his science to very practical use when necessity or diplomacy required. After formulating laws for the lever so complete that no advance was made on them for eighteen hundred years, he stated "Give me a place to stand on, and I will move the earth." To prove his point to the skeptical Hieron, he arranged such a powerful combination of pulleys and levers that he was able singlehanded to pull up onto the beach a large loaded vessel which all the king's men had previously been unable to get out of the water.

It was inevitable that such an intellect should be put to designing engines of war. So long as the peace-loving Hieron lived these constructions served only to create for Archimedes a vulgar fame which he did not desire. But after Hieron died Syracuse was attacked by the Roman general Marcellus; at first by sea and then by land. Archimedes devised huge cranes to reach out from the walls, lift the enemy's ships right out of the water, and dash these ships to pieces against the rocks. He built catapults to throw a veritable rain of large stones on the enemy's land soldiers. And finally, all of his military might defeated by the genius of this one man, Marcellus was obliged to give up the idea of capturing the city by storm.

But the Roman then instituted a blockade which completely shut off Syracuse from all supplies, and in eight months the city was starved into surrendering. Archimedes, studying mathematical figures which he had traced in the sand, was killed by a Roman soldier. This was against the strict orders of Marcellus that the venerable genius should not be harmed, and he erected a splendid tomb in Archimedes' honor. But the greatest of mathematicians was dead, and neither mourning nor honor could bring him back to his figures in the sand.

Cleopatra

Or here we have a character more fabulous than any fable. Her story would be incredible were it not also one of the best authenticated, even as to details, in all our written records. She was such a queen as no Graustarkian imagination would even attempt to make convincing in fiction.

Her name was Cleopatra. A Macedonian Greek by race, she was, due to the conquests of Alexander the Great nearly three centuries before, born in Egypt, in the city of Alexandria which he had founded. By birth she came, at seventeen, to occupy the throne of the Pharaohs. By personality and genius she twice came, during the next twenty years, within striking distance of ruling the world. By fate she came, at thirty-nine, to her end, under such circumstances that her death marked the exact finish of an era and the clear-cut beginning of a new one. The world's longest and most famous attempt at a republican solution to the problems of government ended with Mark Anthony's death and Cleopatra's, after the battle of Actium. With Octavian's victory at Actium there began that Augustan age which, seeking the opposite solution, likewise gave the world its longest stretch of disciplined peace at the price of autocratic dictatorship. It seems almost as though history, aware of the dramatic turning point in its mighty affairs, brought forth a supremely dramatic woman to serve as marker for the event.

At seventeen Cleopatra, co-ruler with her brother Ptolemy XII, was engaged to marry him. This was in accordance with Egyptian royal custom. But melodrama, entering at the very beginning of the lady's historical career, followed it all the way. And along that way the names of famous Romans congregate like stars in a super-movie. First, the great Pompey, last Roman general and statesman in the tradition of Sulla, was assassinated by orders of Ptolemy's minister Pothinus; and Cleopatra herself was banished, that Pothinus' rule as regent for the young prince might be more complete. Then Julius Caesar, who had followed Pompey to Egypt, fought his way to control of the ancient kingdom. The queen had herself smuggled into Caesar's apartment, and converted him into her champion — and her lover.

Even the mighty Caesar tarried nine months in Alexandria, with Cleopatra. Then he established her, with their son, Caesarion, as his guest in Rome. Egypt was hers now, beyond any argument. By foresight, thrift, and skill she was to keep it not only hers, but make of it a rich and powerful treasure house. Henceforth the coin in Egypt's exchequer was never entirely forgotten by any would-be conqueror who gloried in the charms of Egypt's queen.

But a small African kingdom could not satisfy such an imperial Macedonian ambition. Cleopatra dreamed of becoming empress of a united Mediterranean world. With the practicality of her sex she had attached herself to that Roman who was most likely to have the power and the desire to forge such a throne. When Mark Anthony thrice offered Caesar the crown of a king, the general's political sense made him refuse. But the offer would hardly have been made if Anthony had not sensed that the thought was a pleasant one to Caesar. And it seems likely that it was the Egyptian's dream, of combining the Roman West and the Asiatic-African East under one crown, to be shared by Caesar and herself as husband and wife, which now obsessed the Roman statesman. So far and so near to completion had Cleopatra's planning reached when the Roman senators collapsed the bubble by assassinating Caesar.

Despite this failure Cleopatra tried again. A dictatorship over a world-wide empire was clearly in the making, and she had the perspicacity to see it. The assassins and their armies were exterminated; Mark Anthony, Lepidus, and

Octavian succeeded to Caesar as a triumvirate ruling both East and West; Lepidus was eliminated, to make Anthony and Octavian rivals for the sole power; and Cleopatra attached herself to Anthony. He was more passionately devoted to her than Caesar had ever been, and once more her goal was in sight. For a while success or failure hung in the balance.

But fate always tantalized the queen with near success. Throughout the twenty years of her scheming three men appeared who might have brought these schemes to fruition. The first, Caesar, might have succeeded — but was killed too soon. The second, Anthony, didn't have the iron will or the shrewd statesmanship. He and all his hopes were swept aside by the defeat of Actium. And the third, Octavian, who was destined to succeed, would have none of Cleopatra. The princess of eighteen had been irresistible to the fifty-five year old, campaign-aged Caesar. The vivacious woman of thirty had become the inseparable companion of the forty-five year old Anthony, making him forget his former harems and his wives. But the shopworn woman of thirty-nine had no sufficient wiles to snare the youthful and determined Octavian. Her dream of empire was over. There was even the chance that she might be hauled ignominiously to Rome, and paraded as one more exhibit to grace a conqueror's triumph. She saw these things with a clarity of vision which never failed her. And seeing, the famous queen put a poisonous asp to her breast, and died with the same touch of drama that had lighted all her days.

Mohammed

The Arabian peninsula is largely a sandy waste, stretching southeastward from the Mediterranean, between the Red Sea and the Persian Gulf, to the Indian Ocean. For most of the last three thousand years its trackless desert has seemed, to the surrounding peoples, to be an island of barbarism in a sea of civilization. Somewhere into this mysterious and unchartered territory Nabonidus, the last king of Babylon, was wont to withdraw, for his peaceful meditations while his son Belshazzar made futile efforts at staving off the conquering armies of Persia. That was twenty-six hundred years ago. Until very recently, at least, the haunts of the nomadic tribes who dwell in the peninsula were as little familiar to the outside world as in the days of Nabonidus. Only once in all that time has a political power arisen, in the vast stretch between Abyssinia and Mesopotamia, which made its influence felt as far as either. That one time the political power was supported by a world-shaking religious crusade, and Mohammed was its prophet.

A study of the preceding centuries, among the nations and cultures which were affected, makes one feel that the rise of Mohammedanism was the strangest accident in all history. The complete decay of half a dozen different empires had conspired to lay the whole east ready for the conquering sword of Islam. Only through such unwitting preparation of the material could so tiny a spark as Mohammed himself have set off such a mighty conflagration. But the very magnitude of the results makes the pettiness of the man astounding, and himself an object of absorbing interest.

Behold this unknown little merchant, at the age of forty, probably unable even to read and write. He lives in an Arabian town of some twenty thousand population, and owes his moderate prosperity to the fact that he married a widow for whom he had been a camel boy. Nobody even among his neighbors, in this little city of Mecca, suspects him of having any pretensions to greatness; and Mohammed himself at this time would have bargained with life for a few more camels and a slightly larger home. Then behold him eighteen years later, sending out couriers to all the known monarchs of the world, demanding their submission to his teaching and his power. And this was no empty gesture. For within ten more years this demand was enforced, in most cases, by his militant successors. Such a mushrooming of strength and of zeal has not been seen anywhere on the planet before or since.

Mohammed began to preach his new religion when he was about forty years old. It is only a slight exaggeration to say that for years nobody paid any attention to him. His early converts consisted of his wife, Kadija, an adopted son Ali, a slave, Zeid, and one able and faithful admirer, named Abu Bekr. These became the nucleus of a small sect which was saved trouble by its insignificance. But in Mecca there was a meteoric rock, embedded as a cornerstone in a temple known as the Kaaba. This meteorite was worshiped as a god, the big-brother god to all the little gods of Arabia. Much of the trade and prosperity of Mecca depended on the pilgrimages, from all over the peninsula, to worship at this holy stone. Mohammed's preaching ran contrary to this paganism, and in some ten years he achieved the dignity of being considered a threat to the renown and revenues of Mecca. A committee was appointed, representing every family in the city except Mohammed's own, to murder him and erase his new religion.

But about two hundred miles north of Mecca was the rival town of Medina, not quite as large. Torn by internal turmoils, jealous of Mecca and its profits as a shrine of the idolatry which Mohammed was attacking, the citizens of Medina demonstrated that a prophet is not without honor except in his own city. They invited Mohammed to come and rule over them. Sending his followers ahead one by one over a period of two years, Mohammed himself finally left Mecca the very night he was to have been assassinated. He escaped diligent pursuit by taking a long devious route, and arrived as the ruler of Medina — and as a now visible speck on the scene of world politics — on September 20, 622. This flight, known as the Hegira, is used as the basis or starting point of Mohammedan chronology.

It took seven more years, of raids on caravans, of battles which now favored one side and then the other, of treacheries and compromise, before Mecca itself accepted Mohammed, in exchange for being made the pilgrimage center of his new cult. In 629 he returned to the city of his birth, and established it as the capital of his domain. Within three more years this domain extended over all of Arabia. Then Mohammed died. But Mohammedanism, as a religion and as a political force, went on, with the irresistible impetus of a prairie fire.

On the wives and concubines which the prophet added to his entourage, as he acquired the wealth and power to do so; on the revelations from Allah in defense of this domestic life which it was necessary for Mohammed to incorporate into the Koran itself; on his overtures to the Jews and his later severe hostility to them; on the ethical standards and spiritual appeal of the religion which he founded; on the extent to which Mohammed himself was responsible for the characteristics of Mohammedanism; on these and many other aspects of his history, we shall not try to comment here. His life follows a dramatic pattern. The first act covers forty years of our hero's existence as a nonentity. In the second act, for twelve more years, he is a struggling evangelist, grasping at greatness. In the climactic third act he spends the last eleven years of his life as an oriental despot, of steadily increasing power, and with

The Romance Of History

the added advantage of a religion of his own brewing with which to sanctify his deeds. There is no need of Marlowe's mighty line and mightier imagination when fate can concoct such plays.

Catherine I

She was born Marta Skavronskaya, a peasant girl in Latvia, in 1683. She died Catherine I, empress of Russia, the most powerful ruler in Europe, in 1727. Between those two dates is a life so amazing in itself, and revealing so much about the history of eastern Europe with which it was interwoven, that it seems made to order for a great historical novel.

A factual biography of Catherine was attempted by Phil Stong, and published as *Marta Of Muscovy*. It will probably be no surprise to this otherwise excellent writer to hear it said that the attempt failed. For the padding, the repetition, and the confusion of the narrative prove simply that not enough personal details are known about the life of the adventuress herself to supply the meat for a biographical meal. But those few facts which are well established certainly provoke an interest in their heroine which should make her the nucleus of some imaginative masterpiece. Before I get myself sold on that enterprise, let's take a look at those few facts, forthwith.

Marta was one of several children being raised in such poverty and filth as to make the American domiciles of Tobacco Road seem quite presentable, when the bubonic plague reached that section of Europe and carried off her father. Her mother had already died. The little three-year-old orphan was taken into the home of a German Lutheran pastor, Ernest Glück. For the next fifteen years she was treated by the Glücks as one of their own children. Her character was formed in this household. The kind treatment did not include education, for Marta never learned to read and write. But she undoubtedly acquired there many domestic virtues, and a happy reasonableness of personality, which were splendid aids to fate in its design for her future. Then at eighteen Marta married and went away with a soldier, a dragoon in the Swedish army which was occupying her country.

Just what happened during the next months is lost to history. There is even considerable doubt that the marriage referred to above ever took place. For it is fairly clear that Marta became a "camp follower." When the town of Marienburg was captured from the Swedes by the Russians, she was somehow delivered into the hands of Marshal Sheremetiev, the Russian commander, and became his concubine. If the report is correct that she had just previously belonged to a corporal, this was a considerable step up the ladder for a prostitute, as Sheremetiev was one of Peter the Great's ablest generals. Accompanying the marshal while his armies burned and destroyed one Livonian town after another, Marta finally arrived in Moscow with Sheremetiev, about two years from the day she had left Pastor Glück's home. By this time she had certainly become Sheremetiev's friend as well as his favorite, for there is reason to believe that, despite a Madame Sheremetiev somewhere in the background, Marta ran his house in Moscow for him — and ran it well.

Soon, however, the marshal made the mistake of letting his pride and joy be seen by Prince Menshikov, the most powerful man in Russia after the tsar, on the occasion of a visit which the prince paid to the general's quarters. What favor Menshikov gave in exchange for Marta is not known, but it *is* known that immediately thereafter she moved up another step on this strange ladder, and was established as

Menshikov's mistress. He was equally famous as a libertine and as a political schemer, but this brilliantly simple and direct young lady apparently knew how to exert considerable control over his activity in both fields. Also, apparently, Menshikov's ambition was greater than his lust. Recognizing useful qualities of statesmanship in his bedroom companion, the prince gave Marta a few months of educational preparation in a knowledge of European diplomacy, and then arranged to let the tsar discover her. The transfer of her person was duly requested, and made, as expected. The Latvian peasant girl became the "back street" friend of Peter the Great, the vigorous, cruel, able, and absolute sovereign of Russia.

A realistic appraisal of the road Marta traveled would probably indicate that she was now about half way, although the remainder took longer in years and can be briefed in fewer sentences. The next important milestone is the birth, about twelve months later, of a child; the first of twelve whom the Latvian peasant girl bore to Peter during the following two decades. After a while Marta was moved from the German quarter of Moscow to the Kremlin. Despite the fact that the tsar already had a tsarina, and by her an heir-apparent, the ill-fated Alexei, Marta's position changed gradually from that of temporary mistress, to permanent mistress, to publicly recognized consort of the sovereign. Although the chronology is confused, more tangible marks of her rise to power came in due course. Peter was divorced and Marta was made his legal wife; she was made tsarina, under the name by which she is best known to history, Ekaterina (or Catherine) Alexeievna Romanov; she was crowned in an elaborate ceremony as the equal co-ruler of Russia with Peter himself; and finally, on his death in 1725, she ruled alone as Catherine I, empress of Russia. Marta Skavronskaya, peasant, orphan, and prostitute, had set a pace for climbers which few have ever equalled.

The last remark is intended to be anything but derogatory. When it is noted that, by all records and accounts, she was never beautiful; and when it is considered that after bearing six or eight children no woman could have exercised such control by sex appeal over an autocratic monarch who had a well-earned reputation for being the most insatiable libertine in Europe; in light of these reflections it becomes clear that Catherine did not win her way simply as a perfumed wench who afforded pleasure to her warrior husband. Instead, it was her restraining hand on his impulses, his cruelties, and his ambitious dreams for which Peter seems to have loved her — and honored her — most.

Some suggestion of her good sense and diplomatic skill is contained in the fact that Marta kept the friendship and wholehearted support of both Sheremetiev and Prince Menshikov all her life. Some suggestion of her versatility is given by the fact that she fought as one of the most heroic soldiers at the battle of the Pruth, when Peter's career was almost ended by the Turks; and then apparently took the lead in maneuvering for an astounding peace which extricated the tsar from his danger. Apparently she could outdrink, outfight, and outthink most of the men of her day, without losing any of that appealing femininity which is left beyond dispute by her record and her twelve children. And apparently, she had, what must have been an extreme and valuable rarity in Russia, a calm sense of humor, with an ability to laugh occasionally at herself and everybody else. Shakespeare might have said — if he had lived a hundred years later — "She was a woman, take her for all in all, we shall not look upon her like again."

Livingstone

There are pulses in all movement as many a wiser man has pointed out. The progress of the human animal towards enlightenment is by no means an exception. And in the last short stretch of this progress which has been made visible to us by records, two centuries stand out as crests of the waves in such human progress. They are the sixth century B.C., and the nineteenth century A.D.

The fall of old empires and the rise of new pioneer communities, the transition of the center of gravity from a dying autocratic east to a virile forward-looking young west, the attempt of scientific thinking to break through the darkness of accumulated mysticism, the readiness to seize upon and use such new ideas as coinage to facilitate trade and papyrus to facilitate writing; these and many other thrilling aspects of the sixth century before Christ are probably best typified by Pythagoras, struggling vainly at Crotona to establish his religious brotherhood founded on reason.

In the nineteenth century after Christ we have a great widening of all horizons, on the earth and in the skies. Once again science steps eagerly forward, colliding with tradition at every turn. There comes a glory "in the steamship, in the railway, in the thoughts that shake mankind"; exploration and exploitation of all the hidden recesses of the planet; and industrial revolution that insists on changing man's living conditions everywhere to a greater dependence on material comforts; a sanitary-medical revolution that aims to give man control of fortuitous diseases; and a philosophic revolution that puts new gods beside the old ones until all ethical bases are likely to get lost in the shuffle. And the one man who best represents this whole nineteenth century is probably David Livingstone.

Born in a mill village in Scotland, of parents so poor that he himself started to work in the cotton mill when ten years old, David nevertheless found the time and ambition to prepare himself for college. He entered Anderson's College in Glasgow, at the age of twenty-three; was accepted two years later as a candidate of the London Missionary Society; and became a Doctor of Medicine in 1840, when twenty-seven years old. On the eighth of December, 1840, he left England, as an agent of the London Missionary Society, for South Africa, where he was to spend almost all of the remaining thirty-three years of his life.

The details of Livingstone's travels in Africa make extremely interesting reading, especially for the armchair explorer. But we shall pause here only to try to see the historical significance of that work, and the way it fitted so neatly into the pattern of the nineteenth century. He alternated the prayer and preaching of a true evangelist with the scientific observations of an Agassiz. He brought to the African natives Christianity in one hand and medical science in the other. He established church missions to raise the Africans to a religious level with the Europeans, and thus actually established the outposts of empire which brought the blacks under political subjugation of the white races. He respected the ancient prejudices of native chieftains, and transported a steamship piecemeal to Lake Nyasa, four hundred miles inland from the east coast. He familiarized Europe with the size and helplessness of the negro population, and fought the slave trade with every means at his disposal. He was loved as a friend and honored almost as a god, alike by the simplest savage kinglets and by the outstanding scholars of London scientific societies. He combined a sense of humor that never forsook him, and the simple approach of a child, with penetrating depth of intellect and a fervid sense of duty. He lived a life of hardship, suffering, and disease, and was buried in Westminster Abbey with the copious honors of a grateful nation. He was the spirit of Wesley, of Lincoln, and of Darwin, mingled into one synthesis; and to study his biography is to gain a useful and interesting insight into the century which he so nobly, and unconsciously, represented.

CHAPTER VI

The Romance Of History
(Continued)

Somebody once said that ninety-five percent of us are interested only in people, four percent in events, and one percent in ideas — or words to that effect. History treats of all three, with the emphasis varying according to the intellectual fashion and the purpose of the historian. It is worthwhile pointing out here, for the possible four percent, that a sheer love of resounding drama, in either the mass collisions of human millions or the sporadic cataclysms of nature itself, will find much to feed upon in the historical headlines of the last six thousand years. Again, let's put the finger on just a few heterogeneous examples.

Building Of The Great Pyramid

Five thousand years ago last week — or just about — Khufu, Pharaoh of Egypt, decided to build himself a tomb. Only a few miles from his magnificent palace in Memphis was the terraced stone tomb built by Imhotep, for King Zoser, some fifty years before — and now known to us as the Step-Pyramid of Sakkara. This was a beautiful and substantial structure, for Imhotep was one of the great architects of all time. But after all, Zoser had been one of the last scions of a weak and dying strain. He, Khufu, was the founder of a mighty line, the first king of a dynasty that was to rule Egypt forever. His monument, the sepulchre in which his mummified remains would ultimately rest for all eternity, should be in proportion to his greatness; the most massive that ever had been built in the past, or ever would be built in the future. *It was* — at least up till this present writing.

A rocky plateau beyond Sakkara, and some ten miles west of the River Nile, was chosen for the site. The architectural form now known to us as a pyramid was chosen, probably as a further development of what Imhotep and his successors had started. It is unique to this time and place — Egypt of the fourth dynasty and those immediately following. The name comes through the Greeks from the Egyptian word *pi-re-mus*, meaning altitude.

It would be vain and silly for us to try to find anything new to say about Khufu's monument. In the simple fact of its having been built there is ample drama for the most incurable romantic. The selfish daring which could conceive and the arrogant power which could bring to completion so vast and eternal a personal sepulchre make any poetic embroidery by the imagination as superfluous as the proverbial painting of the lily. In this huge pile there are two and one-half million blocks of stone. Some single slabs weigh as much as one hundred and fifty tons. All of them together average two and a half tons each. Yet most of them were brought overland and by boat from the quarries of Arabia, several hundred miles away, as no similar stones were to be found in the valley of the Nile. And they were put into place by the magnificently simple and costly

The Romance Of History

means of building earth ramps to the proper height, and pulling those stones up the inclined planes of such ramps until each could be slid into its proper position. When the fabulous tales concerning the erection of the great pyramid, which persisted throughout three thousand ancient years, are sieved of their exaggeration, it still seems likely that Khufu kept a hundred thousand men employed for twenty years in preparing his final resting place.

Each side of the mighty pile is seven hundred and sixteen feet long. From the bottom edge to the top, measured along the slanting side, is five hundred and seventy-four feet. The vertical altitude, before the nick of time took its slight toll at the apex, was four hundred and eighty-one feet. Six hundred feet directly under this original apex, and hence more than a hundred feet below the ground level of the pyramid, there was cut into the foundation rock the actual chamber where the royal mummy was finally laid to rest. This chamber was reached by a descending passage cut from an opening in the outer surface of the monument, some fifty feet above the ground. The whole structure covers five hundred thousand feet of ground area and contains nearly ninety million cubic feet of masonry.

As Will Durant points out, Khufu and his engineers sought everlasting stability through simplicity of design. Although not quite half as high as the Empire State Building, the Egyptian monument has nearly three times as much cubic volume, and rests on a ground area six times as large. The whole mass, except for its square corners, takes the shape that all of this stone, falling to one spot from the heavens above, would automatically assume in its search for equilibrium. In tune with this plan of architectural fundamentalism was the orientation of the base. Its four sides face exactly north, south, east, and west, with a surveyor's precision. What significance, if any, is to be attached to the further fact that the base also rests exactly on the thirtieth parallel of latitude is a matter left for the historian's surmise or the layman's fancy. Without seeking to find esoteric evidences of more knowledge and more skill than obviously required by the very existence of the pyramid, we still behold sufficient cause for ever-fresh astonishment and admiration. In the record of man's rise from a state of disorganized animal ignorance to some level of organized knowledge and cooperative power, the Great Pyramid is an early milestone. It is a milestone which is likely to stand out for a long time to come because it weighs more than six million tons.

The Destruction Of Nineveh

The sudden and complete annihilation of whole cities was a commonplace in the world thousands of years before the atomic bomb or even modern artillery were invented. In 689 B.C. Sennacherib of Assyria expelled the population of Babylon, burned the city, and turned a canal to flow over its ruins. In 146 B.C. the Romans carried out Cato's injunction that Carthage must be destroyed. After capturing the city, at the end of a perpetration of conscienceless treachery and soulless brutality unmatched in all history, the conquerors sold the survivors into slavery. The city was pillaged, and then burned for seventeen days. Finally, the ground was plowed up and sown with salt. Other instances of man's inhumanity to other men's cities are plentiful in our annals.

But Babylon was rebuilt ten years later, by Sennacherib's son, Esarhaddon, and in another generation was greater than ever — as Assyria was to learn to her sorrow. And Carthage had been only a weaker rival of Rome for a long time before her end. Some such consideration lessens the dramatic effect in the case of these and all similar cataclysms, when they are compared with the destruction of Nineveh. The capital of the Assyrian empire stands alone in the sad glory attached to the height of its fall and the irrevocability of its conversion to a sandy waste.

Picking up the thread a century and a half before, we find that Assyria had already been a great power long enough to have become a decadent nest for interminable civil wars. Then in 745 B.C. an army general named Pulu seized the throne, gave himself the royal name of Tiglath-Pileser III, after one of his country's greatest earlier rulers, and proceeded to prove himself capable of living up to the name. In less than a hundred years more the ambition of Tiglath-Pileser, the organizing ability of Sargon, the impetuous cruelty of Sennacherib, and the statesmanship of Esarhaddon, had made Nineveh the capital of an empire that ruled most of the known world. This power and this throne were inherited, in 669 B.C., by Ashurbanipal, The Great King, the Sardanapalus of Herodotus and the Greek historians. He ruled for forty-three years, amid outward splendor supported by an understructure beginning to crumble at every beam and joint. Over two thousand years later Louis XIV of France, the Grand Monarch, was to present a historical repetition, remarkable for its similarity, over an even longer reign. But the holocaust was delayed for still seventy-four years after Louis' death; only fourteen years after Ashurbanipal bequeathed his sceptre to his inglorious successors, nothing was left of his city or his empire, and the Assyrian nation itself had ceased forever to exist.

How great was the fall of Nineveh, and how comparatively sudden, can be made to appear very strikingly by the presentation of two contrasting tableaux. The first occurs in about the year 640 B.C. — Ashurbanipal celebrated a mighty triumph, ostensibly to show proper gratitude to the gods for their favors. Actually, no doubt, it was to let himself and his people revel in a field day of pride and self-glorification. He had now been king of Assyria for over a quarter of a century. After the revolt of his brother, vassal king of Babylonia, a few years before, had been suppressed, this brother and rival had perished in the flames of his own palace. There was no doubt now that whoever sat on a throne at Babylon did so only as a loyal subordinate of the Great King in Nineveh.

Egypt, first conquered by Ashurbanipal's father, had since revolted and been crushed several times. But the present Pharaoh, Psammetichos, had been put in power by Assyrian legions. Assyrian garrisons along the Nile kept even upper Egypt subject to Psammetichos, and himself — nominally, at least — subject to Nineveh. Tyre and other Phoenician cities had been properly chastised for their wavering fidelity, and all Syria from Edom to Damascus was a part of the Assyrian domain. The kingdom of Urartu, on the north, was allowed to survive at all, only because of its diplomatic servility to Ninevite power. Ardys, King of Lydia, far off across Anatolia, had sent friendly embassies which the court of Nineveh could construe as tenders of submission. Two successive kings of Arabia having revolted and their armies having been annihilated, the suzerainty of Ashurbanipal over that land was at present undisputed. And most important of all, Assyria's one great rival, Elam, whose kings had had the temerity to invade Babylonia itself, was now utterly destroyed. Wherever the Great King looked, from the Southern Mediterranean to the Persian Gulf and the Caspian Sea, he saw only subservient lesser kings, most of whom bore his yoke in name or in very fact. Nor was Ashurbanipal's pride satisfied with this figurative yoke of his friendly dependents. His triumphal chariot was drawn by a very real yoke, to which were hitched four former kings, of Elam and Arabia, who had been his enemies. The Assyrian empire was — or at least then seemed to be — the greatest and most far-flung governmental power the world had so far seen. And Nineveh was the royal seat, the capital, and the mistress of this empire.

The second tableau is presented almost exactly a quarter of a century later, in 612 B.C. Ashurbanipal had died fourteen years before, with his empire tottering around him. The repeated subjugations of Egypt, and then the too costly destruction of Elam, had been a terrific strain on Assyrian military power. Now, in 612, Egypt was already independent under that same Psammetichos who had started as a puppet of Nineveh. Elam destroyed was worse than Elam a rival, for it no longer served as a buffer state against the rising power of the Medes. And Babylonia was having a rejuvenation of national spirit, started by Ashurbanipal's father, which had not really ceased its growth during even the darkest days of suppression by the Great King.

So Kyaxeres the Mede and Nabopolassar of Babylonia formed an alliance to destroy the enfeebled Assyrian tyranny, and marched on Nineveh. Destroy it they did, after one of the great and terrible sieges of history. The last king, Sinshumlishir, his court, his harem, and his palace were all burned together. The whole weakened structure of empire collapsed, completely and with unique finality. Nineveh was made an utter waste, which it has remained for the twenty-five hundred years since. All its provinces and subordinated kingdoms fell apart and were reincorporated into other monarchies. There has been no other vanishing of so great a power, from the scene of political and military struggle, so quickly and so completely, in the records of our visible past.

The Burial Of Pompeii

Fiction writers have invented many imaginary devices to enable us to move backward or forward in time, and see things as they were at a certain epoch in the past or as they should be at some selected date in the future. H. G. Wells, in *The Time Machine*, was able to set his reader down in any century of several thousand, past or future, that the reader supposedly would find most interesting. Edward Bellamy, in *Looking Backward*, transported his readers to America of the year 2000 A.D. simply by letting his hero go to sleep for something over a hundred years in so hermetically sealed a container that all organic processes were held in a state of complete suspension. And anybody familiar with our so-called "funny papers" knows that this mental changing of the coordinates of time and space is commonplace, though not very convincing, in a dozen hardy perennials among the comic strips.

When we leave the realm of fiction, however, and turn to actual fact, we find that nature accomplishes the same result without resorting to supernatural media or scientific hocus-pocus to tax our credulity. It simply dumps a layer of volcanic ash twenty feet to fifty feet deep on top of a thriving town, so suddenly and unexpectedly that all the daily activity of that town is caught as in a movie still, and then preserves everything beneath this impermeable blanket for eighteen hundred years, or until man is ready to look under the blanket and see what his life was like fifty or sixty generations ago. And with splendid dramatic sense nature selects for this purpose, not just any town at random, but one which is a meeting place of the diverse cultures and traditions that make up the synthetic civilization of a world-wide empire. Accomplishing this at a cost of only two thousand lives and the property of only twenty thousand inhabitants shows an economy of sacrifice for purposes of art seldom equalled by the profligate epic poets.

In the year 79 A.D. Titus, the son of Vespasian, sat on the imperial throne of Rome. The boundaries of the mighty empire had not yet reached their extreme limit. That would come some twenty-five years later, under Trajan, when the rule of Roman governors would extend from the north of what is now England, across all western Europe, northern Africa, and eastern Asia, to that valley of the Tigris and Euphrates which had once been Babylonia. But even now, due to ten magnificent years of organizing ability, honest government, thrift, and common sense on the part of the great Vespasian, both Italy and the provinces were enjoying one of those interludes of peaceful prosperity which almost justified the tyranny that enforced it.

Through both the corrupt and the legitimate tributes of government vast wealth flowed in a steady stream from all the provinces to the governing city of Rome. From this center it spread outward again, in a contrary wave, to purchase the necessities, the conveniences, and the exotic luxuries with which the mistress of the world indulged herself. A rich Roman of the patrician class of this era could be forgiven for believing that the world had been created to cater to his desires. A dozen religions flourished, with real faith in none. Morals were, in fact as well as etymology, only accepted customs and conventions, with little ethical foundation. With a lack of interest in exploration, or invention, or any of the facets of scientific thought, which still amazes our renaissance minds, the upper-class Roman divided his attention between politics and the pursuit of pleasure. And yet the very leisure which tempted to excesses bred a philosophy of restraint. Those who did not have to grab joys today, because they felt secure in the availability of similar joys tomorrow, presently learned to value refinement of taste above conspicuousness of consumption. With the result that Roman architecture, Roman literature, and Roman art, creating almost nothing new for themselves, still absorbed into their pragmatic forms much of the best from the heterogeneous cultures which came under Roman sway.

Pompeii was a very old town, probably settled (by Greek pioneers) in that sixth century B.C. when such similar colonies as Sybaris and Crotona were making a Magna Graecia out of Sicily and Southern Italy. It had remained until the time of Titus as one of the chief nuclei of the Greek tradition which so widely influenced Roman civilization. Because of its beautiful location near the Vesuvian Bay, it had become a resort town where wealthy Romans maintained their "summer" homes. Consequently it had more than its share of philosophers and philosophies; of brothels and gaming houses and taverns; of temples, and theatres, and public baths. The Egyptian influence, in the forefront of that Asiatic mysticism which was now beginning to invade Italian minds, had gained its strongest foothold at Pompeii, with a temple for the worship of Isis. And even some few of the little known sect of "Chrestiani," eventually to conquer the empire and its religions, were found among the slaves and poorer classes of this city of the idle and the rich.

Pompeii nestled at the base of Mt. Vesuvius, a volcano which had been quiescent throughout all historical times. On the 24th of August, in the year 79, this volcano came suddenly and violently to life; and there poured forth from its cone such a torrent of molten lava, and steam and cinders and ashes, with all the accompaniment of earth shakings and flashing lightning amid the horrible daytime darkness, as had seldom if ever been equalled in any closely settled section of the planet. Some chroniclers tell us that a large number of the inhabitants were at the amphiteatre, watching a gladiatorial exhibition, when the first volcanic cap was blown into the sky. Certain it is that the light of the sun was completely cut off by unnatural and all too solid clouds before the Pompeiians could gather their wits for escape. And in the tumult, the confusion, and the merciless continuing rain of cinders which followed, one tenth of the residents were buried, dead or alive, under the almost unbelievable layer of volcanic dust. So were their homes, with meals half served; their bakeshops, with loaves of bread displayed for sale; and their public walls, with thousands of messages scratched on them, as varied as those scrawled on fences or on the walls of railroad stations by our contemporary Americans. Bread, furniture, and walls were left caught as in a plaster cast. Within the last hundred years we have been lifting off that plaster cast and seeing once again the properties of the daily scene on which Vesuvius brought down the curtain.

The First Crusade

Fortunately, we are not writing history. We are, instead, writing only an invitation to the study of history. In selecting the First Crusade as one of the attractions which might encourage an occasional reader to accept this invitation, we do not need, or pretend to, the ability to paint a full background picture as a setting for the event. Nor do we accept responsibility for any completeness in our record of the event itself. Our task and purpose is only to make comments, almost at random, which may stimulate the intellectually curious to open a few history books at the right pages and learn more about this remarkable outburst of human energy. It is a surprising movement, to us looking back on it today. It must have been a great deal more surprising to the hundreds of thousands of Europeans who suddenly found themselves taking part in this militant pilgrimage eight centuries ago.

Far more interesting than the Crusade itself is the conjunction of causes which brought it about. Most important, as a prerequisite, is the fact that by the eleventh century all western Europe was finally and completely Christian, at least in name. The missionary movement started by Pope Gregory five hundred years before, the sword of Charlemagne, and the organizing ability of the Church of Rome, had conquered paganism in Europe during the very centuries when ever new droves of pagans were overrunning and conquering Europe itself. The political value of Christianity to kings of the newly forming nations, as a spiritual cement for their feudal domains, had speeded the universality of acceptance and conversion. As the eleventh century drew to a close the shifting boundaries and allegiances and groupings of the political entities still taking shape out of the wreckage of the western Roman empire seemed to offer no promise of anything but a nightmare for future historians. Attempting to untangle the races and their languages presents the ethnologist with the same nightmarish problem. But the fragments were beginning to shake down into some degree of fixation, nevertheless. And already the people of those territories which would later be known to us as England, Ireland, France, Germany, Italy, Austria, Czecho-Slovakia, Yugoslavia, Rumania, Hungary, Bulgaria and Greece, had one great idea and belief in common. They all worshipped approximately the same God, and they all called him

Christ. And suddenly this sense of brotherhood, transcending their numberless and interminable wars with each other, enabled them to rise in one great common purpose. With the leadership of an Abu Bekr to utilize this force, Christianity might have caused that unification of the known world, in the twelfth century, which Mohammedanism had almost achieved in the seventh.

But there was no one great leader, nor ever, for long, any one great purpose. This needed singleness, in both cases, was largely prevented by the number of different motives which had combined to inspire the movement. Let's look at three or four of them.

During all the centuries while the barbarians were conquering segments of the old empire of Rome, and being conquered in turn by the new religion of Rome, the remaining or eastern part of the imperial inheritance was maintaining continuous rule at Constantinople. The powers and boundaries of this Byzantine Empire varied tremendously from generation to generation; but the tradition of deeprooted glory was unbroken. Here was a monarch sitting on the same throne of the Caesars, once occupied by Augustus, and Marcus Aurelius; once occupied, in fact, by that very emperor Constantine, who had moved the capitol of his empire from Rome to this ancient city of Byzantium, now named for himself. Here was a very real title of *Imperator* which all men would accept, even though the power to support the title had decayed so as to be almost negligible.

But in the last half of the eleventh century it looked for a while as though this flickering candle of empire would be snuffed out altogether. For out of those little known regions between India and the Caspian Sea appeared the armies of the Seljuk Turks. Being orthodox Mohammedans, they merely took over the Caliphate of Bagdad, and its possessions. Then, capturing Armenia, they swept across Asia Minor, won a great battle from the emperor's forces, and seized the fortress of Nicaea almost within shouting distance of Constantinople itself. The emperor, Michael VII, appealed to the pope at Rome, Gregory VII, for assistance. Nothing came of it. But the Turks being still there, the next emperor, Alexius, appealed to the next pope, Urban II, and very much came of it indeed.

These appeals were themselves of the nature of diplomatic bombshells. For the subjects of the emperor were Eastern, or Greek Orthodox, Christians, separated irrevocably by doctrine connected with the word *filioque* (which had been added by Charlemagne to the Nicene creed), from the Western or Roman Church. Each party regarded the other as heretics. So the emperor at Constantinople revealed distressing weakness and fear indeed when he appealed for aid to the Patriarch of Rome. And he thereby breathed an ambition into the mind of the pope to extend his own spiritual sway over most of those Christianized eastern domains which had once looked to Constantinople instead of Rome for their religious leadership — and many of which now looked to neither because they had been overrun by the Mohammedan enemy of both.

For the Seljuk Turks had not only swept across Asia Minor to the very gates of Constantinople. They had also turned southward down the Mediterranean, through Antioch and Damascus, and conquered all of Palestine and Syria from another Islamic power which *they* regarded as heretical in the eyes of true Mohammedans. They had captured Jerusalem in 1073. And whereas the more tolerant Islamic rulers who formerly governed these decadent southern caliphates had permitted Christian pilgrims free access to the places made holy by their religion, the Turks reversed this policy abruptly and completely. And in this circumstance Pope Urban found the material for his propaganda that stirred up a continent.

There was other fuel which contributed to the fire. The rule of Egypt also had recently passed into the hands of more vigorous and intolerant Mohammedans. They and the Seljuk Turks to the north now completely blocked the trade routes to India and China which had been making Genoa and Venice rich. So that the full power of those rising cities was thrown behind any movement to cut away the obstacles to their commerce. The Normans, in huge groups of land pirates, were marauding Italy, and were well pleased to turn their freebooting energies to greener pastures farther east. But all of these ambitions and motives were decently covered under the veil of religious consecration to a Christian cause. The rescue of the Holy Sepulchre of Christ from the hands of brutal infidels was the avowed goal of every prince and the inspiring dream of every peasant in the vast throngs who answered the summons of the church.

We have taken several pages to outline why it happened, just to be able to tell in a very few paragraphs what did happen. For it was the amazing uprising and eastward surge itself, of kings and peoples, that would stir any imagination into wanting to learn more about so unusual and so tremendous an event.

On the 26th of November, 1095, Pope Urban II delivered, to a great council of the church held at Clermont, in southern France, the speech which set off the movement. He appealed for a truce to all wars in Europe until the combined arms of all Christians should wrest Jerusalem from the infidels. Complete penance for all past sins could be accomplished by any Christian, prince or peasant, who sewed the red cross to the garment over his right shoulder, and went forth to battle for the cause. With exultant cries of "God wills it" thousands at once took the cross. And then those who were at Clermont scattered over western Europe to preach the crusade to every castle and camp.

Chief among these preachers was Peter the Hermit, a monk who rode an ass from place to place, telling the peasant multitudes of the brutalities he himself had suffered and seen on a pilgrimage to the Holy Sepulchre. The crusading spirit gathered and spread like a vast conflagration. Urban had set August 15, 1096, as the date when the various hosts should depart from their home sectors, for Constantinople as the great general rendezvous. Four months before that date five large groups of impatient peasants had already collected, and would wait no longer for either leadership or plans. Under such inexperienced or mediocre leaders as took charge, these five groups, all starting from somewhere on the French side of the Rhine, proceeded towards Constantinople by the valley of the Danube River. Three of them were destroyed by pestilence, starvation, and the hostility of the Hungarians and Bulgarians, brought on by the Crusaders' own ignorance and rapacity, before they ever even reached Constantinople. Two groups did reach the city, though with greatly diminished forces. Those remnants united to cross the Bosporus and get themselves promptly and completely destroyed by the Turks. By the last of October, 1096, somewhere from a hundred to two hundred thousand crusaders had perished, and the crusade itself had not yet even started.

But it was a different story when the properly organized hosts finally assembled. For despite the lukewarm support of the Emperor Alexius, the jealousies and personal ambitions of the various princely captains, the lack of any overall leadership, the by-no-means-negligible armies of the

Seljuk Turks, and all the horrors and pestilence of unfamiliar desert countries which they had to conquer and cross, this zealous throng did pour across Asia Minor, defeat Turkish armies, besiege and capture well-fortified cities, stand sieges themselves, and eventually, with some fifty thousand left of their decimated ranks, reach and take Jerusalem itself, on the fifteenth of July, 1099. And on Christmas day, in the year 1100, more than five years after Urban made his great speech at Clermont, a Christian kingdom was formally established, under Baldwin I, with Jerusalem as his capital. The drama of the exploit, so unique in history, so different from the usual process by which new kingdoms are forged or stolen, has produced ten thousand romantic chronicles, permeated all modern thinking about mediaeval times, and far overshadowed the actual results in the minds of even the soberest historians.

The Lindbergh Flight

The best of shows can be ruined by a poor reception. And a mediocre show, with an inadequate cast, can be raised to the level of superb entertainment by the contagion of an enthusiastic audience. So, sometimes, do events gain worldwide importance by public reaction to them rather than through the instrinsic elements of the events themselves. The Lindbergh Flight is probably the oustanding illustration of this process in all the records of mass psychology. Not the flight itself, but the excitement which followed, must already be seeming an exaggerated legend to a younger generation which was not present, and which did not share in the vicarious thrill of the young aviator's triumph.

Professor Alexander Magoun, who wrote one of the early histories of aviation, says that Lindbergh was the sixty-seventh man to fly across the Atlantic Ocean. The factual record, stated thus baldly, falls short of fairness to the achievement. But the public recognition of his flight as the first transatlantic hop is just part of an emotional glorification of the whole affair which went equally far beyond the mark. What Lindbergh did was really great, in itself. But the heroic episode was converted into a chapter of world history by the sheer lasting frenzy of public acclaim.

The Orteig prize offer of twenty-five thousand dollars for the first non-stop flight between New York and Paris had been standing, unclaimed, since 1919. Early in 1927 two brave Frenchmen, Nungesser and Coli, had made the attempt in a westward direction. They had dropped somewhere in the ocean, and were never heard from again. In May, 1927, Lieutenant-Commander Richard E. Byrd and his crew, with their plane, the *America*, were waiting at Roosevelt Field on Long Island for favorable weather, to make the attempt from west to east. So were two other well-known aviators, Clarence Chamberlain and Lloyd Bertaud, with their plane, the *Columbia*. These contestants were suddenly joined by an unheard-of man named Charles A. Lindbergh, twenty-five years old, a handsome young Lochinvar out of the west. He had a plane especially built for the Atlantic trip at the expense of some patriotic citizens of St. Louis, Missouri, who had been willing to sponsor his enterprise. He had just flown this plane solo from the Pacific coast to the Long Island starting point. He proposed to fly it, still alone, in one next hop to Paris.

He did. Early in the morning of May 20, after working all night in a drizzling rain to get ready, Lindbergh took off from Roosevelt Field. He flew all that day, all night, and all the following day. The next evening at a little after ten o'clock, Paris time, and thirty-three hours, thirty minutes, after leaving the ground, he landed at Le Bourget

Field. Such is the story, in a simple statement reduced to bare essentials, of the Lindbergh Flight. But when one American newspaper, weeks later, still gave over one hundred columns of space to Lindbergh in one issue, there must have been a lot of "non-essentials" of surprising interest.

There were. It gradually became borne in on the American people that the flight had been no freak. Young Lindbergh had not only put long and able planning, and painstaking care as to every detail, into preparation of himself and his plane for this flight, but it was his habit to proceed with painstaking care in everything he did. His ability to follow his charted great-circle course from Long Island to Nova Scotia to Newfoundland to Ireland to England to France, through darkness and storms and fog, had shown navigational skill that didn't come by just hoping. His estimates of the fuel his plane would need, of what it could carry, and of what his plane would do, had been based on long mechanical and flying experience. His success had been no accident.

His modest behavior, sense of balance and good taste, and refusal to capitalize his notoriety in the cheap ways the public almost had taken for granted — these were of tremendous importance. The fact that Lindbergh was good-looking and unmarried certainly added a romantic touch to his sudden fame. The dramatic exactness with which he "carried the message to Garcia" with no ifs, ands, or buts — he didn't come down in the channel, *almost* to France, or decide to stop in Newfoundland after all to make his trip safer — fired peoples' imaginations. And there were a dozen other factors, some of Lindbergh's making, some growing out of his character, and many with which he had nothing to do whatever, which contributed to the result. We do not propose to re-examine them here. We leave that interesting pursuit for the reader when he goes after the whole detailed story by some of those who have told it better. But we do wish to inspire this further curiosity on the part of the reader by a synopsis of the almost incredible public reaction.

Long before the young flyer reached France every newspaper in the western world was practically standing by for news of his final success, and observations of his passage over Ireland and England were being relayed over thousands of wires. Forty thousand boxing fans, watching the Maloney-Sharkey fight at the Yankee Stadium the evening before, had risen and stood in silent prayer that this brave yound man, winging his way all alone somewhere over the icebergs in the black night of the north Atlantic, would come through and make his goal. As his plane was picked up by observers once again, some eighteen hours later, with the ground of Ireland under him and his goal in sight, the world almost seemed to hold its breath for news that he had made it. He did make it; the other causes began to contribute to the drama; and Fitzhugh Green was probably right that there was let loose "the greatest torrent of mass emotion ever witnessed in human history."

After Lindbergh had been freed from the dangerously tumultuous welcome of the Parisians assembled at Le Bourget, he was taken to the American Embassy. From that point on we must hit just the very highest of the high spots. Beginning with his first informal appearance on a balcony of the embassy the next noon, before a cheering crowd of Frenchmen, the gatherings, the parades, the banquets, and the speeches in his honor steadily climbed in both volume and official significance until they culminated in the welcomes of Washington and New York some three weeks later. The physical stamina of the young hero, in standing up under such an unceasing barrage of organized attention, seemed almost as remarkable as his spiritual stamina in never losing his head.

After being fêted by the President, the Prime Minister, and almost every dignitary of France, Lindbergh was given an official reception by the city of Paris. Half a million people lined the streets! The King and Queen of Belgium made the most of his one-day visit to Brussels, and then he flew to London. The crowd which greeted him at Croydon Airdrome was so huge that thirteen hundred policemen especially selected to maintain order were lost as though they had been "dropped in the middle of the ocean." He visited the King and Queen and Prime Minister, had tea at the House of Commons, went with the Prince of Wales to the Derby Eve Ball, saw the great Derby race from a royal box, and wound up his banquets with one given him by the combined American societies of London. He flew back to Paris for one day, and then to Cherbourg, to board the U.S. Cruiser *Memphis* which President Coolidge had sent especially to bring him and his plane home. He came home, as has been observed by Green, to probably the greatest welcome any man in history has ever received, not excepting all the crowned Caesars and Napoleons who made triumphs part of their stock in trade.

A convoy of four destroyers, two army blimps, and forty airplanes (a lot of planes in 1927) met the *Memphis* as she steamed up Chesapeake Bay late in the afternoon of June 10. And the next day pandemonium broke loose in Washington. Lindbergh was greeted at the gangplank by a large group of cabinet officers and other notables. There was a huge parade which finally landed him on a high stand erected near the Washington Monument, where President and Mrs. Coolidge were waiting. The laudatory speech of the President was quite long for the laconic Coolidge; the simple two-paragraph reply of Lindbergh went far to increase his stature as the ambassador of international goodwill which he was now regarded as being — by millions who three weeks before had looked on him only as a stunt flyer. There followed official dinners, and medals, and honors such as probably no other man has ever received in so short a space of time.

In a few more days the welcome home reached its *crescendo* movement in the reception in New York. For the parade from the Battery to Central Park between three and four million people lined the streets. The houses were so deserted that special instructions were issued to all citizens for protection against thieves. Fifty-five thousand telegrams of congratulation, one of them with 17,500 signatures, were hauled along as part of the parade. And the snowstorm of confetti, tossed out of office windows as a part of the greeting, was found by the street cleaning department to weigh *eighteen hundred tons*!

There are many other details about the phenomenon which are fascinating, and statistics which are amazing. The amount of mail which he received reached such staggering proportions that we doubt if tens of thousands of the envelopes have ever been opened, to this day. At one dinner given the flyer by the city of New York there were four thousand diners. Among the fabulous business offers turned down by Lindbergh was one for seven hundred thousand dollars to appear in the films, and another, for $2,500,000.00(!) for a tour around the world by air.

There was certainly considerable permanent significance in the flight, in the impetus given to aviation. There was certainly a sudden feeling everywhere that the world had become a much smaller place; the one-world consciousness was almost born in those last two weeks of May, 1927. And a volume could be written on the psychological effect

The Romance Of History

of the flight and its repercussions on the domestic American scene. But analysis of such significances is beyond our scope here — as well as beyond our ability — and a further cataloguing of disconnected notes might serve to detract from rather than increase a desire to read the whole story in fuller narrative form. And what we really wish is to encourage such a desire. For here is one of those historical incidents which, when the pages of history seem to be becoming monotonous and dry, suddenly refresh us with drama, romance, and inspiration.

It would be unfair to the hypothetical one percent of the public which is more interested in ideas than in persons or events for us to close this section without extending our invitation to include them also. For the birth, growth, and ramifications of ideas could be used as a framework, on which to hang the flesh of history, just as sensibly as the schedule of reigns and wars and revolutions which is now generally used.

But the invitation will have to be less circumstantial than the two which have preceded it because of my limitations in authorship. It would be easy enough to follow the same pattern of selection as used above. We would take some six or eight mental conceptions which have emerged or re-emerged into the interplay of human thought at reasonably definable dates. They might be, for instance, such diverse ideas as those most readily identified by the following words or phrases: Utopia, totalitarianism, predestination, free and equal, greatest good for the greatest number, and evolution. And we would focus our attention on each of these ideas singly, its birth, development, and final influence, with both events and personalities treated as purely incidental to this exposition.

We would find the first dream of an imaginary state,

ideally governed, making its earliest appearance in the stream of human thought during the first half of the fourth century B.C., in the form of Plato's *Republic*. Then there would be no resurgence of the mirage until the sixteenth century when the title book of the *genre*, More's *Utopia* itself, was published. From that time on there has been a plethora of variations on the theme, including Bacon's *New Atlantis*, Rousseau's *Social Contract*, Campanella's *City Of The Sun*, and Bellamy's *Looking Backward*.

In our cursory examination of the theory and practice of totalitarianism we would begin with Sparta and end with contemporary Russia.

Although we could find a philosophic background for predestination in the determinism of some Greek and even earlier thinkers, it was Calvin who first made the thesis a religious force, with intense impact on the lives and thinking of millions of ordinary men. Beginning with Calvin, therefore, in the sixteenth century, we would have to go backward through the Arabians and forward through the most materialistic monists to suggest the paths down which this thought should be pursued.

Credit or blame for the political conception of simultaneous freedom and equality among men must go to the eighteenth century. It found expression in "*Liberté, égalité, fraternité*," and the preamble to the American Declaration of Independence, "all men are created free and equal." Our job would consist mostly of tracing the idea forward from the time of the French liberals who undermined the *Ancien Régime*.

The ideal of "the greatest good for the greatest number," as the object of all social and governmental activity, was almost an invented creation of a small group of Utilitarian thinkers, led by James Mill, Jeremy Ben-

The Romance Of History

tham, and John Stuart Mill. It would be perhaps the least troublesome of the six to confine within some plausible boundaries of discussion.

With the last idea we obviously could start with its narrower subdivision, organic evolution, and the work of Darwin and Huxley in the nineteenth century. But here again, for even a synoptic suggestion of the history of evolution, we should have to jump all the way back to Anaximander in the sixth century before Christ, and then go forward from Darwin through Spencer and Spengler and the mathematical physicists, to indicate the growth of this idea of evolution until it has come to be all-comprehensive — covering the origin and development alike of the mightiest stars, the smallest amoebae, and the cyclic social organisms into which both recurrently assemble.

But to do more than point a finger at these, or at any six similar offspring of the human brain, would require a knowledge which I do not have and an amount of research I am in no position to undertake. And we can make our point clear without it. It is customary for any of us to go to the pages of history to read as much as we may wish about a particular person. It is equally natural for us to take a certain event as the center of our temporary interest, and to confine our reading to those books, chapters, or pages which will satisfy our curiosity about that event. Intellectual curiosity concerning an idea, sufficient to drive us to look up and study the "biographical" material on that idea, is somewhat more rare — and undoubtedly requires considerably more work and patience to satisfy. But the pleasure of the hunt is often exactly proportional to the elusiveness and stamina of the quarry. And a reading of history from this point of view can make many otherwise dry pages become part of a thrilling picture.

Any invitation is incomplete without the address to which the guest is invited. We may well close this invitation to a reading of history, therefore, with a few comments on where history is to be found. Its formal address, of course, is in those ponderous textbooks, used in schools and colleges, which usually have the word *history* in some phrase or combination of words on the cover which serves as a door. But like many another host, history is more charming and more fun to visit when caught in its less formal and less stately places of abode. In biography, historical novel, poem, and play history loses that monotony of repetition which can sometimes become wearisome in its textbook presentation. Granting that the general chronological thread of the centuries must be grasped, at whatever effort, as a background against which to visualize a particular person, event, or thought, then a delving into details concerning any such particular object of interest will be both more entertaining and more instructive if the mind is allowed to focus on the object as a whole in itself.

Let's try once more to attain greater clearness by using illustration and example. We are sure that any good biography of Nero will leave the reader with a more lasting knowledge of the affairs and events of the Roman Empire in the days of the early Caesars than twice as many pages of formal history of the first century A.D. Charles Kingsley's *Hypatia* is easier reading for most of us than Gibbon's *Decline And Fall Of The Roman Empire*. For at least one tableau of that decline and fall it will leave a firmer imprint on the mind. And Dickens' *Tale Of Two Cities* is every bit as good, for an understanding of what the French Revolution was like to those living through it, as Carlyle's history. For my own part, I confess to having learned a great deal more about our war with Mexico, the northern opposition to this war, and its importance in widening the rift between the two sections of our country, from Lowell's verses which are called, collectively, *The Biglow Papers*, than I ever did from any American history book. And certainly it is more fun to read Shakespeare's plays than it is to memorize the sequence of the Plantagenet kings.

Don't try to take your history straight; at least, not as a steady diet, and unless you have a strong stomach long accustomed to it. You will absorb just as much in the long run by taking a lot of it diluted into historical highballs. You will derive a great deal more pleasure in the process. And the only purpose of reading history that we are talking about here, we repeat once more for final emphasis, is the pleasure of yourself, the reader.

CHAPTER VII

The Romance Of Mathematics

The attitude of many of my readers towards mathematics is undoubtedly that they tried it once and didn't like it. It is chiefly for such readers that mathematics has been chosen as one of our examples for discussion, and that this chapter is being written. If you are one of those who shuts his ears and runs the other way whenever x's and y's get into the conversation, forget your prejudice and bear with us for a few pages, while we try to distill into simple terms the basic conceptions of arithmetic, algebra, geometry, trigonometry, analytical geometry, and the calculus. We'll pause for station announcements now and then, and you can turn me off whenever you feel so inclined.

Mathematics began, and begins, with numbers. The first mathematician was the first savage who was able to tell his companions, not just that he had seen bear, but that he had seen *one* bear or two bears or *many* bears. Note that any number beyond two is still just "many." It was probably long generations after our ancestors learned to count to two before they achieved higher numbers. That is, before they were able to break down the "many" above two into separate exact quantities such as three or four or seven. After a while arrived the next great step. With the aid of the fingers as a guide, it became a common accomplishment to enumerate objects up to ten.

In some early tribes, by using the toes as well as the fingers for markers, the savage obtained a sequence up to twenty, before reaching a jumping-off place or having to start over. A trace of this custom is still preserved in the French language, wherein some of the jumps from zero to a hundred are by twenties instead of by tens; seventy-three being expressed as sixty and thirteen, for instance; eighty being *quatre-vingts*, or four twenties; and ninety-six being given as four twenties and sixteen. This lasting record of counting by twenties reaches back through the Mediterranean migrations to primeval clans, undoubtedly Asiatic and probably beyond the ken of historical research. But it is of provocative interest to find that the Mayas of Central America, in an entirely independent culture flourishing around the first centuries of our era, also used twenty as a base in their highly developed system of numeration.

But after great-grandfather stopped using his feet for grasping branches in trees, he gradually stopped using them for practically everything else except the newly discovered art of walking. The phylogenetic recapitulation of our biological history, which takes place in every individual, shows that at the stage paralleled by babies and small children, early man could still count his toes comfortably by touching them — or even put them in his mouth if he wished to do so; but that he lost this limberness as he acquired erectness, in the course of further development. Until today, when millions of childlike peoples still count on their fingers, the poor toes have lost all convenient usefulness for that purpose.

So running out of fingers sharply limited progress. And higher mathematics for the caveman was the tabulation of things more than ten as ten and one or ten and two or six and ten (sixteen) or two tens (twenty) or four tens and seven (forty-seven). Though in time, because of the

The Romance Of Mathematics

importance of the moon in Mr. Caveman's cosmic reflections, and the constant counting up to twelve moons between the repetition of the seasons, separate names were evolved for one and ten, and two and ten; so that eleven and twelve do not reveal in their present form the mental worksheets by which they were arrived at, as do the numbers immediately above twelve. And as a group quantity, whereby to measure the numerical extent of other aggregations, the unit twelve has been used almost as much even in historical times as the unit ten. The dozen and the gross, or dozen-dozen, is still the most familiar standard, by which to appraise the quantity of goods bought and sold, for huge segments of the global population not yet inundated by the flood of the metric system.

In passing we should also mention that the ancient Sumerians, founders of the first Babylonian empire, used sixty as a base. The reason is unknown but possibly was connected with sixty being the lowest number divisible by both ten and twelve. We have inherited from this source the result, more than five thousand years later, that an hour is divided into sixty minutes and a circle into six times sixty or 360 degrees.

But that's getting far ahead of our story. For as soon as men began to count to any distance at all, and to deal with the numbers which counting added to their mental equipment, the smarter ones began to find ways to combine and separate these numbers, in such manner as to depict faithfully the combination and separation of the sheep or arrows or skins which the numbers represented. And thus in time were evolved those fundamental mathematical tools of addition, subtraction, multiplication, and division with which the modern mathematical sciences have been built. The subdivision of these sciences which still deals with numbers, their manipulation and the relations between them, is known as arithmetic.

The mere idea of abstract numbers, representing tangible things, was enough of a strain on the intellects of our bronze-age forefathers. But in time this mental accomplishment became routine, and there came generations which could tackle the next great problem, of dealing abstractly with *unknown* numbers. Let's illustrate the difference.

A father gives his daughter eighty sheep as a dowry, on condition that the groom supply one-fourth as many. To determine that the groom's contribution is twenty sheep, add this to the eighty, and find that the new flock will consist of one hundred sheep, requires only simple arithmetic.

But suppose the prospective husband announces in advance that he would like to have a flock of one hundred sheep, and the bride's father says: "All right, you contribute your share, and whatever number you supply I'll contribute three times as many, so that the total will make a hundred sheep." Then, unless the problem is solved by trial and error, the higher mathematician of the family (probably the son who will not tend sheep) must reason something like this: "If we take the groom's contribution plus three times the groom's contribution we have four lots equal to the groom's contribution; and these four lots together must be equal to one hundred; hence one such lot, or the groom's contribution, must be equal to one hundred divided by four, or twenty-five; and the father's contribution would consist of three times twenty-five, or seventy-five sheep."

A problem mathematically similar to the above was solved in an Egyptian papyrus dating back to about 1700 B.C. This is, of course, algebra without the benefit of

The Romance Of Mathematics

modern symbols. For basically algebra is simply a method of dealing with an unknown quantity as if it were a known quantity. By establishing the relationships of this unknown with the quantities which are known, and usually by putting these relationships in the form of equations, we are able to find the value of the unknown quantity itself.

We eliminate a great deal of phraseology, and simplify the process materially, by giving the unknown quantity, such as "the groom's contribution," some simpler name, such as x. In our handling of problems like that of Ahmes the Egyptian we would say:

Let x equal the groom's contribution
Then $3x$ equals the father's contribution
Then x plus $3x$, or $4x$ equals the desired total
   of one hundred sheep
$4x = 100$
$x = 25$

Even in such a humble effort as the above we have applied addition, multiplication, and division to an unknown quantity, merely by giving it an identifying symbol. There are, of course, many combinations and specialized forms of the four elementary arithmetical tools. Some of them are known to every school boy, as factoring, getting squares or square roots, or a dozen ways of manipulating and simplifying fractions. The mathematical gropers long ago proceeded to apply all such operations, also, to these algebraic symbols. For it became obvious that almost anything you can do, or know how to do, with numbers, you can also do with an unknown number if you'll just give it a fictitious name like x and go ahead.

One more step completed the foundation of the whole body of processes and theorems which we classify as algebra. Somehow the story comes to mind of the sailor who not only had his little black book of telephone numbers for each port, but had a little red book in which all of his little black books were indexed. The analogy will not stand scrutiny. But algebra not only supplies a means for finding out an unknown quantity, when surrounded by a lot of known quantities; it supplies a great deal of information about unknown quantities in general, without regard to the particular set of facts in which any particular unknown quantity is going to appear.

For by constant use and manipulation of a symbol like x, to represent some quantity whose value was wanted, the mathematicians early discovered that it didn't make any difference whether the x was a nickname for some "groom's contribution" they were temporarily seeking, or stood for any unknown quantity in general. They could work out rules and formulas about it as a generalization, without regard to the particular numbers it might eventually prove to represent in specific problems and applications. By using y and z and other symbols as well as x, they could even deal with two or three or more unknowns at once; though, as in the case of the sailor who might take out two or three or more of his "telephone numbers" at one time, their difficulties did increase considerably with the number of unknowns in tow.

These symbols for unknown quantities are called *variables*, because their ultimate values vary with the conditions in which they are involved. And letting algebra remain monogamously faithful to one variable, for the minute, it so happens that a vast number of everyday problems, most easily solved by algebraic methods, eventually settle into an equation of the form $ax^2 + bx + c = 0$; where a and b and c are the known quantities of the particular situation, but x is the unknown which is causing all the turmoil. So without worrying in the least what numbers may be designated by a and b and c, or what x represents, the algebraists go to work on this statement of affairs, which is known as the general quadratic equation. They first write the equation as $ax^2 + bx = -c$; then divide both sides by a to get

$$x^2 + \frac{bx}{a} = -\frac{c}{a} \; ; \qquad \text{then add} \quad \frac{b^2}{4a^2}$$

to both parts of the equation so as to make the left hand side a perfect square; and then take the square root of both sides, to come out with

$$x + \frac{b}{2a} = \sqrt{\frac{b^2}{4a^2} - \frac{c}{a}}.$$

A little further legitimate juggling reduces this to

$$x = \frac{-b \pm \sqrt{b^2 - 4ac}}{2a}.$$

And we have a value for our unknown friend, x, which will hold, no matter what actual numbers $a, b, \text{and } c$ may turn out to be, or from what set of circumstances the original equation $ax^2 + bx + c = 0$ may have come.

Such algebraic generalizations are usually called formulas. Their use is much older than the symbols which we associate with modern algebra. The Babylonians had established many such formulas several hundred years before the date of the Egyptian papyrus already mentioned. One surprising accomplishment of these Babylonian mathematicians was in dealing with what we call cubic equations; that is, equations such as $ax^3 + bx^2 + cx + d = 0$, and which are not subject to any useful general solution like that above for the general quadratic or second-degree equation. They regularly transformed their cubic equations into the arrangement $x^3 + x^2 = r$, which is more readily handled than any other form through tables of values for r which give corresponding values for x; and they constructed lengthy tables for just that purpose.

Let's look at one more illustration, this time in the domestication of two variables. In trying to connect what we do know with what we do not know, in various situations calling for the application of algebra, it is frequently most convenient to give fictitious names to two or more unknowns, instead of just one. And in the equations, which our assimilation of the facts then produces, we frequently find such combinations as $(x + y)^3$, or the sum of these two variables to the fourth or fifth or some other power. For the low powers it is easy enough to find out what these expansions come to, simply by multiplying them out. But if we needed to know only the seventeenth term, for instance, of $(x + y)^{24}$, it would require all the labor of multiplying $x + y$ by itself, and then the result by $x + y$, and so on for twenty-three times before we could put the result down and pick out the wanted term in this colossal aggregation. So no less an authority than Isaac Newton did all the work in advance, for all future mathematicians and all situations, by taking $(x + y)$ to any unknown power n, and proving that the successive terms of $(x + y)^n$ would always read

$$x^n + nx^{n-1}y + \frac{n(n-1)}{1\cdot 2} x^{n-2}y^2 + \frac{n(n-1)(n-2)}{1\cdot 2 \cdot 3} x^{n-3}y^3 \ldots$$

and so on for as many terms as you wanted, or as the size of a particular n permitted. The dots in the denominators mean simply "multiplied by," as in one times two times three. Still this formula looks forbidding and ferocious, but will always wind up with y^n; and it becomes quite tractable as soon as some actual number is substituted for *n*. It is known as the binomial theorem, or the theorem of binomial expansion. *Bi* means two, *nomial* is from the Latin *nomen*, for name. The formula is applicable to sums of *two* unknowns, two of those fictitious names representing we don't know what, but which we go ahead and work with exactly as if we did.

We haven't room, of course, to give any survey of even elementary algebra. We are trying, instead, to suggest what algebra is about and what it tries to do. This we can summarize by saying that algebra is simply arithmetic applied to unknown quantities, to their manipulation and to the relations between them. Generally speaking, logic has proved and experience has verified that the same rules and processes which hold true for dealing with known numbers in arithmetic will also hold for dealing with unknown numbers in the generalizations which are known as algebra.

While the name algebra comes simply from an Arabian treatise on the subject, written in the ninth century, the name geometry conveys in itself something of its own history. It comes from Greek words meaning a measuring of the earth's surface. Following a statement of Herodotus, the science has usually been considered as an Egyptian invention, mothered by the necessity of resetting boundaries annually after the floods of the Nile.

But Herodotus is frequently more interesting than accurate. When he weighed the various conjectures of the ancients as to what caused those puzzling rises of the great river every summer, he discarded, as the most fantastic and implausible of all, a suggestion that the water came from melting snows far up the river, in the unvisited lands of its source. The conclusion he actually reached was that the sun, by treating the Nile unfairly and hanging around that part of the heavens in the winter time, drew up more water from the Nile during the winter, than from other rivers in other countries, and caused it to run unduly low; whereas in the summer time the sun got busy and drew water from all rivers alike so that the Nile could maintain its natural high level. This was made all the more obvious, according to Herodotus, because the Nile didn't get its waters from rain or snow, as other rivers did, but had to work with a rather bountiful but fixed supply which nature had somehow provided it in the first place.

This digression on Herodotus' lack of perspicacity in scientific matters has seemed worth inserting here, in paragraphs concerned with the beginnings of geometry, to help set the record straight. We know now that the ancient Babylonians had a knowledge of the subject both wider and older than that of the Egyptians. It's true that we have Herodotus' claim to have traveled extensively in Babylonia, his obvious total ignorance of any Babylonian advances in geometry, and his positive statement on behalf of an Egyptian origin of the science. But his authority in this connection can still be brushed aside with a smile when we hold in our very hands the Chaldean clay tablets which refute him. Some of these tablets were already two thousand years old when Herodotus was writing his great history.

It's undoubtedly true, nevertheless, that geometry arose as the measurement of land surfaces. The area of a square plot, or the length of the sides required to enclose a square plot of a given area, must have been one of the earliest problems tackled and solved by the Sumerian wise men. Then came similar achievements with regard to rectangular fields, fields in the shape of right triangles, and eventually polygonal fields of various shapes and numbers of sides.

The Romance Of Mathematics

But the amount of earth needed to build ramparts of certain dimensions, or the depth and width and length of irrigation ditches to hold a certain volume of water, and the size of granaries to contain a given quantity of harvest; these and like practical problems raised geometry from its identity with surveying as rapidly as men's minds could conceive of solving such puzzles other than by the empirical method of trial and error. Until in time the answers were given, not just for specific cases, with known numerical values to work on, but for general cases, where the sides of the triangle or the height of the cylindrical granary were expressed in algebraic unknowns, and the required results were ready at hand for all triangles of whatever dimensions might be applied.

In fact, the practical need for formulas, to take care of the physical problems of civilized existence, frequently caused the *use* of geometry to run far ahead of geometry itself. Consider, for instance, what Professor Bell has called the greatest Egyptian pyramid. It was a purely imaginary pyramid, with a square base, each side of which was a feet long. This imaginary pyramid was cut off by an imaginary plane, parallel to the base, so that the height of the frustum was h feet. The flat top would of course be a square, like the base, but smaller; say with each side b feet long. The volume of such a truncated pyramid, $\frac{1}{3} h(a^2 + ab + b^2)$, was correctly given by some Egyptian genius in about 1850 B.C. But he certainly didn't work this result out mathematically, or prove it except by testing. For the mathematicians never were able to prove it until they could use integral calculus, which arrived on the scene almost four thousand years later. Maybe the Nilotic seer just dreamed this formula in his sleep; but asleep or awake he brought forth a remarkable — and useful — achievement.

Another illustration of the same point is concerned with the Great (and very real) Pyramid of Egypt. When Thales of Miletus was visiting the land of the Nile in the sixth century B.C., his natural curiosity about everything was directed to the height of this huge pile of masonry. So he measured the length of the shadow which the pyramid made at a certain hour of the afternoon, and the length of the shadow made by his upright staff at the same time. By the "obvious" properties of similar triangles, the height of the pyramid was to its shadow as the height of his staff was to *its* shadow; and hence, with the other three facts all known, it was easy enough for Thales to determine the altitude of Cheops' masterpiece. But the first recorded *proof*, or geometrical demonstration, of this equality of ratios between the respective sides of triangles with equal angles did not come until supplied by the followers of Pythagoras about a century later.

This question of proof is worth all the candle we have burned to illuminate it, because it leads us naturally to a clearer understanding of what geometry *is*, and to the distinction between this branch of mathematics and the other branches which we have glanced at so far. Arithmetic deals with known numbers. Algebra deals with symbols representing numbers, and it doesn't make any difference whether they are known or not. But pure geometry deals not with numbers at all, but with *forms*. And whereas the algebraic symbols are but products of man's imagination, or shadows representing substance, the forms of geometry have reality in themselves, and are not dependent for meaning on the fact that they may sometimes be assigned numerical measurements. These forms have certain properties, intrinsic within them, or in their relations to other forms, which are just as real and permanent as the fact that two plus three equals five, but which are not dependent even ultimately on numerical interpretation. With geometry the mathematician acquired entirely new building blocks, besides his old numbers, with which to work and play.

We use "geometric" properties and relationships in every department of human thinking and activity. A circle — any circle, anywhere — has a circumference on which every point is the same distance from one fixed point known as the center. When two straight lines intersect, the angles directly opposite each other at the intersection are always equal. In any right triangle, if we erect a square on each side of the triangle, the surface of the square on the hypotenuse will be equal in area to the sum of the squares on the other two sides. If we take a rectangle and revolve it around one side as an axis we get a "right circular cylinder" or, in plain language, an upright drum. (It might be a tiny shell case, or an oil tank fifty feet high.) If we revolve a right triangle about its altitude as an axis, we get a right cone. Among the properties of such a cone are the fact that its volume is equal to one-third the height times the area of the base; that if you cut across it with a sheet parallel to the base, you get a circle; slant the cutting sheet up or down a bit and you get an ellipse; cut through the cone with a sheet parallel to the altitude and you get a curve known as the hyperbola; with a sheet parallel to one of the slanting sides, you get a parabola; and no matter where or how you cut the cone, with a plane surface, the intersection made by the surface of the cone and the surface of the plane will be one of these figures. The discovery and *proof* of these relationships is part of the business of geometry.

So long as we stick to the forms made by lines, whether curved or straight, on a plane surface — such as this sheet of paper — our work is called *plane geometry*. When we put these lines on the surface of a ball, as of the earth, we have a somewhat more difficult pastime known as *spherical geometry*. When we deal with the forms or solids made by the movement (real or imagined) of surfaces, our field is classified as *solid geometry*. When we get into the mathematics of relativity, dealing with "curved" space (not just curved surfaces), and manifolds of four or more dimensions, we have what Professor Kasner calls "assorted geometries, plain and fancy." But plain or fancy, elementary or advanced, geometry is still a study of the relationships and properties of the forms taken — or which might be taken — by the material phenomena of the universe.

CHAPTER VIII

More Mathematics

Since this book is not billed as an outline of mathematics, or of anything else, it seems better to interrupt the current lecture for a moment and restate our purpose. Our intention is simply to take the wraps off a few random wares, in the museum of formal knowledge, for the inspection of those who have not visited the museum too frequently in the past, or who have been accustomed to spending all of their time in just one particular wing. Having strayed into the mathematics section, in our self-appointed role as guide, we can't very well leave the room without commenting on the three or four more exhibits which are gathered around the entrance. Such comments are not designed to be comprehensive nor scholarly, but merely to stimulate a desire, on the part of our little audience, to visit the same room again, to return with more leisure and better guides to a more detailed scrutiny of the material which it contains. For this reason our remarks concerning even the masterpieces will be casual and brief, lest he who reads may run.

Trigonometry is somewhat like the boy who wanted to be a professional ball player, was trained by his parents to be a preacher, and wound up as bookkeeper in a bank. Out of the ancient need for positional astronomy — to aid navigation, calendar reckoning, and the less legitimate

FIGURE 1

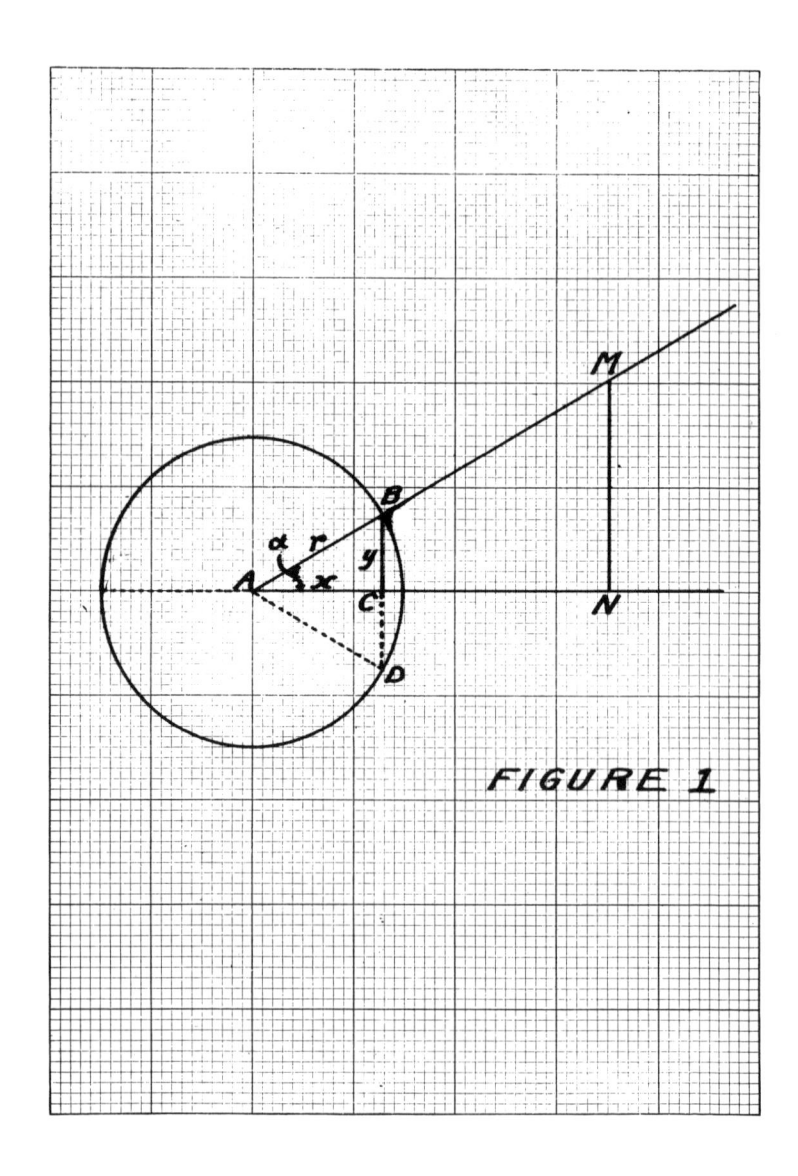

More Mathematics

purposes of astrology — came the necessity for measuring angles. While the word trigonometry means literally "the measurement of triangles," it is, like a politician, concerned chiefly with the angles. And because this early measurement of angles was determined from or in connection with the earth's surface, it was spherical trigonometry, strange to say, which first came out of swaddling clothes and began to perform chores around the mathematical household.

But surveying and architecture required the measurement of angles. too. And whereas our dependence on positional astronomy has steadily declined in modern times, the expanding arts of surveying and of building have increasingly helped to create our present civilization. While the earth's surface is round for the astronomer, it's usually flat so far as the surveyor is concerned, for areas of a size that are in his province. As to the architect, he doesn't care whether it's round or flat, so long as it doesn't wabble under his buildings. *Plane trigonometry*, therefore, or the measurement of angles between lines on a plane surface, became immeasurably more important than spherical trigonometry. So let's draw an angle, and see what the trigonometrician talks about. It will only hurt for a minute.

In Figure 1, above, consider at first just the two lines *AM* and *AN*, and the angle between them, which we shall call *alpha*. We can, of course, define the size of α as so many degrees (out of 360° representing a complete turn around the point *A*). But there is also another way of expressing the magnitude of this angle. For it is easily shown by geometry that no matter where we draw a perpendicular, such as *BC* or *MN*, from one line to the other, the ratio of that perpendicular to the hypotenuse of the triangle which it completes is always the same. Only if we widened or closed the angle between AM and AN would we change this ratio. In other words, the ratio of the distance we have labeled y to the distance we have labeled r indicates or measures one angle and one angle only. In trigonometry we give this ratio a name, the *sine* of the angle.

In fact it is easy to see — and to prove — that the ratios of all three of these distances, y, x and r, to each other remain constant for any angle, α, no matter where we put the perpendicular which we have measured as y. So we give the ratio of x over r the name of *cosine*; the ratios represented by $\frac{y}{x}, \frac{r}{y}, \frac{r}{x},$ and $\frac{x}{y}$ are known respectively as the tangent, cosecant, secant and cotangent. All six of these ratios constitute the *trigonometric functions,* and are the stuff with which trigonometry deals.

The first of these functions to become a mathematical tool was the *sine*, the ratio of the opposite side to the hypotenuse. (In early development y was actually thought of as the *half chord*, or one half of the secant, BD, subtended by the angle 2α, and that conception still enters trigonometric operations in many ways. But we'll have to skip it here.) Now if BAD happens to be a triangle with all sides equal, it is obvious that y is one half as long as r. The ratio of $\frac{y}{r}$ is then $\frac{1}{2}$, or 0.50. The angle, thus determined, as easily shown by geometry, is 30°. But the point is, every possible angle will have some numerical ratio as its *sine*; and every numerical ratio, from 0 to 1, will be the *sine* of some one corresponding angle. As far back as the second century A.D. one Hipparchus, a Greek mathematician of Rhodes, constructed a rudimentary table of *sines*, whereby the angle could be looked up once this ratio was known, and vice versa. Such tables, for all angles down to the fractions of a degree known as minutes and the fractions of minutes known as seconds, with the ratios extended to four or five decimal places, and for all the other five trigonometric functions as well as the *sine,* are today part of the equipment of every schoolboy studying this branch of mathematics.

The direct use of these fixed ratios is still of tremendous importance in a hundred subdivisions of the physical sciences. If we know, for instance, the length of any two sides of any triangle, and the magnitude of the angle between them (through knowing, let us say, the value of its *sine*), then there are simple formulas ready at hand by which to get at the length of the other side, or the magnitude of either of the other angles, or almost anything in reason we might ever want to know about that triangle, from its area to the radius of the circle constructed through its apexes. And this usefulness, representing the contribution of trigonometry in its adolescent stage, is about what the average college student learns to regard as the essence of the subject. We need to look a little further, however, to find wherein lies the greatest dependence of mathematicians on trigonometry today.

We have to go back to algebra a minute, and give meaning to the term *function.* Consider the short story, $y = x^2$. In such a statement of affairs, if x is 1, y also is 1; if x equals 2, y equals 4. We can easily set up a whole table of corresponding values, such as $x = \frac{1}{2}$, $y = \frac{1}{4}$; $x = -1$, $y = 1$; $x = 10$, $y = 100$; and so on for as complete a table as we wish to make. In this equation y is dependent for its value on whatever value or number we assign to x; or in the algebraist's phraseology, y is said to be a *function* of x.

Now we found that we got mixed up with x's and y's in the first place because we had unknown quantities which we could juggle more easily by giving them names. And the algebraists learned in time that they could greatly simplify their juggling, in some cases, by the choice of names for particular unknowns. If they knew in advance, for instance, that a certain unknown quantity would eventually prove to be a perfect square — even though they didn't know what it would be — they might call that unknown x^2 instead of x from the very beginning, and proceed accordingly. Or if the unknown entity was really a difference between two separate unknown entities, they might call it $y - z$, instead of simply x, if such identification would be more convenient for the work to be performed.

As a knowledge of trigonometry became the common property of mathematicians, it was discovered that when the unknown to be dealt with was the ratio between two lengths — as between the height of a pole and the length of the guy rope to support it, for an easy illustration — there were advantages in expressing this unknown not as x, but as the *sine* of x. For whenever the angle x, between the guy rope and the ground, might then be determined, the ratio which they were seeking would be determined at the same time. So they called such an unknown *sin x*, and went on about their algebraic business. After a while adding and multiplying *sin x* and *cos y* (the *cosine* of y), and working out equations containing intricate combinations of these quantities — which were unknown, but could always be recognized as ratios — became as common as similar manipulations with x and y themselves. So that the very name, trigonometric functions, derives from the employment of these terms for this purpose.

Then came a peculiar and unexpected result. Not only did this choice of trigonometric terms to express unknowns prove time-saving for many operations; it enabled the mathematical gentlemen to solve problems and work out generalities which were utterly impossible with the plainer algebraic symbols. We get into waters a little too deep and too rough for this boat, to try to show why this is so. But the function $y = \sin x$, just to suggest an idea, is the simplest periodic function. In plain (and inaccurate) language, the darn thing just repeats itself over and over as we continue assigning values to x. *Sin x* and its complementary partner, *cos x*, constitute a set of what is known as orthogonal functions. Instead of expounding what orthogonal functions are I'll adopt the policy of a teacher I once had who, whenever anybody in the class asked a question she couldn't answer, replied that the class was not far enough advanced for that yet — and you can draw your own conclusions. But because of such helpful properties, these succinct expressions of trigonometric values have become indispensable in numberless mathematical enterprises not even remotely concerned with the solution of triangles. And trigonometry, becoming no more than a system of names for ratios, finds therein its greatest importance.

Analytical geometry is the connecting link between mathematics built on numbers (arithmetic and algebra) and mathematics built on forms (geometry). If that sounds like a mouthful, let's try taking it in a few small bites.

There are many ways of telling the same story. In plain English and arithmetic, we can say that the afternoon sun has reached a point where a man — or any other upright object — is one half as long as his shadow. Telling this story through an algebraic function, we would say that $y = \frac{1}{2}x$, where y is the height of any object, tall or low, and x is the length of its shadow. In the language of trigonometry we would say that the tangent of *alpha* equals $\frac{1}{2}$; or, $\tan \alpha = \frac{1}{2}$, where α is the angle made by the sun's rays with the surface of the earth. The French philosopher and scientist, René Descartes, invented a way to say the same

$y = \frac{1}{2}x$

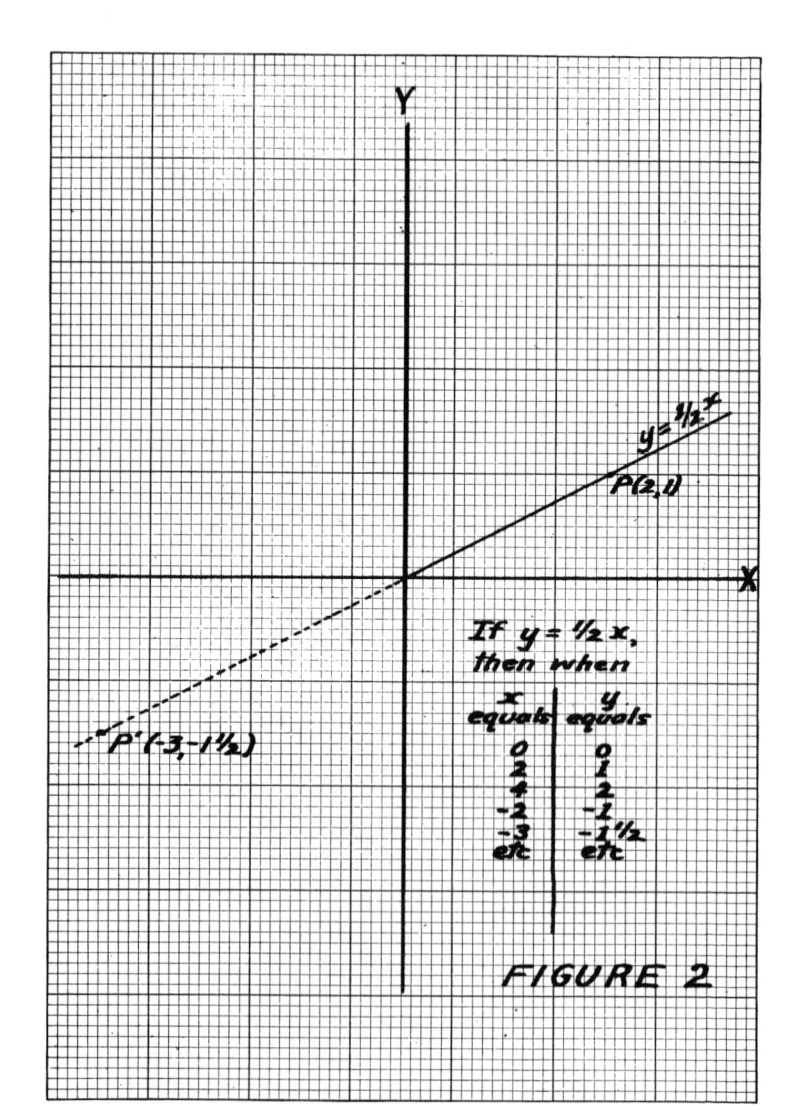

P(2,1)

P'(-3,-1½)

If $y = \frac{1}{2}x$, then when

x equals	y equals
0	0
2	1
4	2
-2	-1
-3	-1½
etc	etc

FIGURE 2

thing by geometry. Pure geometry does not depend, for the validity of its theorems, on numbers or the assignment of measured sizes to its forms at all. But Descartes abandoned the Greek distaste, or even horror, which had prevailed for two thousand years, of associating numbers and metrical divisions with the propositions of geometry; and showed that, by making geometric lines, surfaces, and volumes consist of repeated units of measurement, geometry could be made to tell any story that could be expressed in an algebraic equation. What's more, Cartesian geometry not only tells the same story as algebra with equal precision and comprehensiveness; but the geometric version has marked advantages for many useful purposes.

A simple form of analytical geometry, the two-dimensional *graph*, is used today to picture stock market changes, the progress of sales campaigns, conditions affecting the weather, and the prospects of the Red Sox for winning the American League pennant. The graphical illustration has become an inevitable adjunct of the statistical approach to every field of human activity and interest. Graphs are familiar media of understanding for almost everybody who can understand the printed word. Perhaps it will not now be fatal to their widespread acceptance to let the secret out that graphs are not only "mathematics," but are the very essence of a whole branch of mathematics as important and useful as algebra and geometry themselves. The ordinary sales curve is just a pictorial way of saying that $y = x^2 + 19x + 7$, or of telling some similar story.

On cross-lined paper of equal squares (Figure 2) draw one horizontal and one vertical line, to serve as axes of reference. The point of their intersection is called the origin; it's the starting point for all measurements in any direction. Measurement towards the right from the origin,

$y = x^2$

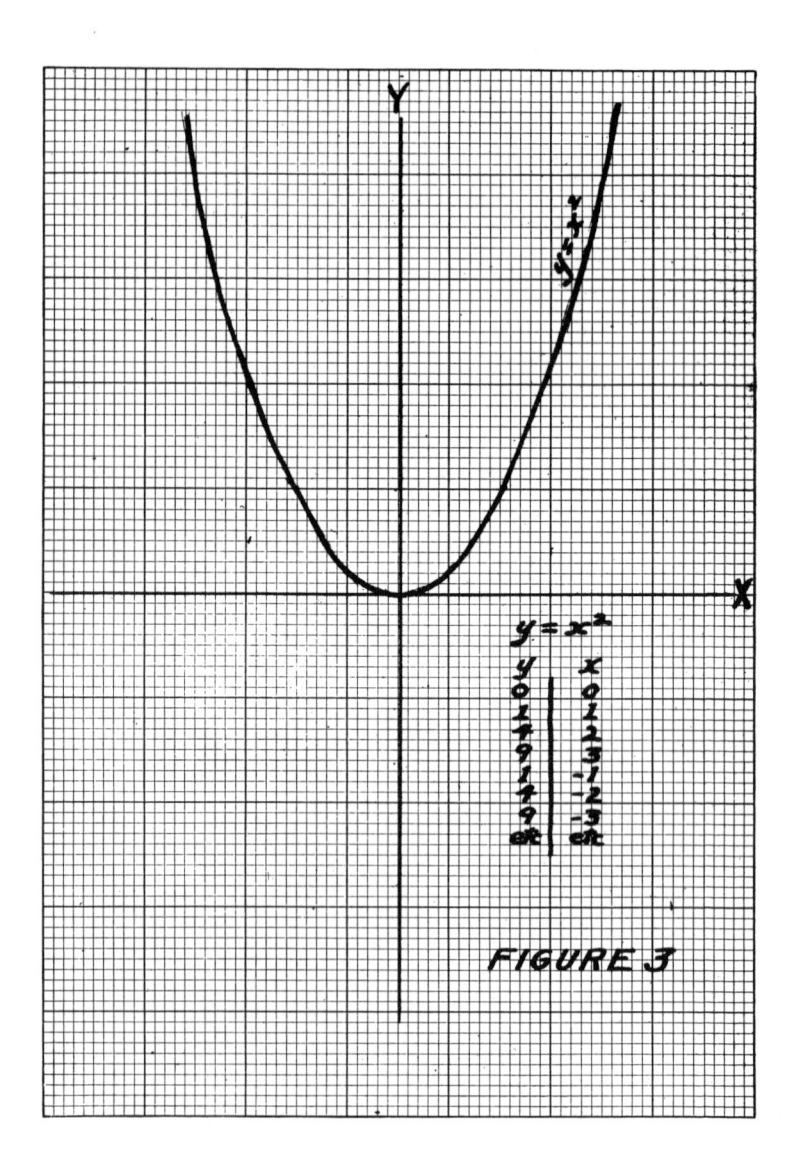

y	x
0	0
1	1
4	2
9	3
1	-1
4	-2
9	-3
etc.	etc.

FIGURE 3

along the X-axis, is considered positive; towards the left is negative. Along the Y-axis, the measurement up from the origin is positive, down is negative. Any point in this plane can now be located exactly by its coordinates along these axes. Consider the point marked P. It is two units out to the right, in the direction parallel to the X-axis; that is, its x-coordinate is 2. It is one unit up, in the direction parallel to the Y-axis, that is, its y-coordinate is 1. At this point x is equal to 2 and y is equal to 1; while these coordinates (2,1) determine this point and this point only, in the plane. Any other x-coordinate, and a corresponding y-coordinate, will determine some other point with equal exactness.

In Figure 2 we have set up a table showing that if $y = \frac{1}{2}x$, then when $x = 2$, $y = 1$; and when $x = -3$, $y = -1\frac{1}{2}$. Experience soon tells us that an equation of this kind is represented by a straight line, and we know that a straight line is determined by any two of its points. So we set up the two points indicated, draw a line through them; and we have a figure which tells accurately, and *continuously*, the whole story or relationship recounted by the algebraic equation $y = \frac{1}{2}x$. For no matter what value we now take for x in that equation, its corresponding value for y will be found on this line. Or, looking at the one practical application with which we started, of the thousands that are possible, we can move a man or a mountain along the X-axis until the top just touches our slanting line, and the length of his shadow will be given by the distance of the object out on the X-axis, or its x-coordinate.

The curve in Figure 3 tells a different story, that $y = x^2$. It is known as a parabola. Any equation of the form

$$y = \frac{x^2}{4a}$$

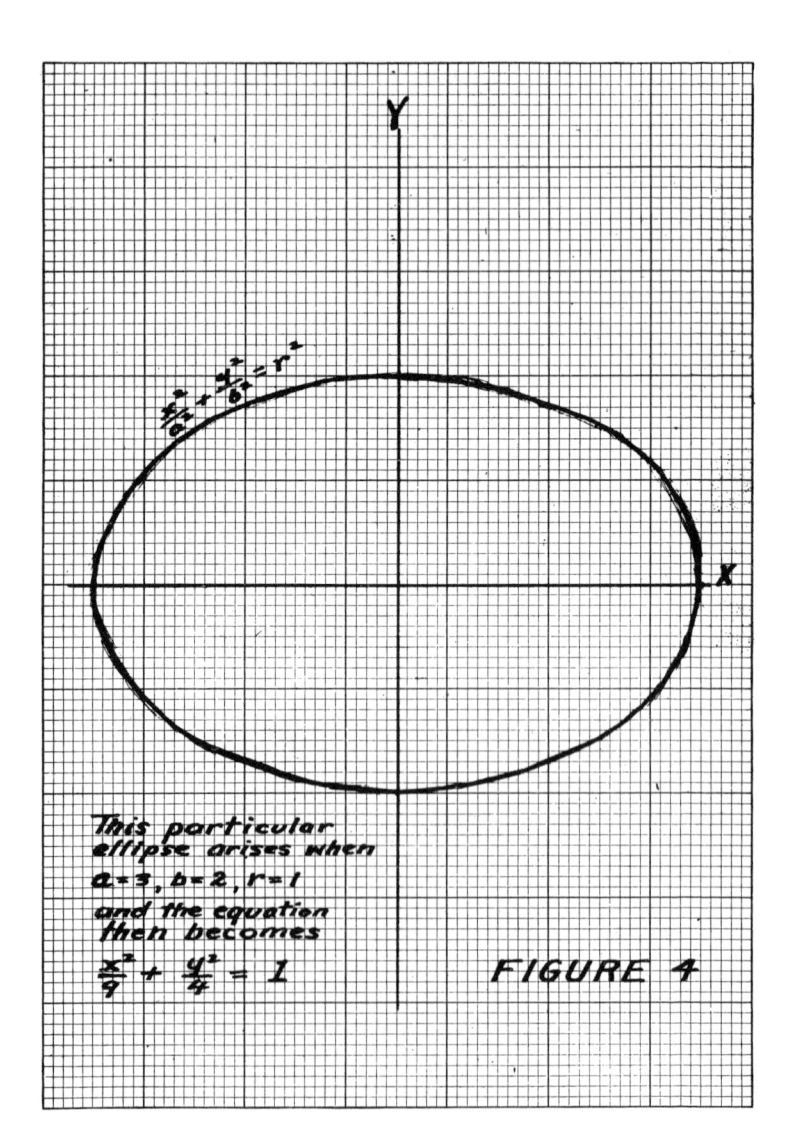

$$\frac{x^2}{a^2} + \frac{y^2}{b^2} = r^2$$

This particular ellipse arises when $a=3, b=2, r=1$ and the equation then becomes
$$\frac{x^2}{9} + \frac{y^2}{4} = 1$$

FIGURE 4

will always give a parabola when put in graphical form, no matter what value a may have. Our sample is merely the particular parabola when a is $\frac{1}{4}$, and the equation simplifies to $y = x^2$. Similarly, if we plot the corresponding values of x and y in $\frac{x^2}{a^2} + \frac{y^2}{b^2} = 1$, we come out with an ellipse: such as that shown in Figure 4, when a is 3 and b is 2. The hyperbola, which looks a bit like two unfriendly parabolas, is given by any equation of the form

$$\frac{x^2}{a^2} - \frac{y^2}{b^2} = 1.$$

You will remember those figures, the ellipse, parabola, and hyperbola, as the intersections made by a plane in cutting across a cone. For this reason they are known as conic sections, and they were studied for two thousand years before the methods of analytical geometry were perfected in the seventeenth century. But because of their usefulness, these three curves have remained a major concern of the followers of Fermat and Descartes. The arches supporting London Bridge are ellipses. The orbits in which the earth and other planets travel around the sun are ellipses. The longitudinal cross-section (through its center) of an automobile headlight is a parabola. The arch of Hell-Gate Bridge in New York is a parabola. The conic sections are a necessary part of the everyday stock-in-trade of the engineers, astonomers, and "pure" mathematicians alike.

But there are an infinite number of other equations which convert in graph-form to an infinite number of other lines and curves. Our old friend, $y = \sin x$, for instance, when plotted by giving enough values to the angle x, looks like its picture in Figure 5, and shows plainly why it is called a periodic function. It may also make clearer the meaning of the word *sinuosity*, as well as

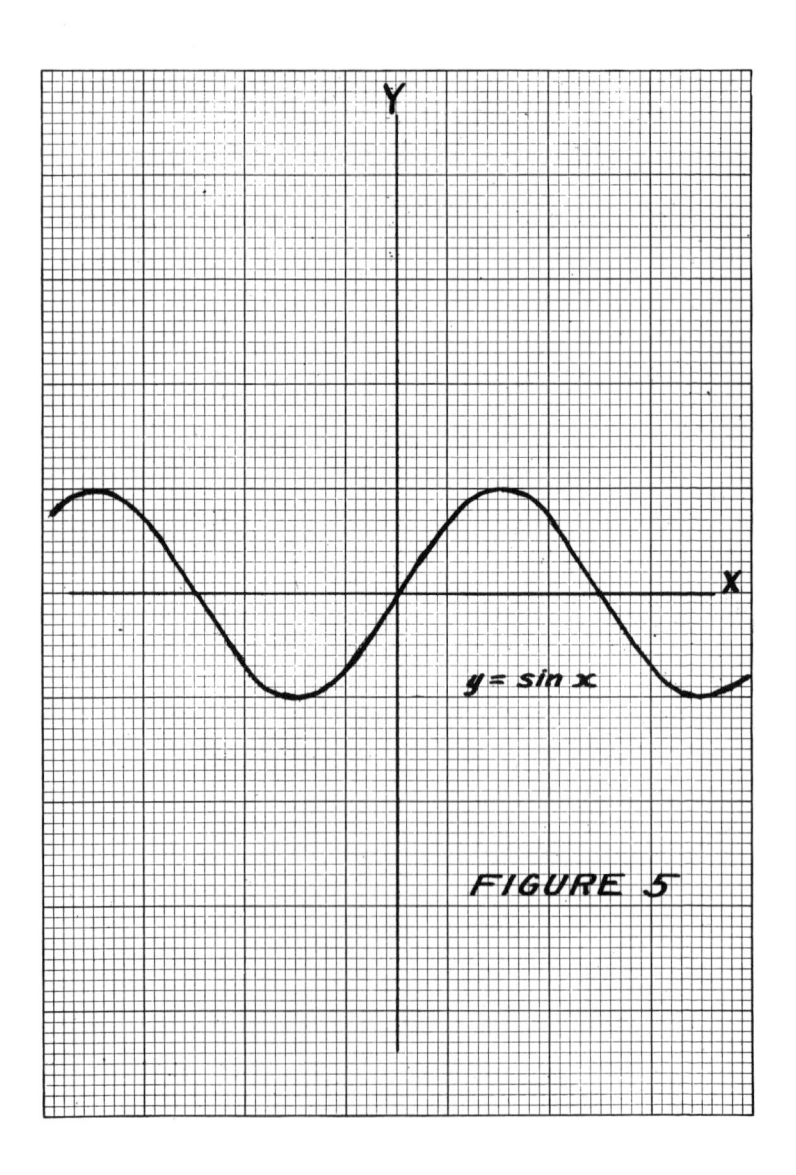

$y = \sin x$

FIGURE 5

indicate why the equation $y = sin\ x$ can be used to represent practically every form of wave motion. In fact, a tuning fork held prong down, and set to vibrating, will trace its exactly corresponding *sine* curve on a sheet of carbon paper dragged under it. The correlation between physical phenomena and the mathematical interpretations of those phenomena seldom escapes from the realm of imagination and materializes into anything so visible.

But converting algebraic equations into curves is not a one-way street. For any circle set down anywhere on a sheet of graph paper with coordinate axes, for instance, it is easy to show, by the relations between x and y at various points on the circle, that the equation $x^2 + ax + y^2 + by + c = 0$ will express the relationship between x and y at all points on that circle, and at points on that circle only; a, b, and c being used here instead of the particular constants which identify a particular circle. And while the process is not so simple in most cases as in that of a circle, it still is usually possible and frequently easy to arrive at the algebraic equation representing any line or curve about which enough facts are known for the curve's story to be told with algebraic definiteness. A great many curves are first introduced to us as the abodes of points satisfying certain conditions. A circle, for example, is the *locus* of all points that are equally distant from another given point called the center. And such conditions can readily be translated into relationships between x and y, when x and y represent coordinate measurements along our set of perpendicular axes. Algebra and analytical geometry are two languages, with freedom of translation back and forth from either one to the other.

Let's look at one of the many advantages derived from this freedom of translation. Suppose we have two separate and rather complicated stories told about the same two un-

known quantities; the first, that $x^2 - 6x + y^2 + 4y - 12 = 0$, and the second that $y^2 = 25 - 5x$. And we want to know what values of x and y will satisfy each state of affairs at the same time. The algebraic approach is to substitute
$$x = \frac{25 - y^2}{5},$$
from the second equation, everywhere that x occurs in the first equation, and thus try to do business with y alone. But this often leads us to forbidding expressions which begin with y^4 and run on through the whole gamut of y^3's, y^2's, and y's. And while it's frequently possible to solve such a fourth-degree equation in one variable, it's also frequently a good idea to find some way to dodge the necessity. M'sieu Descartes invented his analytical geometry partly for the very purpose of handling simultaneous algebraic equations without the benefit of algebra. If we plot the two expressions above on the same axes of reference, the first turns out to be a circle; the second is a parabola which crosses this circle at the point $x = 3.2$, $y = 3.0$ (approximately, and as accurately as we can read the graph-paper dimensions) and again at the point $x = -0.6$, $y = -5.3$. These, then, are the two sets of values for x and y, respectively, which will comply with the terms of both equations at the same time. And while traffic does not move as often in the opposite direction, it's sometimes desirable to determine exactly where two curves cross each other by putting each in the form of an equation in x and y, and then solving these two simultaneous equations algebraically. If geometry can work for algebra, then turn about is certainly fair play.

The reciprocal trade relation thus indicated is, however, only the beginning. Once having found that we could use the figures of plane geometry for very helpful representations of the relationships between two unknowns, x and y,

More Mathematics

it was a simple step to use the three-dimensional figures of solid geometry for similar handling of all sorts of problems in three unknowns, or three dimensions, x, y, and z. If the equation $(x - 2)^2 + (y - 3)^2 + (z - 4)^2 = 25$ be plotted on a set of three-way axes — such as forms the corner of any cube — it will prove to be a sphere of radius 5, and with the center at the point in such cubed-off space indicated by $x = 2$, $y = 3$, $z = 4$. And we can proceed to equations representing the solids made by revolving parabolas, or representing the prolate spheroids laid by an ambitious hen. But these jobs do not always compare favorably with falling off a log, and we doubt if the class is ready for them yet.

Some of our mathematical brethren do not stop even at this point, however. If equations in two variables, x and y, can represent two-dimensional figures, and equations in three variables, x, y and z, can represent three-dimensional figures, why not apply the same rules and operations to the handling of equations in v, x, y, and z, as representing four-dimensional figures, and so on for any number of variables and any number of corresponding dimensions? There is no reason, so long as the results make sense, have logical validity, and serve some useful purpose. It's true that we can make some vague attempt at interpreting and even at visualizing four-dimensional figures, by considering the fourth dimension as time. A three-dimensional block or object is moving through the fourth dimension, time, in much the same way that a two-dimensional plane moves through a third dimension to generate the block. And many even of the "practical" conceptions about dimensions will hold for the fourth. Beyond that the manifolds in five or more dimensions may be useful for certain mathematical manipulations, and these manipulations may have logical validity; but for the layman they do not make sense. And even the mathematician who can solve problems in an n-dimensional manifold, and can deduce quite accurately many geometrical properties of n-dimensional space, will be the first to admit that, literally, he doesn't know what he is talking about. We can only say in leaving this exhibit that if any of our readers do have a yearning to delve into the mathematics of four or more dimensions, then analytical geometry supplies an excellent entering road. Where the road leads to depends on who follows it, and is something you'll have to find out for yourselves.

Hitting only the high spots in our rapid-fire survey of elementary mathematics, we have now arrived at our last assignment. And any mathematician in our audience is undoubtedly holding his breath, waiting to see how we go about trying to elucidate in a few simple paragraphs the methods and purposes of the calculus. All we can say is that he'll probably choke to death; but if the patient reader wishes to hang on we'll do our best.

The inclusive term, the *calculus,* comprehends two divisions, differential calculus and integral calculus. Historically, the second division would require attention first, since it was at least foreshadowed by the "method of exhaustion" of the Greeks; and kept bobbing up, almost to the surface and ready to be discovered, for two thousand years thereafter. While differential calculus wasn't discovered at all. It was deliberately invented by both Leibnitz and Newton (their respective followers have been fighting ever since over who was first), as a means of solving problems in which they were interested and which would not yield to any other tools. But there are sound logical reasons for having students tackle differential and integral calculus in that order today, and we'll follow the usual procedure.

More Mathematics

Let's go back to our familiar and particular relationship between two unknowns, stated algebraically as $y = x^2$, and geometrically in the curve above (Figure 3). It's obvious from either form of the story that when x changes y also changes, and much faster. If we start with x equal to 3, when y equals 9; and if x then changes by one unit, so that x equals 4, then y changes by 7 units, for y is now equal to 16. If we start at $x = 5$, $y = 25$, however, and increase x by one unit, to equal 6, then y is increased by 11, for it now equals 36. In other words the *ratio* of the changes in x and y vary with the point at which such changes are made. Geometrically, this is merely pointing out that the slope of the curve does not remain the same (the curve would be a straight line if it did) but steadily changes as the value of x is increased. The job done by differential calculus is simply to determine the ratio of the change in y to a corresponding infinitesimal change in x at any and all points of the curve, or for any and all values of x in the equation. The importance of this job, for further tasks to be done in both pure and applied mathematics, can hardly be overestimated.

That there is no other means of ascertaining this ratio cannot be understood without a digression concerning two terms which permeate all mathematical thinking. They are *discrete* and *continuous*. When a boy drags a stick along a fence of upright palings, the clattering noise which the stick makes shows that the fence is made up of *discrete* units of wood, with intervals between; and not of a *continuous* board which would give no such intermittent sound. The notes struck on a piano keyboard are separated in pitch by discrete intervals, those on a violin string may be made to flow into one another in a continuity without breaks. Our everyday numbers, as first brought forth by our ancestors for counting, represent discrete quantities such as seven apples. But the numbers representing tomorrow's weather will not, because temperature is changing by non-discrete amounts all of the time. A flea that hops from point to point along a line does so by discrete stages; but a point that moves smoothly along a line is continuous in its motion. No matter how small a segment of the line we choose as a unit, the point passes through an infinite number of smaller segments in going over that unit. An exact discrete unit, as the smallest definite measure of its motion, is impossible to conceive.

After this lecture we go back to an earlier statement whose significance was not stressed at the time. Using nothing but the language of arithmetic, we can know of the relationship between two quantities that when $x = 1$, $y = 1$; $x = 2$, $y = 4$; $x = 10$, $y = 100$; $x = 2\frac{1}{2}$, $y = 6\frac{1}{4}$; $x = 3.1$, $y = 9.61$; and so on for a table of a thousand or a million corresponding values, if we wish to go to that trouble. Yet even after a table of billions of such values was contructed, there would still be more billions of values for x whose corresponding values for y would not be stated for us. But in the algebraic account of this relationship, $y = x^2$, or in the geometric translation into a curve on a system of coordinates, we have the *continuous* relationship between x and y determined for any and all possible values. After the acquisition of discrete numbers, and the ability to count by discrete intervals, this ability to cope with continuous measure has been the most important achievement in that division of human mental progress which we identify as mathematics. Contemporary scientists are the first to ridicule Sir James Jeans' epigram that God was a mathematician; but it is worth noting that as the phenomena of the universe are both discrete and continuous, so are our mathematical conceptions for dealing with them. One system is a reflection of the other, and Jeans saw both in the mirror.

More Mathematics

Let's return, however, to the patient parabola, $y = x^2$. And skipping the equivalent approach by the algebraic path, let's see the method and meaning of the job done by differential calculus in adding details to this geometric story. We have below (Figure 6) the same curve once more, this time on a larger scale. Let's take for consideration the point P, where the x-coordinate of the curve is 4 and the y-coordinate is 16. We can readily see that when the x-coordinate increases to 5, the y-coordinate increases to 25. That is, as an average for that whole distance along the curve, the change in y is nine times as great as in x; the *ratio* of the change is 9. But when the increase in the x-coordinate is only 0.5, to 4.5, y increases from 16 to 20.25, or by an increment of only 4.25. The ratio of this increment of y to the corresponding increment of x is less than 9; it is 8.5, to be exact. And our important question is not as to what is the average ratio of the change over a given distance, but the exact ratio at any fixed point such as P.

Now instead of increasing x by 1, or even by 0.5, let's take smaller and smaller increases. Such an increment is known as Δx (*delta x*). Let Δx equal only 0.1, for instance. Then y will be equal to $(4 + 0.1)^2$, or 16.81; and the increase in y, known as Δy, is only 0.81. The ratio of *delta y* to *delta x* is now .81/.10, or only a little over 8. And if we take smaller and smaller increments of x, we find that the ratio $\frac{\Delta y}{\Delta x}$ approaches nearer and nearer to 8. Until finally, by the theory of limits — proof of which we haven't time to discuss here — we arrive at the conclusion that since the ratio of *delta y* to *delta x* at the point P approaches 8 as a limit, as *delta x* is taken smaller and smaller and approaches zero, then the actual ratio of $\frac{\Delta y}{\Delta x}$ at P is

FIGURE 6

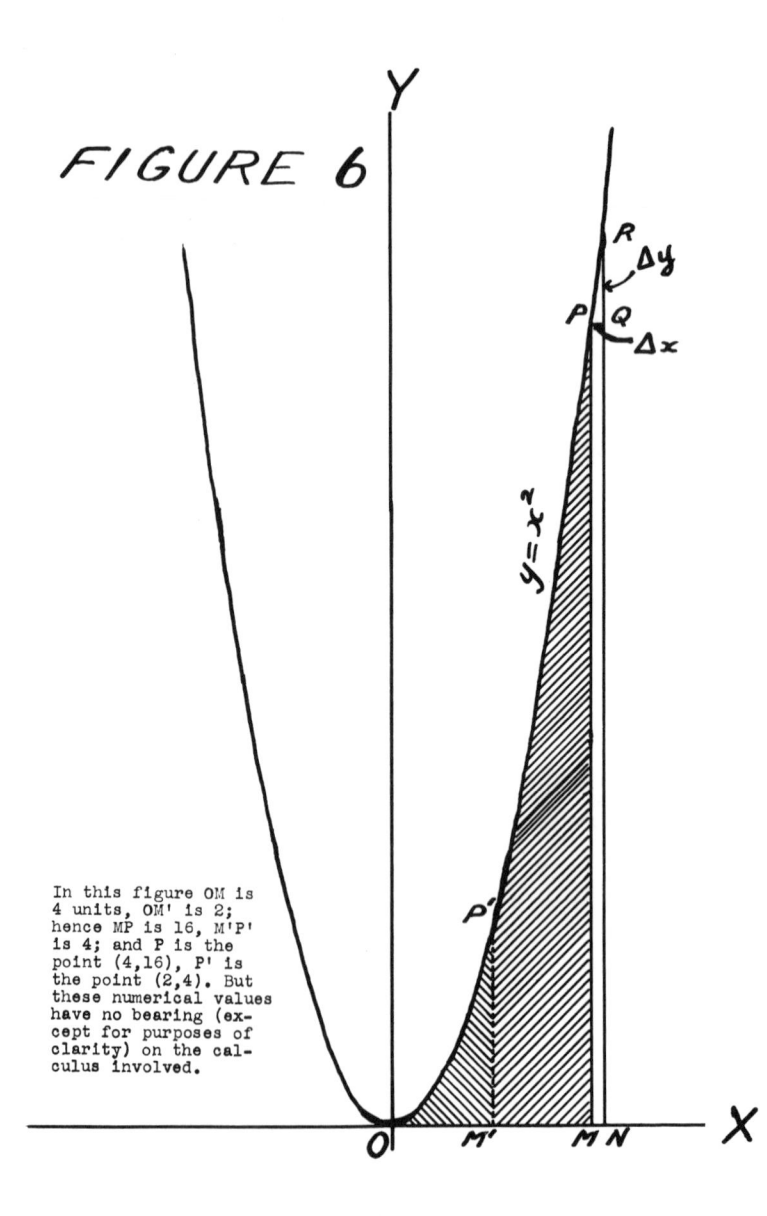

$y = x^2$

In this figure OM is 4 units, OM' is 2; hence MP is 16, M'P' is 4; and P is the point (4,16), P' is the point (2,4). But these numerical values have no bearing (except for purposes of clarity) on the calculus involved.

exactly 8. That is, in the curve $y = x^2$, at the point where $x = 4$, y is changing $2x$ times or 8 times as fast as x.

By similar trials we would find that at the point $x = 3$, y is changing $2x$ or 6 times as fast as x. And that *at all points*, whatever x may be, the ratio of the change of Δy to Δx is equal to $2x$.

The limit of this ratio of Δy to Δx, as Δx approaches zero, is known as the derivative of the curve or of the function (it's a new function *derived* from the old one), and is written $\frac{dy}{dx}$. For the equation $y = x^2$, we have just seen that $\frac{dy}{dx} = 2x$. For the equation $y = x^3 + 6$ we would find that $\frac{dy}{dx} = 3x^2$ (the constant 6 vanishes, because it has no bearing on the slope at any point). For the equation $y = \sin x$, $\frac{dy}{dx} = \cos x$.

Certain patterns, readily converted into useful formulas, become quickly discernible. But half the problem of differential calculus is still the finding of the derivative of particular curves and functions.

Using these derivatives, after they are found, is the privilege not only of the calculus but of all other branches of mathematics and its allied sciences. Let's look at just one simple illustration. The distance covered by a freely falling body in a given number of seconds is determined by experiment as $s = \frac{1}{2}gt^2$, where s is the space or distance fallen, t is the time in seconds, and g is the acceleration due to gravity, often imprecisely called the constant of gravitation, equal approximately to 32.2 feet per second per second. Now the ratio of the change in s, or the distance, to the change in t, or the time, at any fixed instant, would be the velocity of the falling body at that same instant. That is, $\frac{ds}{dt}$ in the equation above, and velocity, or v, are synonymous terms. But by analogy with our operation on $y = x^2$, or by use of the widely known formula which gives for the general equation $y = ax^n$ the derivative, $\frac{dy}{dx} = nax^{n-1}$, we can readily see that $\frac{ds}{dt}$, in our equation for the falling body, is equal to 2 times $\frac{1}{2}$ times g times t. Hence

$$v = \frac{ds}{dt} = gt$$

is the desired expression to tell us how fast the body is falling nine seconds or nine hundred seconds after it starts. And to be struck by the use of derivatives, it is by no means necessary to look at a falling body. This ratio of the change in one quantity to the change in another quantity with which it is somehow connected enters into (among a few thousand other things) the pitch of propeller blades, the path of a projectile, the degree of curve in a railroad track, the measure of the elasticity of steel, and the compilation of tomorrow's weather report.

It is derivatives which have been worked out in advance, or which can be found as wanted, that the engineers employ to such advantage. But higher mathematics makes a great deal of use of derivatives even before they are found. For just as we saw that we could, for convenience, call an unknown not simply x, but $sin\ x$, or any of the trigonometric functions, so we can also include in the arbitrary name of our unknown some knowledge we do have about it, by labeling it $\frac{dy}{dx}$, and dealing with this unknown, thus named, in numberless manipulations. There is a whole division of mathematics, known as differential

More Mathematics

equations, concerned with the algebraic handling of $\frac{dy}{dx}$ in endless combinations and expansions. But that province is out of bounds under our present command.

In contemporary understanding and practice integral calculus is simply or primarily the reverse of differential calculus. But no one would have expected the embryo to turn out that way, during its twenty centuries of incubation. In order to see what integral calculus does, instead of how it does it, we might find it worth while to go back and look at the fumbling towards this accomplishment which was engaged in by the Greeks, the Chinese, and many others, long before the days of Leibnitz and Newton.

In Figure 7 we have a circle with radius equal to 1. We inscribe in that circle a square, *ABCD*. In the right triangle *AOB* the square of the hypotenuse *AB* is equal to the sum of the squares of the other two sides, each of which is a radius and hence equal to 1. So *AB* is equal to the square root of 2. The other sides of the square are the same length, the area of the square is thus $\sqrt{2}$ times $\sqrt{2}$, which equals 2; and we know that the area of the circle, of radius 1, must be larger than 2. Now draw *AE* and *BE* to the central part of the arc *AB*. We have an isosceles triangle, *AEB*, whose base is known to be $\sqrt{2}$. It is fairly simple by geometry (even the Greeks could do it) to determine that the area of the triangle *AEB* is .207, and that the area of all four similar triangles erected on the four sides of the square is 4 times .207, or .828. Hence the area of the eight-sided polygon which might be inscribed in the circle is 2 plus .828, or 2.828; and the area of the circle must be larger than that. By then erecting the isosceles triangle *AFE*, and computing its area, we can arrive at the area of a regular inscribed polygon of sixteen sides. We can continue

FIGURE 7

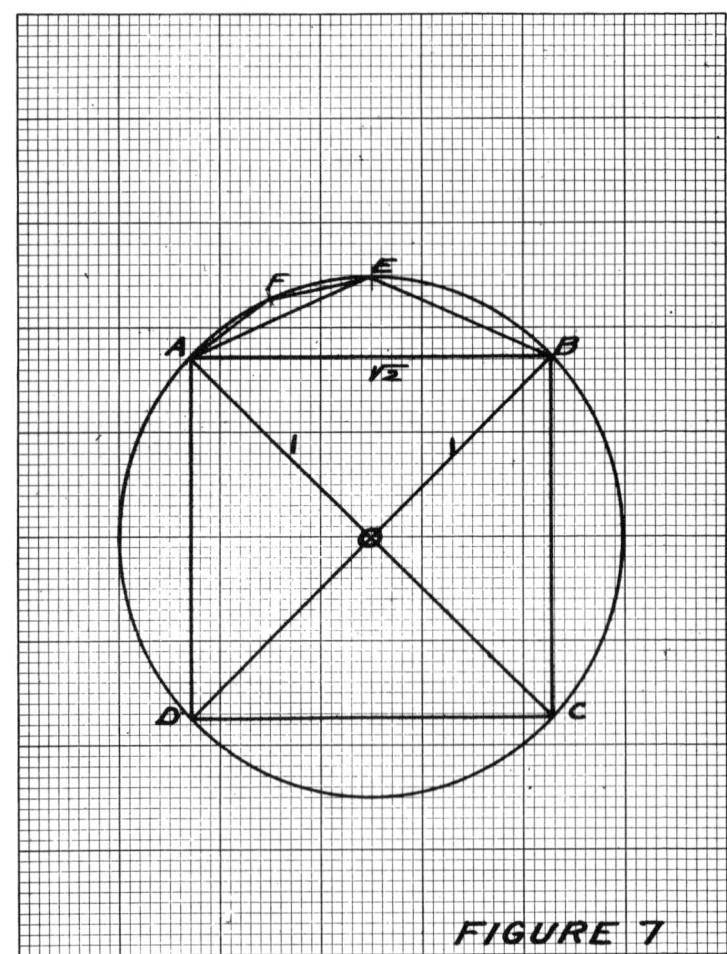

More Mathematics

to regular polygons of 32 sides, then 64 sides, and as far as we wish to go; and by calculating the area of each we come closer and closer to the true area of the circle in which they are enclosed.

By this "method of exhaustion" many peoples had computed the area of a circle of unit radius, long before calculus was imagined, as being in the neighborhood of $3\frac{1}{7}$. Even the Egyptians had worked out the rather peculiar valuation $\frac{256}{81}$, or $\frac{4^4}{3^4}$, which in our decimal system is just short of 3.1605. This is not too bad an approximation to the value of $\pi(pi)$ that is accurate to four decimal places, namely 3.1416, which is in general usage today. And if you had not realized that the kind of work described above was primarily for the purpose of finding the value of π, you can be sure that the Greeks did.

They called this exercise (and others of quite a different nature with the same objective), by the famous and intriguing name of "squaring the circle." For as early as Hippocrates in the fifth century B.C., the Greek geometricians were aware that the areas of different circles were proportional to the squares of their diameters. We express the same thing more completely when we say that the area of any circle is πr^2, r being its radius. If the radius is 1, then the area of that circle equals π, which is what the Greeks were seeking. Also, while the operation we have just described is known in modern mathematics as a converging infinite series, and is not the method of integral calculus, it does clarify — we hope — the kind of thinking, of need, and of purpose, which eventually led both Newton and Leibnitz to develop this great mathematical tool.

For the process was one of summing up the smaller and

smaller triangles inside the circle, far enough to arrive at a total of the area to whatever degree of accuracy was desired. The very integral sign, ∫, from which this branch of mathematics gets its name, was originally just an elongated S, meaning sum. And finding the very real sum, or integral, of an infinite number of infinitesimal pieces, is what calculus does, even though the above procedure falls far short of the way calculus does it.

So let's now see how and why integration, in practice, becomes the reverse of differentiation. The reasoning is a bit slippery, so hang on tight. In Figure 6 suppose we are interested in the shaded area between the X-axis, the right wing of the parabola, and a perpendicular drawn to the X-axis from a point P. P can be identified as any point having an x-coordinate and a y-coordinate such that these values of x and y will satisfy the equation $y = x^2$, for the point lies on that curve. The length MP is obviously the y-coordinate, OM the x-coordinate. We can call the area OMP simply U. Now let's move from P up to R, so that the outward movement, MN, is very small (though greatly magnified in the figure). If OM equals x, then MN is a slight increment or Δx, QR is the slight increase in y, or Δy; and we have a new actor on the scene, the increment in the area U, or ΔU. Delta U is, of course, the area $MPRN$. Now when we make MN smaller and smaller — that is, let Δx approach zero — ΔU approaches simply the rectangle $MPQN$ as its limit. But the area $MPQN$ is simply MP (or y) times MN (or Δx), or $y\Delta x$. We have, therefore, that ΔU approaches $y\Delta x$, or that $\dfrac{\Delta U}{\Delta x}$ approaches y, as a limit, as Δx approaches zero. But in the last section we saw that under these circumstances the theory of limits tells us that $\dfrac{dU}{dx}$ actually equals y, at the point P.

More Mathematics 145

There is one more step, resulting from the fact that in all affairs connected with this parabola y is always equal to x^2; so we can substitute accordingly and arrive at the statement that $\dfrac{dU}{dx}$ equals x^2.

What this means, in less symbolic language, is that the *rate of change* of the area under the parabola, with respect to the change in the length of the X-axis which is covered, is always equal to x^2; and this is true, no matter at what point the change is considered.

But here we have wound up at just the opposite end from where we started in the last section. There we had a function, of which we wanted to know the derivative. Here we have, and know the value of, a derivative $\dfrac{dU}{dx}$. It's equal to x^2. What we'd like to know is the original U from which this new function could have been derived. Put in the more usual form of what is known as differentials, we have $dU = x^2\,dx$. We want to know what we had to differentiate, in the first place, to get $x^2\,dx$. Trial and error shows us, if we are familiar with the pattern taken by differentials, that $\dfrac{x^3}{3}$ plus any constant is the expression. That is, the integral of $x^2\,dx$, or $\int x^2\,dx = \dfrac{x^3}{3} + C$.

In other words, by finding the rate of change of the area generated between the curve and the X-axis, with respect to the change in x, we came out with the differential of the area U, before we found out U itself. And in fact, by reversing the process learned in differential calculus, we were then able to ascertain that this area U was equal to

$$\dfrac{x^3}{3} + C.$$

But ordinarily we are not interested in the whole area generated by a curve in question. Let's say we want to know the area between the curve, the X-axis, and the perpendiculars where x equals 2 and x equals 4. Then C, which is known as the constant of integration, disappears, although we'll have to skip the geometrical reasoning involved and plead time as our alibi. (C simply has the effect of moving the whole curve up or down a given amount on the Y-axis, and thus of adding a *constant* amount to the shaded area at all times. Hence, when this same amount is both added and subtracted, the net result is the same as if C didn't come to the party.) For then $\frac{x^3}{3}$ represents an area U, of which $dU = x^2 dx$ is true, when $x = 4$, or when the line MP has moved out four points along the X-axis; and $\frac{x^3}{3}$ also represents a corresponding area U', when the line MP' has moved out only two points. Subtracting the lesser from the larger gives the area $M'P'PM$. That is, substituting these values of 4 and 2 in $\frac{x^3}{3}$, and subtracting one from the other, we get $\frac{64}{3} - \frac{8}{3} = \frac{56}{3} = 18.67$ as the area in question. If we are interested in the whole shaded area, then we have to find U, always equaling

$$\frac{x^3}{3} + C,$$

between the boundaries when $x = 4$ and when $x = 0$. This, by substitution again, is

$(\frac{64}{3} + C) - (0 + C) = 21.33$ square feet, or square inches,

or whatever measurement we were dealing in. And if you got lost somewhere back there near the third fork in the

More Mathematics

road, don't worry about it; many a college freshman has done the same thing, and never has gone back to see where he went astray.

Merely because we have used the determination of an area for purposes of illustration, however, it is not to be supposed that the application of integral calculus is of such limited scope. Differential calculus told us how to find the rate of change, with respect to each other, of two mutually interdependent variables, no matter what such variables represent. Integral calculus tells us how, if we know the rate of change and one of the variables, to find the other. Nor does it stop with two variables nor two dimensions. Applying the same principle to three dimensions, it is as easy for anybody familiar with integral calculus to work out in his head that the volume of a sphere with radius r is $\frac{4}{3} \pi r^3$ as it is for an ordinary high school boy to find mentally that the square of 24 is 576. And there is no other known way to calculate the exact volume of a sphere! Not without good reason has the calculus been called "the most powerful instrument ever invented for the mathematical exploration of the physical universe."

CHAPTER IX

More Mathematics
— Towards The Deep End

Figures of speech are not rationed. We can wear one out and discard it as often as we please. Let's have mathematics cease to be a museum, therefore, and become a pond. One end is quite shallow, with a gently sloping bottom. We can wade in and splash around and see how we like the water. How far we then explore the pond depends on whether and how well we learn to swim. There are boats — like this one — to give you a ride over the surface; but somehow you never see as much nor have as much fun, being a passenger, as when going it the hard way and with only your own powers to keep you from drowning.

The water of this pond presents one continuous medley of images, as if the whole cosmos were suspended just above it. For mathematics is the mirror of the universe. There is nothing real in mathematics, but all realities are reflected in it. The moving shadow shapes, of which our pond is full, are of two sorts. These are arithmetical numbers and geometric forms, most of which can transpose themselves, while we are watching, from one form to the other. There are hybrid shapes, half-completed transformations, everywhere we look. In the shallower parts of the pond, at least, it is not difficult to find the image which represents any familiar phenomenon. When we get into deeper darker waters, where the shadows may not blur but our own vision does, the task becomes steadily harder. But always, in shallow water and deep water alike, the more intriguing reverse problem is largely beyond our powers. The physical interpretations which we are able to make of the mathematical shadow shapes, and the relations between them, are so obviously but a child's beginning, towards identifying the forces and formulating the laws which these shapes represent. The first job, of translating a physical problem into mathematical terms, belongs to the engineer. The second job, of looking at and studying mathematical images until they finally come to have meaning in the physical world — or more meaning than they already had — is the job of the pure mathematician. Let's disguise ourselves as pure mathematicians and wade in a little way.

One image that we see everywhere, interlocked with almost every other number, form, and pattern, has been given the name of *pi* (π). "Ah, ha!" we say, "that's one we know. When it takes the shape of numbers, it's 3.14159... plus. On assuming its more honest geometric form of a circle and a diameter, it's even easier to recognize, for that's exactly what this *pi* represents: The ratio of the circumference to the diameter, of all the circles of the universe. No wonder we see this *pi* in so many places in the pond."

But then we look a little while longer. We see strange combinations of numbers that somehow finally remind us of *pi*. One of them is this peculiar series: $1 - 1/3 + 1/5 - 1/7 + 1/9 - 1/11 + 1/13 - 1/15 + 1/17 \ldots$ etc. We examine it more closely and find that we are looking at one-fourth of *pi*. The further we carry out this procession before computing it and multiplying by four, the more accurate number of decimals we shall have reached for *pi*. We then find any number of similar "convergent" series which

Towards The Deep End

converge on *pi* as their equivalent; another well-known one being 2(2/1 x 2/3 x 4/3 x 4/5 x 6/5 x 6/7 x 8/7 x 8/9 x 10/9 x 10/11 ... etc.). If any of our party is in doubt, he should work out either series. Here is the circle-to-diameter value of *pi*, to check against, for twenty decimal places; 3.14159265358979323846....

"That's funny," we are saying to ourselves, when a fellow who has been further out in the pond comes swimming back to join our group. He turns out to be an actuary for a life insurance company. "What do you think?" he says. "That image you call *pi* turns out to be a part of all our formulas, by which we determine what proportion of a group of people will be alive at a given time. Now what on earth has the ratio between a circle's circumference and its diameter to do with the number of people who stay alive?"

Standing near us is an experienced swimmer who has been out in the middle of the pond many times. "Maybe you have the cart before the horse," he remarks. "Maybe it's just incidental that this *pi* pictures the ratio of the circumference of a circle to its diameter. For one sure thing is that *pi* is very much at home in the whole field of probability." You might try this surprising illustration: Take a table top and draw parallel lines on it, of any width apart just so the distance is greater than the length of the needle you are going to use. Then drop a needle repeatedly on the table from some distance above, and record the number of times it falls across a line and the number of times it comes to rest not touching a line. You will find that the probability of the needle lying across a line involves *pi* as a factor.

Many doubting Thomases have rushed out to try this experiment. One (the Italian mathematician, Lazzerini, in 1901) dropped his needle over three thousand times. He found that the result gave *pi* correctly to seven decimal places. Why? Well, so far as we know, the question had not been answered up till breakfast time this morning. What is the nature of the unifying thread that binds all these relationships together? What is the complete and real *pi*, of which these are but dimly glimpsed manifestations? If you have two or three lifetimes to spare, you might apply one of them to the problem and be very happy in the job.

Our ape-like ancestors didn't really invent the integral numbers 1,2,3,4,5, etc. They merely discovered these shadows of reality on their earliest rambles along the shore of the mathematical mirror-pond, and invented names for them. We got along with just these numbers for countless generations. But after a while we discovered *fractional* numbers, such as 1/2, 1/5, 2/7, 11/234, etc.; and negative numbers, such as -1, -7, -43 1/3, which the Greeks would not play with because they couldn't think of any way to measure such numbers in their geometry, but which the more mystic Chinese and Hindus used without any such practical scruples. And we have been discovering new kinds of numbers ever since. There are *irrational* numbers, such as the square root of 2. You can never express them exactly in integers, or as the ratio between integers, no matter how long a fraction you attempt for the purpose. The square root of 2 can be wrapped up for handling, however, by treating it as x in the equation $x^2 = 2$. But there are *transcendental* numbers which cannot even be expressed algebraically; one of these is our old friend pi. There are *imaginary* numbers, such as the square root of minus 1, which is called i for convenience. There are *complex* numbers, such as $2 + 3i$, which have tremendous usefulness for certain divisions of higher mathematics. There are also *transfinite* numbers, but please ask some-

Towards The Deep End

body else what they are. There is an old story about the farmer, resting on a bench in the public square of a small county-seat town, who startled his companions by drawling: "Well, if I had as much money as I know where the court house is, I'd be rich." If the mathematicians had as much money as they know numbers to count with — there'd be more mathematicians.

But if you think we have all the numbers we need, or have learned all there is to know about them, you are preeminently mistaken. After thousands of years we still know so little about the integral numbers themselves that their properties and the relationships between them are eternally hinting at laws of nature which we have not yet fathomed. Every problem solved but opens up a dozen new ones, and results which seem purely idle and useless theory today have a strange habit of becoming the very backbone of *practical* and necessary mathematical operations tomorrow. For the kind of parlor pastime dealt with, consider the following étude.

We all know that $3^2 + 4^2 = 5^2$; the Greeks even used this fact, converted into a right triangle of string with sides of 3, 4, and 5 units respectively, for laying out right angles in their architecture and surveying. We can see that $5^2 + 12^2 = 13^2$; we can find many similar combinations. In fact, it is readily obvious that $x^2 + y^2 = z^2$ has an endless number of possible solutions where x, y, and z are all positive integers. But what about $x^3 + y^3 = z^3$; that is, two numbers such that, when you take the cube of each and add those cubes together, the result will be the cube of some other whole number. Try it. But don't try too long. For strange as it may seem, there isn't any answer; it has been mathematically proved that there are no whole numbers to fit the requirements.

It's worthwhile stopping to see what this means in

"real" life, instead of in the shadow-existence of the numbers. It means that you can take a square with a side five units long, chop it up into the twenty-five little squares, chop up another square with a side twelve units long into its hundred and forty-four little squares, and reassemble all these combined pieces into one exact and complete square again. And that there are plenty of other teams of squares which you can thus reshuffle into one new and larger square. But that nowhere in all the universe are there two cubes, of whatever size or material, that can be cut up into their respective little unit cubes and then have these combined little unit cubes reassemble exactly into one large cube again. If you are ever playful enough to arrange cubical lumps of sugar into a big cube with six lumps to each direction, you will have 216 lumps. Another larger cube beside it, with eight lumps to the side, would contain 512 lumps. If you then sweep both these cubes with your hands into one pile, and try to erect a new cube on nine units as the length of a side, you will come out just one little lump of sugar short of being able to complete the structure. For 216 plus 512 equals 728, while 9^3 is 729. Similarly, if you mix together the lumps from a cube with nine units to the side, and from one with ten units to the side, and start to work on a new cube with twelve units to the side, you will complete your beautiful new block entirely — and have just one annoying little lump of sugar left over. But you'll never get the lumps to come out even, no matter how long you try nor with what sized cubes. For x^3 plus y^3 can never equal z^3, in integral numbers.

What about $x^4 + y^4 = z^4$? This is impossible, too. The same is true for the sum of the fifth powers of two numbers; that sum *cannot* equal the fifth power of another number. But by this time we no longer know what it means. What about $x^{3001} + y^{3001} = z^{3001}$? Now we

Towards The Deep End

don't even know whether it's true. We think it's still impossible, but we can't be sure. For there is a strange bit of history connected with this problem. The great French mathematician Fermat, who would have given the world analytical geometry if Descartes hadn't done so, and who practically founded the modern theory of numbers, had a habit of making notes on the margins of books he was reading. He would frequently assert that he had found a proof for so and so; and while he never bothered to give these proofs, they always turned up later to support his assertion. With one exception. This was his famous entry that he had found a positively beautiful proof that $x^n + y^n = z^n$ was impossible for whole numbers when n was greater than 2. Maybe he had; but nobody else has ever been able to do so in the three hundred years since. It has been proved for individual cases, all the way up to $x^{707} + y^{707} = z^{707}$. But despite the fact that the greatest mathematicians have tackled Fermat's Last Theorem, that prizes up to twenty thousand dollars have been offered for any such proof, and that immediate fame in the scientific world beckoned as a reward to any amateur who might be successful, the question is still unsettled as to whether Fermat was mistaken or whether any such general proof is possible. You might try your hand at it some lonesome Saturday night. It will certainly keep you out of mischief.

A prime number is one which has no factors other than 1 and itself. The first few are 1,2,3,5,7,11,13,17,19,23,29, 31,37,41,43,47,53,59, etc. Euclid proved — what looks rather obvious to the layman — that there are an infinite number of primes. But how can you tell whether a number is a prime or not? More work has probably been put on that problem than on all other mathematical problems combined. What about 4294967297, just for an illustration? One of the greatest mathematicians *guessed* that it was a prime, because $2 + 1$, $2^2 + 1$, $2^4 + 1$, $2^8 + 1$, and $2^{16} + 1$ were all primes, and this number was $2^{32} + 1$. He was wrong, however, for the number is divisible by 641. Prime numbers, like prime beef, are sometimes hard to recognize, even when you know the source from which they came.

Depending on how far out you go into the mathematical pond, you can find these number-images in patterns and combinations of any desired degree of complexity. Consider, for instance, the proposition that *every* odd square number, 9 .... 25 .... 49 .... 81 .... etc., has 1 left over when you divide it by 8. Any high school boy should be able to prove it as a general theorem. Consider the proposition that 27 equals 25 plus 2 is the *only* case in the whole range of integral numbers where the cube of one number is equal to the square of another number plus 2. A good college math teacher could prove it. Consider Goldbach's thesis that *every* even number is the sum of two primes, or Riemann's Hypothesis, if you can even understand what Riemann's Hypothesis is in the first place. (I can't.) Nobody can prove them. In the theory of numbers and in the whole range of higher arithmetic you can choose any kind of water you wish while you are learning to swim.

But the geometric forms deserve a little attention, too. Those nearest the shore, such as points and lines and squares and circles, seem so familiar that we seldom realize how little we know about them, or how small a fraction we understand of what they signify. A little further out we get to studying a sphere, and find that it has the greatest volume in proportion to its surface of any possible geometrical body. And all of a sudden we know why rain drops are round and why molten lead, poured from

Towards The Deep End

sufficient height, will break up into round shot. The pressure of the atmosphere, working on all points alike of these yielding little "chunks," of water or of lead, naturally forces each one into that form which has the least possible surface. Among all sorts of conic sections, mixing into everything, we find a lot of beautiful ellipses. Some of them, along with other diverse duties, act as models for the solar system. Shimmering a bit vaguely in a thousand snake-like forms are sinusoid curves, the shadow-land representations of sound waves and light waves and electric waves and probably of dozens of kinds of waves that we do not yet even know exist.

Way out in the middle, surrounded by four-cusped hypocycloids, tractices, and pseudo-spheres we find a strange curve known as the catenary. It represents a relationship between two variables such that the rate of change between them, at any given instant, is equal to the integral of the dependent variable except for a constant multiplier; in mathematical terms, the derivative and the integral of the function are both always the same, except for the effect of the constant. This may not sound like much help when we find that the function is

$$y = \frac{a}{2}\left(e^{\frac{x}{a}} + e^{-\frac{x}{a}}\right).$$

But take your watch chain with two hands, and let it dangle between them; take one end of a rope for jumping, while your son takes the other; or hang a freely suspended rope-ladder bridge from one tree to another across a stream; in every case you will have a catenary. If you want to know anything accurate about the hang of the chain or the rope or the swinging ladder you'll have to dissect that stubborn function to find it out.

Not all of the swimmers in our pond are mathematicians, by any means. Over there in a cove is a very practical-looking fellow, watching a lot of exponential curves which keep shifting themselves back and forth into number-shapes known as logarithms. He's a manufacturer of slide rules. Those fellows swimming around the schools of polyhedrons are geologists and chemists; interested, among other things, in crystallization. A little to the right of center (no politics implied) an intent group is learning all it can about some shadows that look like arrows of all lengths and sizes. That is a group of engineers concerned with vector analysis. And the whole middle of the pond is full of very young fellows talking a strange language about electronics.

Passing by all these "practical" men, however, and swimming boldly towards the far end of the pond, we find the shadows getting more vague and the water murky. (In fact the whole figure of speech is getting murky.) Of the comparatively few swimmers who seem to be at home in this deep water, some call themselves physicists, some mathematicians, and some philosophers. In many cases it's hard to tell whether the shadows here are number-shapes or form-shapes; in most cases their connection with reality has been guessed only dimly and in part. Here is the home of parallel lines that *do* meet; of *curved* space — fifty-seven varieties; of sticks that fall up instead of down because the probability in favor of gravity finally runs out. Most of the numbers roundabout have some such identification as transfinite Alephs, or even "classes of all classes that are similar to a given class." But there are still plainly recognizable some good old integral numbers, which would look encouragingly familiar if they were not so terribly large. For some swimmers in these waters are looking for shadow-expressions with which to count and measure either extremely great or extremely small realities. And of course the smallest number you can think of is merely the largest number with a 1 put over it. The numbers needed for appraising such matters are usually expressed as simply powers of 10; 10^{19} or 10^{37} or — a famous number —

$$10^{10^{34}}.$$

To escape the monotony of such exponential nomenclature, Professor Kasner has invented the terms *googol* and *googolplex*. The first is a 1 with a hundred zeros after it; the second is a 1 with a *googol* of zeros after it. That last one really does stagger the imagination. It seems that we are going to have adequate terms in which to express our national debt for a great deal longer.

These largest numbers are just as finite (and accurate, if accuracy is desired) as those which comprise the multiplication table of our childhood days. For a fascinating exactness is the province and purpose of mathematics. There is no difference in kind between these numbers and the few digits employed by our barbarian ancestors; only a difference in our ability to reach up and use them.

We have epitomized, in our mirror-pond metaphor, that property of mathematical conceptions of representing so faithfully some body of the tangible phenomena and natural laws which make up our environment. This property has frequently led even the best of mathematicians to extravagant confusion of reality with the mere symbols of reality. Pythagoras built an influential religious brotherhood on the belief that numbers were the ultimate essence of all things. Plato contended that God always geometrized. Leibnitz discovered that with the binary system, using two as a base instead of ten, he could recreate all mathematics with just the two symbols 1 and 0; and became so entranced with this discovery that he conceived of 1 as being God, the zero nothingness, and the possible combinations of 1 and 0 — or God working on nothingness — as expressing the entire universe. And even some of our contemporary mathematician-philosophers have shown a tendency to lose their mathematics in the haze of their philosophy.

We are not proposing any statute making it illegal for mathematicians to philosophize, or vice versa. We have had too many great contributions to mathematics from men like Pascal and Descartes. The true philosopher should, like Bacon, "take all knowledge [including mathematics] to be his province." And the dreamland of speculative philosophy has an undeniable attractiveness of its own. But our invitation extended in these chapters is a little less broad. We have hoped to suggest that the interplay of mathematical symbols, *per se*, from the smallest cardinal numbers to the monstrous figures of astronomy, from the line and circle to the one-sided surface of a Möbius band or its equivalent in four-dimensional space, is more interesting than crossword puzzles and more entertaining than the usual offerings in the movie or radio bill of fare. If we can entice a rare skeptic here and there to wade far enough into the pond, we'll baptize a few converts yet. And like most evangelists we can honestly offer such converts neither material gain nor the acclaim of their fellow men, but only a spiritual delight in the work being done.

CHAPTER X

Invitation To Poetry

One of the fundamental appeals of poetry is the compression of vast forces of thought into the capsule of a few simple looking words.

When Will Durant finishes his monumental story of civilization, and if the remaining two volumes live up to the promise of the first three, he will have presented — for those who care to see — a complete and convincing picture of how the present is always but a product of the past. To do so he will have used five thousand printed pages.

H. G. Wells, much less lucidly because he was primarily a propagandist rather than a historian, nevertheless left the firm impression, at the end of fifteen hundred pages, that all our present civilization, for better or for worse, is but an inheritance accumulated for us by our ancestors.

Sinclair Lewis, in the preface to *Main Street*, in a few lines that are almost poetry, wrote:

> Main Street is the climax of civilization. That this Ford car might stand in front of the Bon Ton Store, Hannibal invaded Rome and Erasmus wrote in Oxford cloisters.

But Alfred Tennyson said it in seven and one-half measures of trochaic verse:

I the heir of all the ages, in the foremost files of time.

161

The earliest beginnings of civilization, to which we can reach fumblingly through archaeology and language, took place in Central Asia. Vaguely, as through a glass, darkly, we can trace the movement of the centers of civilization westward to the northern shores of the Persian Gulf, along the Tigris-Euphrates valley, and to the flooded marges of the Nile; then more clearly across the Mediterranean, to the Grecian archipelago and the Italian and Iberian peninsulas; across Europe, in the full light of recorded history, to the British Isles; and finally, beyond question, to the American continents. That, despite all our patriotic pride, the movement will continue, is as inevitable as that the sun will rise tomorrow. And only a cataclysmic conversion of the whole planet into gases by the runaway release of atomic explosions, or some other force let loose by man in his learned ignorance, will prevent the fulfillment of Macaulay's prophecy. He anticipated that a curious traveler from New Zealand, proudly conscious of his own position in the forefront of enlightenment, would some day survey from the wreck of London Bridge the ruins of a departed civilization.

Ten thousand erudite volumes have painstakingly analyzed this rise and fall of nations, the transmission of cultures, and the migration of races. But Bishop Berkeley has summed them all up in one pentameter line:

Westward the course of empire takes its way.

The promise of a heaven, with peace and happiness everlasting, has loomed large among the moral forces activating the conduct of human life, for more than two thousand years. It has been particularly important in the appeal of the Christian and Mohammedan religions. Consequently the glories and the ecstasy of this life after the resurrection have been painted by the greatest poets and described in detail by the imaginations of the greatest preachers. But just what heaven could or should be like must still vary considerably with the temperament and desires of the individual human being before whom its promise is spread.

In the second line of an old Baptist hymn, however, written by J.M. Black, there is an assurance that transcends all of these conflicting hopes, and holds forth a thought which must strike with a mighty impact any intellect that can accept the realistic directness of its meaning. Its powerful simplicity is, to my mind, unsurpassed by any verse, in the poetry of any language. "When the trumpet of the Lord shall sound," this hymn begins, "and time shall be no more,"

And the morning breaks, eternal, bright, and fair.

Just try to grasp what the word *eternal* means to a fundamentalist, in that connection; think of the most beautiful morning you can remember, when all the world was bright and fair; and then try to grasp the idea of such a morning lasting forever, with neither storm nor cold nor heat nor night ahead. Perhaps you can't be converted; perhaps you do not even like the prospect of monotony which may leap to your mind. But certainly the poet has summarized here, in just eight words, a great deal of what thousands of religious martyrs have lived for and died for over the last twenty centuries.

Thinking is one thing; translating thought into action is something entirely different. Sociologists who like to parade sweeping generalities sometimes assure us that the East, with thousands of years of philosophic contemplation as a setting for the individual thinker, is as far ahead of the West in the sheer power of mental processes as our Western American culture is ahead of India and China in development of the mechanical arts. Some historians will make the same distinction between the ancient world and the modern. For, twenty-four hundred years before Darwin, Anaximander arrived at a firm belief in organic evolution, by a maximum of brilliant reasoning from a minimum of scientific observations; fifteen hundred years before Watt, Hero of Alexandria made a steam-engine — as a toy; and there are few, indeed, of the most far-reaching conclusions of contemporary metaphysics which were not propounded by ancient philosophers. But in most cases it still remained for the nineteenth and twentieth centuries to convert these surmises into scientific formulations which could be used as the basis of progress, and these toys of the brain into the working tools of human life. However terrible may be the uses to which our achievements are put, it is still the unique glory of our present age that we have not only the Einsteins and Russells who can carry pure thought into depths that startle us, but also the Curies and Comptons who can convert these thoughts into radioactive forces that change and shake the earth.

The discussion of these two categories of human endeavor, and the consideration of their relative values, has permeated philosophical writing throughout more books than any one man could ever read. But for any man or any people who may wish to indulge in self-appraisal, the ultimate demarcation and summation of the two capacities was put in the form of a one-line question, in Nathalia Crane's beautiful prize-winning poem on Lindbergh's flight:

> You fly the wings of logic — can you fly the wings of lead?

There are few of the great sweeps of human thought or emotion that have not been crystalized by some poet in a single line. When his subordinates ask the conqueror Tamburlaine why he is willing to sacrifice everything for power, Marlowe lets him add up all the drives of ambition in one mighty verse:

> Is it not passing brave to be a King,
> And ride in triumph through Persepolis?

When the timid Macbeth asks Lady Macbeth to consider what may happen if they fail, Shakespeare lets her voice the final answer of that form of courage which weakens at no obstacles and wavers at no crimes to achieve its end:

> But screw your courage to the sticking-place,
> And we'll *not* fail.

The contention of the moralists that just retribution somehow ultimately follows every act of man has been distilled out of a million sermons of a hundred different religions, into one authentic line of purest poetry from the King James version of the Christian Bible:

Whatsoever a man soweth, that shall he also reap.

There is one school of thought, ranging from a monistic material determinism to a Calvinistic spiritual faith, that man is not a free agent. The whole argument is comprehended in Fitzgerald's translation of Omar, in one sentence of resignation:

> And the first Morning of Creation wrote
> What the Last Dawn of Reckoning shall read.

There is a contrary school of thought that somehow, whether within a supreme cosmological purpose or as merely an accidental sentience amid an infinity of insentient accidents, each man has the power of decision over his own actions. Perhaps the boldest expression of belief in, and acceptance of, this responsibility lies in Henley's boast:

> I am the master of my fate:
> I am the captain of my soul.

The age-old and irreconcilable conflict between these two philosophies is reduced by Sidney Lanier to eight measures of poetry:

> The yea-nay of Freewill and Fate,
> Whereof both cannot be, yet are.

Then the question arises as to why we should feel called on to solve these problems, or any problems. What accident of evolution was it that put in this human animal the force of ambition? Why should we yield to such an urge, the origin and reason of which remains utterly unknown to us? Why toss our little lives onto the bonfire of an inscrutable purpose? Maybe it would be better to avoid ambition of either the mind or the heart; to turn aside from the struggle to merge battling convictions as well as from the struggle to surpass or to control battling men; to accept life as merely a warm and pleasant interlude, and death itself as a fitting curtain at the end of our inconsequential personal dramas. Walter Savage Landor gives epigrammatic expression to a whole philosophy of renunciation in four famous lines:

> I strove with none; for none was worth my strife.
> Nature I loved and, next to Nature, Art;
> I warmed both hands before the fire of life;
> It sinks, and I am ready to depart.

But, as Longfellow said, these mighty thoughts suggest life's endless toil and endeavor; and poetry is not confined to such martial strains. It speaks a varied language, to match our every mood. In many forms it appeals chiefly to our ear, as music; in others, to the intellect, as mathematical, rhythmical beauty; again, it stirs the emotions, as an expression of our deepest sorrows and joys and aspirations. Let's glance first at the work of those poets for whom O'Shaughnessy speaks, in his famous ode:

> We are the music-makers,
>   And we are the dreamers of dreams.

From Samuel Taylor Coleridge we offer the opening lines of his *Kubla Khan*:

> In Xanadu did Kubla Khan
>   A stately pleasure-dome decree:
> Where Alph, the sacred river, ran
> Through caverns measureless to man
>   Down to a sunless sea.

From Sidney Lanier, consider the first (or any) stanza of his *Song of the Chattahoochee*, the song the mountain stream seems to be singing as it rushes downward to the plains and the sea:

> Out of the hills of Habersham,
> Down the valleys of Hall,
> I hurry amain to reach the plain,

> Run the rapid and leap the fall,
> Split at the rock and together again,
> Accept my bed, or narrow or wide,
> And flee from folly on every side
> With a lover's pain to attain the plain
>> Far from the hills of Habersham,
>> Far from the valleys of Hall.

For the most famous *tour de force*, in representation of the sounds of gurgling water, the student should read Southey's *The Cataract Of Lodore*, which is too long to be quoted here in full, and which loses much of its force in any fragment. But abandoning such onomatopoeic efforts, and going ahead with other examples of sheer musical delight, we select from a dozen suitable melodies of Edgar Allan Poe the last stanza of *To One In Paradise*:

> And all my days are trances,
>> And all my nightly dreams
> Are where thy gray eye glances,
>> And where thy footstep gleams —
> In what ethereal dances,
>> By what eternal streams.

From Shelley's ode *To A Skylark* let's read aloud such stanzas as these:

> Higher still and higher,
>> From the earth thou springest
> Like a cloud of fire;
>> The blue deep thou wingest,
> And singing still dost soar, and soaring ever singest.
>
> In the golden lightning
>> Of the sunken sun,

O'er which clouds are bright'ning,
   Thou dost float and run;
Like an unbodied joy whose race is just begun.

Sound of vernal showers
   On the twinkling grass,
Rain-awakened flowers,
   All that ever was
Joyous, and clear, and fresh, thy music doth surpass.

Teach us, sprite or bird,
   What sweet thoughts are thine:
I have never heard
   Praise of love or wine
That panted forth a flood of rapture so divine.

What objects are the fountains
   Of thy happy strain?
What fields, or waves, or mountains?
   What shapes of sky or plain?
What love of thine own kind? What ignorance of pain?

Waking or asleep,
   Thou of death must deem
Things more true and deep
   Than we mortals dream,
Or how could thy notes flow in such a crystal stream?

We look before and after,
   And pine for what is not:
Our sincerest laughter
   With some pain is fraught;
Our sweetest songs are those that tell of saddest thought.

Teach me half the gladness
   That thy brain must know,

> Such harmonious madness
>   From my lips would flow,
> The world should listen then, as I am listening now.

For a calm and stately cadence listen to Alfred Noyes' *In The Cool Of The Evening*, of which this is the first stanza:

> In the cool of the evening, when the low sweet
>   whispers waken,
> When the laborers turn them homeward, and the
>   weary have their will,
> When the censers of the roses o'er the forest aisles
>   are shaken,
> Is it but the wind that cometh o'er the far green hill?

Or for lilting rhythm and happy impetuous rhyme, almost all of Alfred Noyes' *The Barrel Organ* is worth quoting, but we shall have to suggest nearly two hundred lines with just two short selections:

> The cherry-trees are seas of bloom and soft perfume
>   and sweet perfume,
> The cherry-trees are seas of bloom (and oh,
>   so near to London!)
> And there they say, when dawn is nigh and all
>   the world's a blaze of sky,
> The cuckoo, though he's very shy, will sing a song
>   for London.
>
> Come down to Kew in lilac-time, in lilac-time,
>   in lilac-time;
> Come down to Kew in lilac-time (it isn't far
>   from London!)

And you shall wander hand in hand with Love in summer's wonderland,
Come down to Kew in lilac-time (it isn't far from London!)

There are short staccato measures, as in Thomas Buchanan Read's *Drifting*, of which almost any stanza will serve as an example:

> Yon deep bark goes
> Where traffic blows,
> From lands of sun to lands of snows; —
> This happier one,
> Its course is run
> From lands of snow to lands of sun.

Or verses of bass and guttural majesty, such as the opening lines of Milton's sonnet *On The Late Massacre In Piedmont*:

Avenge, O Lord, thy slaughtered saints, whose bones
   Lie scattered on the Alpine mountains cold;
   Even them who kept thy truth so pure of old,
When all our fathers worshipped stocks and stones,
Forget not . . . .

And because the procession could be endless, we should bring it to a close. Lines that suggest Milton's "linkèd sweetness long drawn out" seem fitting for the purpose, and none could be more perfect than the opening stanza of Gray's *Elegy*:

> The curfew tolls the knell of parting day,
>   The lowing herd winds slowly o'er the lea,
> The plowman homeward plods his weary way,
>   And leaves the world to darkness and to me.

Obviously, every worthwhile line of poetry, no matter how melodious, contains thought as well as music. When we segregate the various appeals of poetry, it must be with a clear recognition that these attributes overlap in every example chosen. All we can try to do by such arbitrary sorting of quoted passages is to highlight one characteristic of poetry at a time, by grouping together selections in which that characteristic seems to be emphasized.

Our language is full of beautiful short lyrics which tell a story; of grief or joy, of triumph or despair. There are stories to express every reflection on human life and its impenetrable destiny. The poets thus put for us, more forcefully, poignantly, and precisely than we can ever do in prose, the thoughts for which we grasp in our contemplative moods. In the following pages we gather together a few illustrations of such sermons in lyrical form.

Many of us, still groping in later years towards the long, long dreams of our youth, are startled to have Thomas Jones, Jr. express our thoughts so well for us in eight lines as simple as these:

> Across the fields of yesterday
>   He sometimes comes to me,
> A little lad just back from play —
>   The lad I used to be.
>
> And yet he smiles so wistfully
>   Once he has crept within,
> I wonder if he hopes to see
>   The man I might have been.

We have read of tyrants who planned, or even constructed, mighty monuments to symbolize and immortalize their power. We know how time eventually converts the walls of their cities to dust, and their very names to oblivion. But let Shelley tell the story in his *Ozymandias Of Egypt*:

> I met a traveler from an antique land
> Who said: Two vast and trunkless legs of stone
> Stand in the desert. Near them, on the sand,
> Half sunk, a shattered visage lies, whose frown
> And wrinkled lip and sneer of cold command
> Tell that its sculptor well those passions read
> Which yet survive, stamped on these lifeless things,
> The hand that mocked them and the heart that fed;
> And on the pedestal these words appear:
> "My name is Ozymandias, king of kings:
> Look on my works, ye Mighty, and despair!"
> Nothing beside remains. Round the decay
> Of that colossal wreck, boundless and bare,
> The lone and level sands stretch far away.

The unbelievable finality of death has weighed upon all human minds at some time, and upon some human minds at all times. But the metamorphosis of a living organism, capable of love and laughter, into a mere collection of inorganic chemical elements, has never been put with more tragic succinctness than in the conclusion of Wordsworth's stanzas *To Lucy*:

> A slumber did my spirit seal;
> I had no human fears:

> She seemed a thing that could not feel
> The touch of earthly years.
>
> No motion has she now, or force;
> She neither hears nor sees;
> Rolled round in earth's diurnal course,
> With rocks, and stones, and trees.

Allegories of life, in prose and poetry, have been written repeatedly from the earliest days of recorded thought. In the nineteenth century, especially in America, there was something about the *Zeitgeist* which prompted an outpouring of such allegories in lyric verse. Longfellow, in *Excelsior*, and Lanier, in *The Song Of The Chattahoochee*, glorified a sense of Duty as the supreme motivating force, driving youth (or river) on to fulfillment of its destiny. Holmes, in *The Chambered Nautilus*, pictures growth and the aspiration to growth as a more natural dispensation, permitted alike to the shell of the crustacean and the soul of the mammal by a generous deity. But Poe, finding a loophole for once in his morbid fatalism, romantically promises that each of us, in our journey known as life, may reach the golden land of our dreams, if we only have the imagination and courage to ride toward it with sufficient boldness and unshaken faith. Of all these poetic personifications of that groping forward and upward which we associate with the strange passage between birth and death, I like his *Eldorado* best:

> Gaily bedight,
> A gallant knight
> In sunshine and in shadow
> Had journeyed long,
> Singing a song,
> In search of Eldorado.

> But he grew old —
> This knight so bold —
> And o'er his heart a shadow
> Fell, as he found
> No spot of ground
> That looked like Eldorado.
>
> And, as his strength
> Failed him at length,
> He met a pilgrim shadow:
> "Shadow," said he,
> "Where can it be —
> This land of Eldorado?"
>
> "Over the mountains
> Of the moon,
> Down the valley of the Shadow
> Ride, boldly ride,"
> The shade replied,
> "If you seek for Eldorado!"

The artistic world — like many another — is full of sham and pretense. Playwrights veer from ridicule of war to glorification of war, depending on the current fashion among their fellow-intellectuals. Poets cry out in dolorous self-pity over woes which would vanish at the first touch of common sense and honest effort. But real depth of feeling can never be faked, and the products of such artificial fervor omit a faint glow, because of the light of timeliness which is reflected on them, and then become recognizable as dead coals to be swept away in the next generation's rubbish. Or so Henry Van Dyke assures us with convincing sincerity in *The Valley Of Vain Verses*:

> The grief that is but feigning,
> And weeps melodious tears
> Of delicate complaining
> From self-indulgent years;
> The mirth that is but madness,
> And has no inward gladness
> Beneath its laughter, straining
> To capture thoughtless ears;
>
> The love that is but passion
> Of amber-scented lust;
> The doubt that is but fashion;
> The faith that has no trust; —
> These Thamyris disperses,
> In the Valley of Vain Verses
> Below the Mount Parnassian,
> And they crumble into dust.

The contempt of the cavalier spirit for the cruel intolerance of Puritanism; the clash between the conception of life as a pleasure and the conception of life as a painful duty; these are far older than Roundhead and Cavalier. They go back to the first moralist and sinner contemporary with each other. Most poetry on the subject has always been partial to the sinner; even Milton found great difficulty in restraining the tendencies of his muse to get over on the Cavalier side of this philosophical fence. But few writers have compressed so much biting scorn of the cold self-righteous judges, and such understanding sympathy on behalf of the romantic sinner, into so few lines, as Katherine Lee Bates in her short narrative poem on the hanging of *Sarah Threeneedles*:

Invitation To Poetry 177

By the grim grace of the Puritans she had been brought
   Into their frigid meeting-house to list
Her funeral sermon before the rope ran taut.
   Soft neck that he had kissed!

Through the narrow window her dazed blue eyes
     could see
   The rope. Like a glittering icicle it hung
From the hoar cross-beam of the horrible gallows-tree.
   His arms about her flung!

Two captive Indians and one Guinea slave,
   Hating at heart the merciless white God,
In the stubborn ground were hacking her shallow grave.
   Sweet April path they trod!

Her shivering neighbors thrilled to the fierce discourse
   Of the minister, who thundered the dire sting
Of a sinner's death till his vehement voice went hoarse.
   She heard love's whispering.

And still she stood while the frozen communion bread,
   That the preacher broke ere he poured the chilly wine,
Rattling into the plates, her judges fed.
   Her food was more divine.

   Those of us who burn with a fever to roam the far places of the earth are inclined to look with scorn upon the more placid citizens who do not have the desire to leave their comfortable homes or the courage to upset the regular routine of their lives by distant travels. But few could express this scorn more pungently in a whole volume than Ruth Comfort Mitchell has done in the fourteen lines of her sonnet, *The Travel Bureau*:

All day she sits behind a bright brass rail
Planning proud journeyings in terms that bring
Far places near; high-colored words that sing,
"The Taj Mahal at Agra," "Kashmir's Vale,"
Spanning wide spaces with her clear detail,
"Sevilla or Fiesole in spring,
Through the fiords in June." Her words take wing.
She is the minstrel of the great out-trail.
At half past five she puts her maps away,
Pins on a gray, meek hat, and braves the sleet,
A timid eye on traffic. Dully gray
The house that harbors her in a gray street,
The close, sequestered, colorless retreat
Where she was born, where she will always stay.

Since the last half of the eighteenth century the oppression of the poor by the rich has loomed increasingly as a theme for poets as well as more practical preachers. When O'Shaughnessy said that three men with a new song's measure could trample an empire down, he was not exaggerating unduly, as the *Marseillaise* had already proved. And while it has usually remained for the demagogues to upset states and kingdoms by playing on class distinctions, and while it is such prosaically solemn gentlemen as Rousseau, Marx, and Lenin that the revolutionists have usually revered as their gods, the poets have frequently blown on the smouldering embers of social unrest with blasts so seemingly gentle but persistently effective as to make themselves important apostles of discontent. Thomas Hood's *The Bridge Of Sighs* and *The Song Of The Shirt*, Edwin Markham's *The Man With The Hoe*, and Margaret Widdemer's *God And The Strong Ones* come readily to mind; each worth more towards improving the social conscience than a dozen tracts by some long-haired anarchist whose thinking all ends with a barricade in the streets. And the most compelling sermon for the alleviation of working conditions of the poor that I have ever read, in prose or poetry, was compressed into just four lines by Sarah N. Cleghorn in the following quatrain:

> The golf links lie so near the mill
>   That almost every day
> The laboring children can look out
>   And see the men at play.

Our contemporary world seems to be reeling to ever madder music, and moving at an ever faster pace. We can't keep up with it. We rush to make more money to spend, and then lose our sleep to find ways to spend it. Sun and sky and stars, mountain, forest, and sea, are just names for parts of the environment in which we do our treadmill race. We are in no mood to become acquainted with these friends. Our religion has little faith, and less promise of future happiness on this earth or in a heaven to come. Perhaps we'd all be happier as simple pagans, ignorantly trembling before the gods of thunder, and leisurely thrilling to the daily glories of sunrise and the mystery of moonlight on the water. So have declared a thousand sages, each of his contemporary world, from the Stoics of ancient Greece to the nostalgic farm boys turned philosophers of modern America. But never has the thought been put more incisively, convincingly, or beautifully than by Wordsworth in that justly famous sonnet with which we close this section of our poetry parade:

> The world is too much with us; late and soon,
> Getting and spending, we lay waste our powers:

> Little we see in Nature that is ours;
> We have given our hearts away, a sordid boon!
> This sea that bares her bosom to the moon,
> The winds that will be howling at all hours,
> And are up-gathered now like sleeping flowers;
> For this, for everything, we are out of tune;
> It moves us not. — Great God! I'd rather be
> A Pagan suckled in a creed outworn;
> So might I, standing on this pleasant lea,
> Have glimpses that would make me less forlorn;
> Have sight of Proteus rising from the sea;
> Or hear old Triton blow his wreathèd horn.

In our arbitrary isolation of the strings of human reaction played upon by poetry, we name last that string which the poets pluck most often. Clearly, the appeal to our emotions is the most widely recognized function of those who deal in rhythmic cadences and rhyme. In the "sea without a shore, of human joys and wonders and regrets," there is no wave nor trough on which the poets have not turned their searchlight, to make it stand out more clearly with the illumination and the shadows they have cast around it.

The field of illustrations is coextensive with our whole treasury of verse. Let's narrow our choice, therefore, to stanzas which express or intensify the particular emotion of romantic love, and select a few examples to show how the music makers put our purest or most passionate thoughts for us, into combinations of word and sound that we could never achieve ourselves.

It is not alone the twentieth-century dramatists, leading sophisticated lives in penthouses on top of Manhattan

Invitation To Poetry 181

skyscrapers, who look with longing on the simple pleasures of pastoral scenes; it is nothing new for urban celebrities harried by the pace of their ambitious lives to write wistfully — and almost convincingly — of the joys of love and life in a rural setting, where the contented toiler and his virtuous wife pursue the even tenor of their ways. Even in the England of good Queen Bess, almost four hundred years ago, courtiers interrupted their rivalry for advancement with rivalry in verses, painting the delights of an Arcadian existence. One of these outpourings still remains today the best-known version of this nostalgic dream. It's Christopher Marlowe's *The Passionate Shepherd To His Love*:

> Come live with me and be my Love,
> And we will all the pleasures prove
> That hills and valleys, dales and fields,
> Or woods or steepy mountain yields.
>
> And we will sit upon the rocks,
> And see the shepherds feed their flocks
> By shallow rivers, to whose falls
> Melodious birds sing madrigals.
>
> And I will make thee beds of roses
> And a thousand fragrant posies;
> A cap of flowers, and a kirtle
> Embroidered all with leaves of myrtle.
>
> A gown made of the finest wool
> Which from our pretty lambs we pull;
> Fair-lined slippers for the cold,
> With buckles of the purest gold.

> A belt of straw and ivy-buds
> With coral clasps and amber studs:
> And if these pleasures may thee move,
> Come live with me and be my Love.
>
> The shepherd swains shall dance and sing
> For thy delight each May morning:
> If these delights thy mind may move,
> Then live with me and be my Love.

Even in the days of Marlowe and Sidney and Greene, however, there were clear-eyed scoffers to point out the flaws in this idyllic picture. Sir Walter Raleigh penned *The Nymph's Reply To The Passionate Shepherd*, in which, for sound reasons, the nymph said "No." But perhaps the best argument, to our modern ears, for a little more common sense in our poetic imaginings of romantic bliss, has been presented very unpretentiously by Nathaniel Parker Willis in *Love In A Cottage*:

> They may talk of love in a cottage,
>   And bowers of trellised vine, —
> Of nature bewitchingly simple,
>   And milkmaids half divine;
> They may talk of the pleasure of sleeping
>   In the shade of a spreading tree,
> And a walk in the fields at morning,
>   By the side of a footstep free!
>
> But give me a sly flirtation
>   By the light of a chandelier, —
> With music to play in the pauses,
>   And nobody very near;
> Or a seat on a silken sofa,

> With a glass of pure old wine,
> And mamma too blind to discover
> The small white hand in mine.
>
> Your love in a cottage is hungry,
> Your vine is a nest for flies, —
> Your milkmaid shocks the Graces,
> And simplicity talks of pies!
> You lie down to your shady slumber
> And wake with a bug in your ear,
> And your damsel that walks in the morning
> Is shod like a mountaineer.
>
> True love is at home on a carpet,
> And mightily likes his ease; —
> And true love has an eye for a dinner,
> And starves beneath shady trees.
> His wing is the fan of a lady,
> His foot's an invisible thing,
> And his arrow is tipped with a jewel,
> And shot from a silver string.

Lest we grow facetiously out of tune, however, with the mood of youthful desire, let's turn to a selection "in praise of her" by one of the most impassioned of all our poets of love. Whereas Milton, the Puritan and scholar, wrote love poetry that we might have expected of Byron (had Byron been that good), the drinking cavalier, Edgar Allan Poe, wrote love poetry that we might have expected of Milton. Passion pure and undefiled has never had an abler or more devoted laureate. We have already quoted, in another connection, the last stanza of Poe's *To One In Paradise*, but will still offer here the first stanza, because it sums up so beautifully the totality of worship felt by youth for its chosen mate:

> Thou wast all that to me, love,
>   For which my soul did pine:
> A green isle in the sea, love,
>   A fountain and a shrine
> All wreathed with fairy fruits and flowers,
>   And all the flowers were mine.

Perhaps the past tense makes this seem more heartfelt, because we are all aware of the tragic death of Poe's young bride, which so affected his life thereafter. But here is another selection from Poe, *To Helen*, in the present tense, with all the exaggerated and hopeful ardor of the lover who sees peace and happiness ahead.

> Helen, thy beauty is to me
>   Like those Nicaean barks of yore,
> That gently, o'er a perfumed sea,
>   The weary, wayworn wanderer bore
>   To his own native shore.
>
> On desperate seas long wont to roam,
>   Thy hyacinth hair, thy classic face,
> Thy Naiad airs, have brought me home
>   To the glory that was Greece
> And the grandeur that was Rome.
>
> Lo! in yon brilliant window-niche
>   How statue-like I see thee stand,
> The agate lamp within thy hand!
>   Ah, Psyche, from the regions which
>   Are Holy Land!

Invitation To Poetry 185

If there seems something inescapably stilted and self-conscious about Poe, however, even in his most successful rhythmical creations of beauty (his own phrase), let's read aloud, as calmly and simply as we might sit listening to an organ, this prothalamic prayer by Jean Ingelow:

> One morning, oh! so early, my belovèd, my belovèd,
> All the birds were singing blithely, as if never they
>   would cease;
> 'Twas a thrush sang in my garden, "Hear the story,
>   hear the story!"
>   And the lark sang, "Give us glory!"
>   And the dove said, "Give us peace!"
>
> Then I hearkened, oh! so early, my belovèd,
>   my belovèd,
> To that murmur from the woodland of the dove,
>   my dear, the dove;
> When the nightingale came after, "Give us fame to
>   sweeten duty!"
>   When the wren sang, "Give us beauty!"
>   She made answer, "Give us love!"
>
> Sweet is spring, and sweet the morning, my belovèd,
>   my belovèd;
> Now for us doth spring, doth morning, wait upon
>   the year's increase,
> And my prayer goes up, "Oh, give us, crowned in
>   youth with marriage glory,
>   Give for all our life's dear story,
>   Give us love, and give us peace!"

Or let us pause for a different and shorter prayer, by a maiden about to surrender her whole life into the keeping of the man she is marrying. It is called *The Door*, and is by Mary Carolyn Davies:

> The littlest door, the inner door,
>   I swing it wide,
> Now in my heart there is no more
>   To hide.
>
> The farthest door — the latch at last
>   Is lifted; see.
> I kept the little fortress fast.
>   — Be good to me.

Fitzgerald's translation of Omar makes him say that heaven is but the vision of fulfilled desire. Not the fulfillment itself, be it noted, for Omar was too cynically wise to believe that the fulfillment could ever approach the heights which anticipation had painted; but the *vision* of this fulfillment. While most of us cling to the hope that for some mortals, sometime, somewhere, there are dreams which come true without losing any of their lustre, the poets who grow ecstatic over love's fulfillment always do so in advance of the event. Even when there may be a narrative describing the scene as something in the present or as the past, we find that the poem is named *Prothalamion*, showing that what is described is merely the scene as it is expected to be. Omar could take a sad I-told-you-so kind of pleasure out of the fact that there are few if any post-nuptial rhapsodies on the poets' wedding nights.

But the vision lends itself to poetic treatment, of every degree of enthusiasm and aphrodisiac imagery. Among the best examples, it seems to me, of such poetry in praise of Eros, is one surprisingly unhurried in rhythm and rhyme and action. It is as though these lovers felt such assurance of continued happiness together that even the ecstasy of the nuptial hour melted into a calm and supreme content. Not unexpectedly, the title is *Prothalamion*, and it is by Francis Brett Young.

Invitation To Poetry

When the evening came my love said to me:
    Let us go into the garden now that the sky is cool,
The garden of black hellebore and rosemary,
    Where wild woodruff spills in a milky pool.

Low we passed in the twilight, for the wavering heat
    Of day had waned, and round that shaded plot
Of secret beauty the thickets clustered sweet:
    Here is heaven, our hearts whispered, but our lips
        spake not.

Between that old garden and seas of lazy foam
    Gloomy and beautiful alleys of trees arise
With spire of cypress and dreamy beechen dome,
    So dark that our enchanted sight knew nothing but the
        skies.

Veiled with soft air, drenched in the roses' musk
    Or the dusky, dark carnation's breath of clove;
No stars burned in their deeps, but through the dusk
    I saw my love's eyes, and they were brimmed with love.

No star their secret ravished, no wasting moon
    Mocked the sad transience of those eternal hours:
Only the soft, unseeing heaven of June,
    The ghosts of great trees, and the sleeping flowers.

For doves that crooned in the leafy noonday now
    Were silent; the night-jar sought his secret covers,
Nor even a mild sea-whisper moved a creaking bough —
    Was ever a silence deeper made for lovers?

Was ever a moment meeter made for love?
    Beautiful are your closed lips beneath my kiss;

And all your yielding sweetness beautiful —
Oh, never in all the world was such a night as this!

A parallel selection which we offer for this same mood is of a different tempo. It almost trembles with the urgency of passion. Strange to say, it was written by a woman, Laurence Hope. As the patient reader may already be well aware, Laurence Hope was the pseudonym of an English woman, the wife of Major-General Nicholson, and was stationed with him in India for many years. She became imbued with the philosophy of India, especially as it regarded women as the slaves and playthings of men. If this seems to be an exaggerated comment, please recall that the Hindu practice of suttee required the wives and concubines of a dead chieftain to burn themselves to death in his funeral pyre, on the theory that their usefulness was now gone; and then note that at the very time the British were trying to stamp out this practice, Mrs. Nicholson, at the age of thirty-nine, committed suicide on the grave of her husband.

Most of her love poetry, however, was written from the point of view of the man. And perhaps because of her acquired belief that woman's one great duty and glory lay in catering to the passions of her lord and master, she has once or twice raised the near-erotic almost to the sublime, by the pure intensity of the passion portrayed and by the beauty of her verse. Passing over the equally famous *Choti Tinchaurya* (also known as *The Bride*), we offer her *The Garden Of Kama*. Kama is the Indian god of love, corresponding to Eros in the Greek Pantheon:

The daylight is dying,
The Flying Fox flying,
   Amber and amethyst burn in the sky.

Invitation To Poetry

See, the sun throws a late,
Lingering, roseate
   Kiss to the landscape to bid it good-bye.

The time of our Trysting!
Oh, come, unresisting,
   Lovely, expectant, on tentative feet.
Shadow shall cover us,
Roses bend over us,
   Making a bride chamber, sacred and sweet.

We know not Life's reason,
The length of its season,
   Know not if they know, the great Ones above.
We none of us sought it,
And few could support it,
   Were it not gilt with the glamour of love.

But much is forgiven
To Gods who have given,
   If but for an hour, the Rapture of Youth.
You do not yet know it,
But Kama shall show it,
   Changing your dreams to his Exquisite Truth.

The Fireflies shall light you,
And naught shall affright you,
   Nothing shall trouble the Flight of the Hours.
Come, for I wait for you,
Night is too late for you,
   Come, while the twilight is closing the flowers.

Every breeze still is,
And, scented with lilies,

> Cooled by the twilight, refreshed by the dew,
> The garden lies breathless,
> Where Kama, the Deathless,
> In the hushed starlight, is waiting for you.

In my humble opinion, and letting the critics faint where they may, this is the best love poem in the English language. Certainly, the two lines,

> Oh, come, unresisting,
> Lovely, expectant, on tentative feet,

say as much, and say it as beautifully, as we could expect of two lines in any language, or by any poet.

But romantic love is not all passion, and most romantic poetry approaches the altar more obliquely. Much of the best lyric singing is designed to crystallize more subtle and more gentle reaches of thought and feeling. How, for instance, could anyone express gratitude for renewed joy in life more compactly, more sincerely, than Jessie B. Rittenhouse in *Debts*:

> My debt to you, Belovèd,
> Is one I cannot pay
> In any coin of any realm
> On any reckoning day;
>
> For where is he shall figure
> The debt, when all is said,
> To one who makes you dream again
> When all the dreams were dead?

> Or where is the appraiser
> > Who shall the claim compute
> Of one who makes you sing again
> > When all the songs were mute?

If we allow to the poet license to achieve emphasis by turbulent exaggeration and a tempestuously sweeping meter, we find in Ernest Dowson's *Impenitentia Ultima* a cry of painful guilt and regret that reaches our sympathy by its very hopelessness, while it sways our senses by the music of its lines:

> Before my light goes out forever, if God should
> > give me choice of graces,
> > I would not reck of length of days, nor crave
> > for things to be;
> But cry: "One day of the great lost days, one face
> > of all the faces,
> > Grant me to see and touch once more and
> > nothing more to see!"
>
> For, Lord, I was free of all Thy flowers, but I
> > chose the world's sad roses,
> > And that is why my feet are torn and mine
> > eyes are blind with sweat,
> But at Thy terrible judgment seat, when this my
> > tired life closes,
> > I am ready to reap whereof I sowed, and pay
> > my righteous debt.
>
> But once, before the sand is run and the silver
> > thread is broken,

Give me a grace and cast aside the veil of
    dolorous years,
Grant me one hour of all mine hours, and let me
    see for a token,
    Her pure and pitiful eyes shine out, and bathe
        her feet with tears.

Her pitiful hands should calm and her hair
    stream down and blind me,
    Out of the sight of night, and out of the reach
        of fear,
And her eyes should be my light whilst the sun
    went out behind me,
    And the viols in her voice be the last sound
        in mine ear.

Before the ruining waters fall and my life be
    carried under,
    And Thine anger cleave me through, as a child
        cuts down a flower,
I will praise Thee, Lord, in hell, while my limbs
    are racked asunder,
    For the last sad sight of her face and the little
        grace of an hour.

And for the closing place of honor, in this too thin sheaf of pages from the poetry of love, we choose Amelia Josephine Burr's *To Her — Unspoken*. The feeling here is too deep, and the expression too sincere, to admit of any doubt:

Go to him, ah, go to him, and lift your eyes
    aglow to him;
    Fear not royally to give whatever he may claim;

Invitation To Poetry

> All your spirit's treasury scruple not to show to him.
>   He is noble; meet him with a pride too high
>   for shame.
>
> Say to him, ah, say to him, that soul and body sway
>   to him;
>   Cast away the cowardice that counsels you
>   to flight,
> Lest you turn at last to find that you have lost
>   the way to him,
>   Lest you stretch your arms in vain across a starless
>   night.
>
> Be to him, ah, be to him, the key that sets joy
>   free to him;
>   Teach him all the tenderness that only love
>   can know,
> And if ever there should come a memory of
>   me to him,
>   Bid him judge me gently for the sake of long ago.

In finishing this chapter on poetry with so much left unsaid, we owe perhaps our humblest apologies to Edward Lear, Lewis Carroll, W.S. Gilbert, Guy Wetmore Carryl, and the other "nonsense" poets.

A little nonsense now and then is not only relished by the best of men, but by some of us who are not so good. There is a singing quality about Lewis Carroll's *The Walrus And The Carpenter* or Edward Lear's *The Owl And The Pussy-Cat*, which seems to me to give them an irresistible charm. And even many people who at first find more serious poetry boring can gradually see themselves being drawn into a wider browsing, through the enjoyment they get out of the material which Burton Egbert Stevenson classifies under *The Kindly Muse, The Mimics, Glints O'Sunshine,* and *Just Nonsense.*

But there are so many points of departure for "fresh woods and pastures new" in the realm of poetry, that we must call a halt to our travels altogether. If any reader is so kind as to pay attention to direct advice from a long-winded dabbler, this is the place for me to put it. So I have several pieces of such advice to give.

First, do not memorize poetry. It is usually a waste of time, and certainly is the last way to learn to love the poets.

Second, do read poetry, and try to understand it. When we read a short story — unless by one of our more esoteric moderns — we remember the plot, because we understand it. To the extent that we really grasp what the poet is saying, all that he is saying, we remember that, too. We are able to repeat it, at least in our own words. And since the greater the poem, the more concise and meaning-laden is each word of the poet, it is surprising how soon we find ourselves, after rereadings in which the full sense becomes clearer every time, able to tell the poet's story in his own words — and with a feeling of sharing with him his deepest thoughts.

And finally, may I be pardoned for injecting a very personal comment, with sincerity as its only excuse. In a busy life of many ups and downs, with interest scattered over business and family and books and games and travel, I have derived more pleasure from my long friendship with the poets than from any other source. If I can persuade even a few other struggling mortals to make a closer acquaintance with "the mighty minds of old," and even with the lesser minds who are no further away than our bookshelves and an easy chair, I shall have done a little something to express my gratitude.

Invitation To Poetry

The reading of poetry is not necessarily, as many believe, either the profession of a pedant or the pastime of a recluse. It is not the mark of an introvert, any more than a love for music, or chess, or mathematics. And it leads not just so much further into a world of books, but — through absorption of the thinking of so many diverse minds on all the phenomena of life and the universe — to a greater awareness of the pulsing forces, clashing ideologies, and infinite complexes and aspirations which make up the throbbing world of which we are a part. As Angela Morgan points out, in her beautiful poem, *Kinship,* quoted below, the nature of our daily job has little bearing on the extent to which any of us may reach out across time and space with our thoughts:

>   I am aware,
> As I go commonly sweeping the stair,
> Doing my part of the every-day care —
> Human and simple my lot and my share —
>   I am aware of a marvelous thing:
>   Voices that murmur and ethers that ring
>   In the far stellar spaces where cherubim sing.
> I am aware of the passion that pours
> Down the channels of fire through Infinity's doors;
>   Forces terrific, with melody shod,
>   Music that mates with the pulses of God.
> I am aware of the glory that runs
> From the core of myself to the core of the suns.
>   Bound to the stars by invisible chains,
>   Blaze of eternity now in my veins,
>   Seeing the rush of ethereal rains
> Here in the midst of the every-day air —
>   I am aware.

    I am aware,
As I sit quietly here in my chair,
Sewing or reading or braiding my hair —
Human and simple my lot and my share —
  I am aware of the systems that swing
Through the aisles of creation on heavenly wing,
  I am aware of a marvelous thing:
Trail of the comets in furious flight,
Thunders of beauty that shatter the night,
   Terrible triumph of pageants that march
   To the trumpets of time through Eternity's arch.
I am aware of the splendor that ties
All the things of the earth with the things of the skies,
   Here in my body the heavenly heat,
   Here in my flesh the melodious beat
   Of the planets that circle Divinity's feet.
As I sit silently here in my chair,
   I am aware.

CHAPTER XI

Old Books And New Reviews

It was long ago pointed out that of the making of books there is no end. There isn't even a pause. If all the books which rolled from the presses of this country alone last year were stacked side by side on one shelf, the shelf would have to be eighty miles long. If only one book of each title were used, the shelf would still be one hundred and fifty yards long. And the number of titles printed since Gutenberg set up his first press in Mainz, nearly five hundred years ago, would reach a discouraging total. All of us, young or old, who can read, are eternally faced with the problem of selection.

This chapter of pointers on books, mostly of the past rather than of the present, is offered, therefore, despite considerable misgiving. Before thus rushing in, where critics fear to tread, the author would like to reach an understanding with any reader who may be so flattering as to use these pages, even partly or occasionally, as a guide to his own reading. That understanding is simply that neither in form nor purpose is this list a critical survey. The hundred books mentioned below do not constitute a skeleton of knowledge, of any or all subjects. They are certainly not considered by me to be the hundred "best" books, whatever that might mean. If the old argument about which ten books you would choose for your sole companions on a desert island were revised to permit a hundred volumes instead, these are by no means the hundred books this author would, at the present stage of his ignorance and desires, either choose or recommend.

The basis of the list here made is far more personal. These are simply the one hundred books, out of some two or three thousand that have given me pleasure, which I should be most sorry to have missed. This chapter is a purely casual series of comments on books that I have either liked most, or been most glad to have read for what I got out of them. It is simply a random and incomplete and intimate reminiscence of remembered high spots in thirty years of miscellaneous browsing.

My one and only qualification as a critic is that my taste appears to have been reasonably orthodox. For that reason, in listing some of the books that I have enjoyed, I can hope that any reader who may thus be encouraged to pick up this or that volume will also have a fair chance of enjoying it. To this end I promise you honesty in stating what I have really thought about any masterpiece or trifle, alike, and not what the literary or scientific pundits have decided I should have thought.

In so informal a guide to reading pleasure a studied order or organization of the material becomes not only unnecessary, but undesirable. Except for a few broad divisions, therefore, to save the time of some seeker in a particular field of knowledge, no classification of the works discussed here has been attempted. For convenience, we can follow roughly the chronological parade of the authors across the centuries, but even that arrangement may be called to mind more often by its breach than by its observance. So let's stop building defenses, and talk about books.

GENERAL PROSE LITERATURE

1. CERVANTES: DON QUIXOTE. A more complete identification is, *The Life And Achievements Of The Renown'd Don Quixote De La Mancha*, by Miguel de Cervantes-Saavedra. It leads this subdivision simply by the time of its appearance — about 1600.

Few books have ever had so direct and considerable an influence. *Don Quixote* practically laughed knight-errantry, and an exaggerated pseudo-chivalry that was still hanging on in Europe, right out of existence. Not even the most penniless second son of the most pompous grandee could see such mediaeval posing as anything but ridiculous after Cervantes painted this picture.

Besides having the indicated historical value, Don Quixote is easy and enjoyable reading. The befuddled but idealistic Don, his lean nag, Rozinante, and his down-to-earth squire, Sancho Pança, move on from one silly adventure to another with the pace of a fairy tale.

My copy is Ozell's revision of the English translation by Peter Motteux, published by Modern Library.

2. DANIEL DEFOE: ROBINSON CRUSOE. This is too well-known to need any comment here. The theme of man-alone-on-a-desert-island seems so commonplace today that we do well to remember it had a literary birth and a beginning in this creation of Defoe. *Robinson Crusoe* is still one of the most delightful books in all literature.

My copy is an unabridged edition published (many years ago) by R.F. Fenno & Company, N.Y.

3. JONATHAN SWIFT: GULLIVER'S TRAVELS. The travels include *A Voyage To Lilliput*, *A Voyage To Brobdingnag*, *A Voyage To Laputa* and *A Voyage To The*

Houyhnhnms. The first of these, in particular, describing the author's experiences in a land peopled by human beings less than six inches high, has become a part of the background of universal conversation and consciousness.

Intended as a satire on the stupidities and hypocrisies of mankind, *Gulliver's Travels* has achieved tremendous and perennial fame as a simple adventure story. As either satire or adventure, it is one of the great works of world literature.

My copy is a one-volume publication of Modern Library, which also contains *A Tale Of A Tub* and *The Battle Of The Books* by the same author.

4. LE BARON DE MONTESQUIEU: THE PERSIAN LETTERS. Montesquieu's greatest work was a long and obviously profound essay on *The Spirit Of Laws*. But I can't list it here for the simple reason that I have never read it. The critics who start sneering at me for having omitted Montaigne's *Essays*, or Descartes' *Discourse*, or Rousseau's *The Social Contract*, or a dozen other famous masterpieces of pre-revolutionary France, will have to be pacified with the same answer.

The Persian Letters is a satire, held together by a flimsy thread of romance, on the governments, morals, and manners of France and Western Europe in the early eighteenth century. It is told through the letters to and from two Persians who have left the land of seraglios to visit the lands where monogamy is at least the ideal. The author bribes his readers to wade through comments on laws and customs by interlacing chapters which are sometimes as spicy as even a Frenchman could desire.

My copy, which also contains Montesquieu's *Considerations On The Causes Of Roman Greatness And Decay*, was published in Paris by Didot Frères in 1853. (With

Old Books And New Reviews

regard to French, at least, I practice what I have preached above, by never reading translations.) But an English translation is available in any good library.

5. VOLTAIRE: CANDIDE. Leibnitz, famous as a philosopher but much greater as a mathematician, had propounded the thesis that "everything is for the best in this the best of all possible worlds." Voltaire gave rein to his disgust at such casuistical nonsense, in a satirical novel of the adventures and mishaps of a man who believed it. Irving S. Cobb did the same thing a hundred and fifty years later in one short but brilliant anecdote ending, "Lord, this is getting plum' ridiculous."

My copy of *Candide* was published by Fortic, Paris, and also contains *Zadig* by the same author.

6. EUGÈNE SUE: THE WANDERING JEW: It has been thirty years, at least, since I read this long novelized chain of romantic melodrama. The impression it made is still more vivid with me today than that of a great many hundreds of books I have read since. It is a story of plots and intrigue, kept to a very earthy level despite a supernatural base, that would make most of our present-day spy-fiction seem fleshless by comparison. I should be sorry to have missed it.

My copy (an English translation — I was not up to the French when I read this) is a one-volume edition published by A.L. Burt Company.

7. SIR WALTER SCOTT: IVANHOE. Here is sheer romance in the older and more chivalrous tradition. To many of us, when our world was still young, this was romance at its best.

My copy, one of The Windermere Series, with illustrations by Milo Winter, is published by Rand, McNally & Company.

8. JAMES FENIMORE COOPER: THE DEERSLAYER. Having read and enjoyed all of Cooper in my youth, it is difficult for me to pick just one title to represent him here. But certainly I can allot him only one niche, at the expense of other authors and other books which I would thereby have missed in this imaginary elimination. So selection of the *The Deerslayer* is purely an idiosyncrasy of personal preference. This is, as certainly most of my readers already know, a highly colored story of the "cowboy and Indians" type, when the "cowboy" side was taken by the pioneer settlers of the American colonial period. The characterization is artificial, but the action moves swiftly and the interest never lags. Also, Cooper is worth reading particularly for a special reason. He has always been one of the most widely popular American authors on the other side of the Atlantic, and for a hundred years the ideas of Europeans concerning our country and ourselves have been greatly influenced by their reading of Cooper's tales.

My copy of *The Deerslayer*, with pictures by N.C. Wyeth, was published by Charles Scribner's Sons in 1929.

9. RUDOLPH ERICH RASPE: BARON MUNCHAUSEN. Here are tall tales than which there are no taller. The Baron earned for himself a reputation of being the greatest liar in all fact or fiction. Until that reputation is taken away from him by some even more arresting and more fanciful effort, his boastful account of his amazing exploits makes itself well worth reading.

Baron Munchausen himself was an actual character, an honored German diplomat. These tales attributed to him, or at least the tales of his Russian expedition which constitute the kernel of the modern expanded versions, were written by a German adventurer and swindler named Raspe.

My copy is one of the Lotos Series, published in 1889 by Trubmer & Company of London.

10. WASHINGTON IRVING: THE SKETCH BOOK. Who would want to miss the tale of *Rip Van Winkle*, or *The Legend Of Sleepy Hollow*?

My copy is a volume of the Longmans' English Classics series, published by Longmans, Green & Company.

11. CHARLES DICKENS: A TALE OF TWO CITIES. Here's a heroic tale of danger and romance and sacrifice during the terrible days of the French Revolution. It is perhaps the least typical of all Dickens' works, but I enjoyed it the most.

My copy is one volume, including also *Sketches By Boz*, of a complete set of Dickens published many years ago by John W. Lovell Company.

12. CHARLES DICKENS: DAVID COPPERFIELD. I have never been to England, but I *have* read Dickens. This may be even better than making the trip, for Dickens gives us the England of the first half of the nineteenth century, before world wars, class struggles, and a collapsing empire had changed the serenity of its ways.

David Copperfield is the success story of an other and calmer age. Here is the realm of the pompous and penniless Mr. Micawber, always waiting for something to turn up; of the arch hypocrite and "'umble" villain, Uriah Heep; of Peggotty and the angelic Agnes; of the beloved Dora and the upright David himself; all characters that live as vividly and surely as any that breathe in the pages of fiction. This is the most popular work of one of the world's most popular authors.

My copy is one volume of the same set of Dickens' works referred to above, published by John W. Lovell Company of New York.

13. ALEXANDRE DUMAS: THE COUNT OF MONTE CRISTO. Let's concoct a recipe for the most exciting possible piece of adventure fiction. First we'll take a happy young man, on the eve of his wedding, and have him crookedly and unjustly condemned to a foul dungeon of a prison. Then after great suffering we'll have him engineer a hair-raising and successful escape, taking with him the secret of a fabulous treasure, which has been passed on to him by a dying fellow prisoner. Then we'll have this treasure prove real, and come into the possession of our escaped hero, who now masquerades as a tremendously wealthy nobleman, entirely above suspicion, in the very city where live the selfish friends who sent him to prison. Next, leisurely, inexorably, with a lot of oriental savoring of the pleasure of being a guiding hand to fate, our hero takes his deserved revenge. Put this all together as one smoothly connected, convincing story — and if you are a genius the result may be half as interesting as Dumas made it. To my mind, reading "Monte Cristo" for the first time is one of life's memorable pleasures.

My copy is an ancient six-volume set, published by Calmann-Lévy of Paris.

14. ALEXANDRE DUMAS: THE THREE MUSKETEERS. Athos, Porthos, and Aramis are the three musketeers in the service of Louis XIII of France. It is the period when that monarch and Cardinal Richelieu play chess with

each other every evening, after engaging in intrigues against each other every day. Duels are fought at the drop of a handkerchief — preferably a lady's handkerchief — and by none more readily, or more politely, than by these guardsmen of the king. But the youthful and swashbuckling D'Artagnan, a Gascon apprentice musketeer, is the hero of this famous romance, which has been called "the best-known novel in the world." For this last and other reasons I should hate to have missed it — but my enthusiasm is only lukewarm, nevertheless.

Although I do not recommend an abridgement in this instance, my copy is such an abridgement, nevertheless, published by Ginn & Company, for school use, in 1904. There is an excellent edition in English, translated by Philip Schuyler Allen, illustrated by Milo Winter, in the Windermere Series by Rand, McNally & Company.

15. CHARLES KINGSLEY: HYPATIA. Throughout the period of Roman greatness the fountainhead of Greek culture and tradition remained not on the mainland of Greece nor on the islands of the Aegean, but at Alexandria, in Egypt. Even in the fifth century, when barbarians were already trampling all over the western empire, Alexandria was still a center of learning and philosophy.

Kingsley epitomizes the best of Greek paganism through his beautiful heroine Hypatia, based on a half-legendary woman mathematician. He shows both the ennobling aspects of the growing Christian faith, and the corruption it had already reached under Cyril, the quite historic archbishop of the city. And he introduces a band of fearless marauding Goths who do not have the slightest understanding of Greek paganism *or* of Christianity. The result is a book which does not hold the interest too well through either its action or characterization, but which presents a tableau from history, with great erudition and probably more than usual accuracy. This is definitely not "escape" fiction. If you have a lot of troubles on your mind you are likely to forget the book even while reading it, and find yourself thinking about the troubles. But if you have the calm leisure, and sufficient interest in the ancient thoughts and days, you will enjoy it.

My copy is from the thirteenth edition, published in 1882 by MacMillan & Company of New York.

16. VICTOR HUGO: LES MISÉRABLES. Such was already the fame of the author, and the public expectations with regard to the book, that *Les Misérables* was first published simultaneously in France, Belgium, England, Germany, Spain, Italy, Russia, and the United States. This was in 1862. The expectations were fulfilled and the author's fame increased. This is an epic in prose.

Jean Valjean, the reformed criminal turned humanitarian, and Javert, the personification of law, unforgiving and incorruptible even by pity, are the protagonists through over twenty-five hundred pages of rambling plot and digressive dissertations. But the result is a powerful and enthralling *story*, nevertheless. If you have never read it, do so.

Although I do happen to own a complete copy in both French and English, this is the only case throughout this list where I recommend an abridgement. For at least a first introduction to the stupendous work I would suggest the excellent schoolbook edition by Flora Campbell, published by D.C. Heath & Company.

17. HARRIET BEECHER STOWE: UNCLE TOM'S CABIN. This book exerted a tremendous influence towards precipitating the American Civil War and bringing

about the abolition of slavery. It is the story of slave life in the old South.

Practically every reading list published since *Uncle Tom's Cabin* appeared has felt obliged to include it, because of the novel's epoch-making qualities, and has then apologized for doing so with the suggestion that it was literary trash. I think the book had to have a lot more worth than that, as sheer literature, or it would never have achieved its influence. Personally, I enjoyed it as a story — and so, I believe, will you.

My copy is the Everyman Edition, published by E.P. Dutton & Company.

18. EDGAR ALLAN POE: COLLECTED STORIES. Poe not only created the modern short story form, but wrote mystery stories which have never been surpassed by the thousands of writers who have used that literary medium since his day. The morbidness of his imagination has tinged many of them with so much horror, gloom, and despair that they are saved from oblivion only by the artistry with which the effect is achieved. But *The Gold Bug* escapes these critical objections, by the adventure interest and skillful suspense which make it one of the most widely known stories in all literature. *The Murders In The Rue Morgue* is a piece of detective ratiocination that carries the reader along breathlessly to a surprising and yet entirely satisfactory, and inevitable, conclusion. *The Purloined Letter* is a gem of simplicity and of psychological penetration that no reader ever forgets. And these, and many others, are all masterpieces of their kind.

My copy of the stories is contained in a complete set of *The Works of Edgar Allan Poe* in one volume, published by Walter J. Black, Inc., New York. It is an excellent edition.

19. ALPHONSE DAUDET: TARTARIN OF TARASCON. If Cervantes had been twice as witty, and had lived two hundred and fifty years later, he might have written this story of the great armchair hunter and his experiences when fame forced him to action. This is one of the most delightful satires ever written, not even spoilable by being used as a textbook for all the beginners' French classes in the world.

My copy, with the French title of *Tartarin de Tarascon*, is an ordinary school-text edition, well edited by Leon P. Irvin, and published by Henry Holt and Company.

20. ALPHONSE DAUDET: TARTARIN IN THE ALPS. The same hero as above now becomes a great mountain climber, with considerable inner reluctance, and with equally hilarious results.

My copy, *Tartarin Sur Les Alpes*, was published by Calmann-Lévy of Paris, and was picked up at a second-hand bookstore in this country.

21. ALPHONSE DAUDET: SELECTED SHORT STORIES. The nature of this personal list makes any apologies for allotting three numbers to Daudet unnecessary. But I should be prepared to defend the selection, even on a much more critical basis. Certainly some of his short stories are among the best ever written.

Most of the numerous editions of selected stories by Daudet, used as textbooks in first or second year French classes in this country, contain pieces from both his *Monday Tales* and *Letters From My Mill* (he was living in an old windmill when the letter series was written.)

My present copy, *Neuf Contes Choisis*, edited by Victor E. François, is a school book published by Henry Holt & Company.

22. RALPH WALDO EMERSON: ESSAYS, FIRST SERIES. In another connection, in another book, I have expressed my humble opinion that the most profound single sentence in all American literature is Emerson's

> Line in nature is not found;
> Unit and universe are round.

This sentence is from one of his poems, rather than the essays, but supplies a splendid sample of the compactness and penetration of his thought.

The best known of these essays are *Compensation, Self-Reliance,* and *Friendship.* The essay on *History* is excellent. The one entitled *The Over-Soul* should be read by anybody who is interested in Emerson as a leader of the Transcendentalist movement; of that strange attempt of Yankee minds to transplant and remold Hindu philosophy so that it might become an indigenous part of American intellectual growth. Emerson makes his greatest contribution to the movement in this dissertation, and in his famous short poem, *Brahma.*

The essays are not easy reading — for that matter neither is much of his poetry — and their philosophic generalization is out of date today. But if you wish to follow a great mind at work, and are willing to do a little mental work yourself in order to keep up, then by all means read them.

My copy is a very old one, part of a two volume set also containing *Essays, Second Series*, published by Donohue, Henneberry & Company of Chicago.

23. WILLIAM MAKEPEACE THACKERAY: VANITY FAIR. Many people rate this as the best novel ever published. I do not, but I concede them ground for

argument. It is the story of an English adventuress-social climber, who would be willing to sell her soul — and her body — to become Lady So-and-So, with fifty thousand pounds a year. The characterization of this heroine, Becky Sharp, is so detailed and excellent that half the literate world feels personally acquainted with her. If you have not also already made her acquaintance, then do so without delay.

My copy was published, goodness knows when, by John Wurtele Lovell of New York; but the book is available in many well-edited reprint series.

24. NATHANIEL HAWTHORNE: THE SCARLET LETTER. The cold self-righteousness of the Puritan spirit lay heavy on colonial New England. Hester Prynne, beautiful and full of life, came from the old world to a Massachusetts town, ahead of her unloved, scholarly old husband. More than a year later she gave birth to a daughter, whose father she refused to identify. For this crime the judges, in their "mercy," condemned her to wear forever on her bosom the Scarlet Letter A, signifying adulteress. Her husband appeared, unknown to all but herself; and made it his life mission to seek out and inflict morbid revenge upon the man who had betrayed him. It proved to be the young minister, who was regarded as the holiest preacher of the settlement. Out of this material, and the psychological gloom of the setting, Hawthorne weaves a dramatic tragedy.

Here is one of America's greatest novels, from every point of view — including interest-holding qualities for the casual reader.

My copy is part of *The Novels And Tales Of Nathaniel Hawthorne*, published by Modern Library.

25. GEORGE ELIOT: ROMOLA. I am willing to grant that George Eliot wrote "greater" novels than this, by almost any critical standard. But it is the one of her works I should be most sorry to have missed, nevertheless. The scene is Florence, in the days of Savonarola, but it is not the excellent re-creation of one historical time and place which buys for this novel its number in my list; nor is it the presentation of evil unalloyed in a human character. It is the convincing picture of the conscious, gradual, and inevitable failing of a man's mental capacities which makes Romola stand out in my memory as a work of tragic greatness.

My copy is a very old one, published by William L. Allison, New York.

26. ROBERT LOUIS STEVENSON: TREASURE ISLAND.
> Fifteen men on the dead man's chest —
> Yo-ho-ho, and a bottle of rum!

Meet Jim Hawkins, and Captain Smollett; Ben Gunn and Long John Silver; behold the dead man's chest, and the buried treasure itself.

Somebody has said that men are only boys grown tall. Perennial popularity of this yarn of adventure, with men of all ages, is good evidence that somebody was right. This book is a romantic boy's daydream brought to life in realistic fiction.

My copy is Volume VIII, in *The Works Of Robert Louis Stevenson*, published a long time ago by Peter Fenelon Collier, New York.

27. ROBERT LOUIS STEVENSON: DR. JEKYLL AND MR. HYDE. This story of a man with two entirely distinct

and opposed personalities was told by Stevenson long before *schizophrenia* became a common term even in the jargon of the psychologists. Dr. Jekyll is a useful and honored citizen; Mr. Hyde is a murderous beast. But they are both the same man. The story is sufficiently good reading to be worth your time, aside from the fact that its dual character has passed into the background of our language.

My copy, which also contains Stevenson's *Prince Otto*, was published by A.L. Burt Company.

28. EDWARD BELLAMY: LOOKING BACKWARD. This is one of the "Utopia" books, sugar-coated with a Jules Verne plot and an unconvincing romance. But it is well worth reading for two reasons. One is that, especially since the push towards socialism given us by the New Deal, this prophecy made by Bellamy in the 1880's as to what America would be like in the year two thousand shows some startling signs of having been darn good guessing. In the second place, the sale and influence of the book was so large, in its own time, that this work itself constitutes one of the great and early pushes given America in the leftward direction. Marx and Engels were the heavy-browed intellectuals of a foreign philosophy; Bellamy was a man you might meet on the street, talking in terms any American could understand about production and distribution. His *Looking Backward* furnished the material out of which sophomoric liberals were cutting their mental clothes for a generation.

My copy is published by Houghton Mifflin Company.

29. JULES VERNE: TWENTY THOUSAND LEAGUES UNDER THE SEA. The fantasy of one generation frequently becomes a commonplace of the next. That great

invention of a creative imagination, the submarine, on which Jules Verne's hero made his adventurous journey, is no longer either a dream or a mystery. And this account of the voyage of the *Nautilus* suffers from the fact that science has now made some of its wonders commonplace, and others ridiculous. Jules Verne has become outmoded for mid-twentieth century reading. But I am very glad to have enjoyed this tale in my youth, nevertheless.

My present copy, illustrated by W.J. Aylward, was published by Charles Scribner's Sons in 1936.

30. WILKIE COLLINS: THE MOONSTONE. Here is practically the grand-daddy of all detective novels. And although the family has now grown to the point where they seem just about ready to take over all first-run publishing in the English-speaking world, squeezing all other literature into an odd-lots-of-paper business, very few of the offspring of this generation have the stuff of which grandpa was made. For inventiveness and airtightness of plot, for careful and consistent characterization, and above all for suspense and sustained interest on the part of the reader, *The Moonstone* could give cards and spades (whatever that may mean) to at least ninety-nine out of one hundred of the mystery-murder novels now pouring from the presses in such a broad stream. If you like to wonder about who stole the jewel of fabulous worth, and how the guilty party could have a perfect alibi, then take a week off — it is about what you will need — and read Collins' masterpiece.

My copy was published by The Century Company, New York.

31. SIR ARTHUR CONAN DOYLE: ADVENTURES OF SHERLOCK HOLMES. To the best of my knowledge

there was no book published by Doyle under that title, but he wrote several detective novels and collections of stories around that master of deduction, Sherlock Holmes, and his stooge, Dr. Watson. A great many reprints and assortments of these yarns have been made, and are still appearing.

While it seems to me that Doyle stood on the shoulders of Gaboriau, and — to paraphrase Lowell — took full advantage of the fact that Poe before him had written, his great appeal and popularity is evidenced by the present public regard of Sherlock Holmes as the prototype of all fictional detectives. Although the Sherlock Holmes stories and a 1912 movie both make us laugh today at just the spots where they should prove most seriously exciting, both are well worth reading or seeing for one time, anyway.

My collection is *The Complete Sherlock Holmes*, published by Doubleday, Doran & Company, Inc.

32. GEORGE BARR McCUTCHEON: GRAUSTARK. The upright and democratic American who stumbles into a romance with the beautiful princess of some imaginary — and usually Balkan — European kingdom, and winds up by marrying the princess despite hell, bewhiskered counselors, thousand-year-old traditions, and high water — this story has been told, with all varieties of fairy tale trimmings, in hundreds of books by almost as many authors. But most of them, plus the later works of McCutcheon himself, are still just *Graustark* in different dress. If you like this kind of fanciful and ivory-towered romance — I do — or have read ten thousand detective books and need to vary your escape fiction, then McCutcheon's books will take you back into a Europe before the first World War — as it never was, but as many an American farmer boy thought it ought to be.

My copy was published in 1903, by Grosset & Dunlap.

33. EDWARD NOYES WESCOTT: DAVID HARUM. The hero was a horse-trading old skinflint, completely honest according to his own lights, and equipped with such a combination of shrewdness, sentiment, and common sense that he has come to be regarded as the "typical" American of the late nineteenth century. The author was himself a small-town banker; and this novel, which was his only book and was published posthumously, probably contained a considerable amount of autobiography. *David Harum* is still fun to read, and will add its contribution to your knowledge of what our country was like in grandfather's time.

My copy was published by D. Appleton & Company in 1899.

34. FËDOR M. DOSTOEVSKI: THE BROTHERS KARAMAZOV. This book probably represents the Russian mind, spirit, and environment of the late nineteenth century, to just about the same extent that *David Harum* was the portrait of a typical American and his background. Dostoevski's book is a monumental tome, permeated with gloom, about people who know that the heavy hand of fate will always crush them in the end. Wescott's book is a few hundred unpretentious pages, tinged with a sardonic humor, about people who know that, basically, they have the world by the tail. Even poverty, American style, is a temporary misfortune, to be worked out of in a year, or a decade, or a generation. Poverty, Russian style, is something inherited, like haemophilia or feeble-mindedness, and inevitably to be passed on to the next generation and the generations thereafter.

As an artist, Dostoevski undoubtedly deserves top rank. I am glad to have looked into the dark Russian cellar, and suggest that *The Brothers Karamazov*, or *Crime And*

Punishment by the same author, is an excellent trap door through which to take this look. But for me one or two glimpses is enough, and I'm glad to get back onto pages where the world looks bright, or at least possible, once more.

My copy is an English translation by Constance Garrett, published by Modern Library.

35. RUDYARD KIPLING: KIM. Returning (by a middle stage) from the oppressive mental atmosphere of the Russian to the light-heartedness of an American scene untortured by past defeats, we might read this chiaroscuro romance by Kipling. For in it the East and West do meet. This is the thrilling adventure story of a boy with a Western mind, and of Irish ancestry, who is raised as a native in India, and trained from early childhood to be an agent of the British secret service.

The veneer of modernization, of railroad trains and English laws, lies thin and superficial over a teeming India soaked with immemorial customs and superstitions. Young Kimball O'Hara roams from the south to the hills and back again; ostensibly, and to some extent sincerely, as the menial disciple of a Tibetan holy man seeking escape from the Wheel Of Life. But simultaneously he is a skillful player of the "game," a trusted and resourceful member of a small fraternity that thrives on danger and intrigue.

In my own mind, after some thirty years since I read it, *Kim* remains somehow pigeonholed in the same slot with *Treasure Island*. And this is in praise of both.

My present copy was published by Doubleday, Page & Company in 1924.

36. MARK TWAIN: TOM SAWYER. This completes the journey of the last few titles, and brings us back home

with a vengeance. For Mark Twain is as American as the Mississippi River, on which he spent a good bit of his life.

You have probably read *Tom Sawyer* anyway. If not you *must*. So there is no need of my saying any more about it. This title has been chosen to represent Mark Twain, because it is probably both the best-known and most typical of his works. But I like *A Connecticut Yankee At King Arthur's Court, The Prince And The Pauper*, and *Innocents Abroad* (Part I — the second part isn't worth reading), all better. If you do not enjoy them also, and almost everything else this author ever wrote, then our tastes just do not agree and you had better not pay much attention to my advice concerning books to read.

My copy is one volume of the Author's National Edition of *The Writings Of Mark Twain*, published by Harper and Brothers, New York.

37. O. HENRY: STRICTLY BUSINESS. In my personal and humble opinion, Edgar Allan Poe deserves full credit as the man who planted the seed of the short-story form in English literature. But the man who, next in line, cultivated the crop most assiduously and successfully, was O. Henry. His stories have a snap and sparkle, a constant twist of phrase and turn of mind, which make their every page a delight. When to these characteristics there is frequently added a depth of feeling and sincerity of human sympathy, conveyed with such a subtle touch that you blink to find them there, the result is a flower of fiction which should not blush unseen, nor waste its sweetness on library shelves.

Not being able to assign twelve or more numbers to O. Henry, to match each one of the volumes in a usual edition of his works, I have selected here *Strictly Business*, because it contains a particular story, *The Municipal Report.*

38. O. HENRY: THE FOUR MILLION. This title has been chosen, for the second of the two allotted to this author, because it contains the story *Mammon And The Archer.* This story, the one cited above, and *The Gift Of The Magi,* which also appears in *The Four Million,* seem to me to furnish a taste of O. Henry at his best. If you follow me this far, I hope they will induce you to read a hundred more of his stories.

My copy of this book, as of Number 37 above, is one volume of a complete set of O. Henry's works published by Doubleday, Page & Company in 1910.

39. LEWIS CARROLL: ALICE IN WONDERLAND. "The time has come," the walrus said, "to mention one of the most unique and surprising books since the Egyptians started growing papyrus." (If the walrus didn't say that he should have.) This is sheer nonsense, made so carefully consistent that the reader finds himself at times almost swallowing the plot. And yet it never loses the whimsical flavor of nonsense, nor the humor which is a natural component of the whole conception.

Lewis Carroll, whose real name was Charles Lutwidge Dodgson, was a well-known and serious mathematician; he was also an ordained minister, and the son of a practicing clergyman. He was so strait-laced that he refused ever to see again a friend who once told a vulgar story in his home. This watch-and-ward society attitude did not interfere with his sense of humor; and apparently his training in rigorous thinking as a mathematician helped to create that precision of style which makes both his prose and his light verse seem so perfectly finished down to the last sound and syllable.

Alice In Wonderland and the sequel, *Through The Looking Glass*, were written for a child, and are supposedly books for children. But very few grown people ever get old enough not to enjoy them; and nobody pretending to literacy in the English-speaking world can afford not to have read them. Otherwise, he will miss the reference and the point in too much of our daily conversation.

My copy, with illustrations by A.E. Jackson, was published by Garden City Publishing Company, New York.

40. THOMAS WOLFE: LOOK HOMEWARD, ANGEL. Longfellow said that the thoughts of youth were long long thoughts. Thomas Wolfe was still a young man when this, his first and greatest novel, was written; and he succeeded in getting most of these long long thoughts of youth into this one book. It is a story of an American country boy, from an uneducated family, who is touched by a genius for which there seems no reason other than purest chance. Driven by his own inner fire, he outgrows geographically and mentally his family, his community, his state, and eventually most of his countrymen. He finds occasional moments of happiness or triumph, but also much doubt and despair in the process. My own insignificant opinion is also shared by many of our greatest writers and critics, that this novel will grow in stature over the decades, and outlive almost any other written in our generation.

The book was frankly autobiographical, to a startling extent; which makes it so much more of a pity that the author died at the early age of thirty-eight. His best-known other books are *Of Time And The River*, and *The Web And The Rock*.

My copy of *Look Homeward, Angel* is published by Modern Library.

41. S. S. VAN DINE: THE BISHOP MURDER CASE. Having talked about Poe and Gaboriau and Doyle, in the field of detective fiction, I cannot deny my personal taste to the extent of leaving out Van Dine. He certainly will not live as long as the others; and is, in fact, already being both laughed at and forgotten. But this is a list, if I may be pardoned for repeating it, of books which I myself would be most sorry to have missed, because of the enjoyment they gave me. And certainly *The Bishop Murder Case* belongs in any such honest list.

Van Dine's real name was Willard Huntington Wright. He was a profound thinker and author, and noted as both a literary critic and art critic before he began writing detective fiction. So that his erudition slops over quite heavily, and purposely, into this new field. Philo Vance, his detective hero, talks like a cross between Oswald Spengler and Oscar Levant. But the result is — or was — extremely entertaining fiction, for those who like mystery stories, nevertheless.

My copy is a reprint edition, published by Grossett and Dunlap, New York.

42. PEARL BUCK: THE GOOD EARTH. What Dostoevski did for Russia, and Mark Twain (with a few dozen others) did for America, Pearl Buck did for China in this long novel of a Chinese farm family. Raised in China, so that she knows thoroughly the color of every clod of ground she talks about, she is nevertheless an American. Hence she was probably able to interpret Chinese life to our western minds much better than any Chinese himself could have done.

Although her Chinese characters, too, are bound down by the weight of centuries, the American reader can come to know them, love them, and feel that he is living with them, in a way that is impossible with Russian characters, at least for this particular American. You will enjoy *The Good Earth*, and also be glad at the end that you have read it.

My copy is the reprint edition published by Pocket Books, Inc.

43. SINCLAIR LEWIS: MAIN STREET. A little more than a quarter of a century ago the American public was slapped in the face by this book, so hard that they barely stopped talking about the slap before World War II came along to distract their attention. James Fenimore Cooper, a hundred years before, told us Americans that we were provincial, ill-mannered, and uninspired. The only result was that we all got mad with Cooper. Sinclair Lewis didn't bother to tell us anything. He merely held up a picture of Gopher Prairie, as a typical town, for everybody to look at. So we all heaped honors and royalties on Sinclair Lewis, while taking a quick glance back in the mirror every few minutes to see if he could possibly mean us.

The Americans in *Main Street* are the children and grandchildren of those Mark Twain wrote about, but they are becoming a great deal more self-conscious, through now rubbing elbows more closely with each other and the rest of the world. Lewis has almost a microscopic eye and memory for details, of scene and of character, which make his pages a pleasure, and a constant surprise, to read. *Main Street* and *Babbitt*, especially, by this author, should be a part of your literary background and mental outlook as an American.

My copy is published by Harcourt, Brace & Company, New York.

44. KENNETH ROBERTS: OLIVER WISWELL. So far as

interest in the romance, or even in the characters, goes, this novel leaves me very unexcited. But as history, it is a masterpiece. And since it is history which otherwise might never have been written, and certainly would never have been written so clearly and convincingly, I should be very sorry indeed to have missed the book.

This is the story of the American Revolution, as seen through the eyes of the American Tories, loyal to England, who opposed the Revolution, fought against it, and migrated to Canada or other British dominions after their cause was lost. It will surprise you — and correct a lot of erroneous impressions created, quite naturally and inevitably, by the patriotic authors of our history school books.

My copy was published by Doubleday, Doran and Company, Inc.

DRAMA AND POETRY

45. FIFTEEN GREEK PLAYS: EDITED BY LANE COOPER. The "most modern" of the Greek playwrights was Aristophanes. In fact, his humor and satire so amaze us with their smart freshness that we rub our eyes in disbelief that such lines could possibly have been written twenty-three centuries ago. You would hardly be surprised to find the signature of George Kaufmann at the end. Of his eleven comedies still extant, *The Frogs* is probably the favorite.

The other three most famous Greek playwrights were Aeschylus, Sophocles, and Euripides. They were all three roughly contemporary with each other, antedating Aristophanes by about one generation; and were all three writers of tragedies. *Oedipus, King of Thebes*, by Sophocles, written with powerful artistry, is the story of the king who was condemned by fate to kill his own father and marry his mother; and who discovers, in the course of the play, that through his very efforts to escape this dread prophecy, he has unwittingly done both. It has stood pre-eminent as a tale of psychological horror for twenty-four hundred years, and even supplied the term "Oedipus complex" to our present-day language of psychology.

Aeschylus and Euripides are important and interesting, not only in themselves, but because of the lasting and tremendous influence they have had on other poets and dramatists ever since. A great many of the stories of Greek mythology reached their fixed and permanent forms in the plays of these tragic dramatists, and have served as source material in the literature of every Western culture since that time.

My copy of the best-known works of each of the playwrights mentioned above is contained in a one-volume edition of *Fifteen Greek Plays*, published by Oxford University Press, New York.

46. VERGIL: THE AENEID. A parenthetical explanation, and apology, is probably due here to some readers who may be discovering with horror that Homer is obviously being omitted entirely. The answer is simply, I am sorry to say, that I have never read either the *Iliad* or the *Odyssey*. This is a lapse which I hope to rectify sometime before I finish my next thousand mystery novels.

In the meantime, since this must remain a personal record, the first great epic poem on which I can comment is *The Aeneid*. I read it in school, as a task in Latin translation, as has almost everybody else. Despite even this unfavorable approach, I still remember much of it with pleasure (though not in Latin). I have dipped into English translations a few times since. Despite its digressiveness and many other faults, there is a stately sweep which must appeal tremendously to any reader who has a natural liking for the epic form of poetry, as it happens that I do. For this reason, as well as its great influence on so much literature since Vergil's time, I should be very sorry to have missed it.

The copy on my library shelf is the Everyman Edition of the translation by E. Fairfax Taylor, published by E.P. Dutton & Co., Inc.

47. PLAUTUS AND TERENCE: PLAYS. In the panoply of full names, these two Roman playwrights are Titus Maccius Plautus and Publius Terentius Afer. Terence was born about the time Plautus died, not long after 200 B.C. They are grouped together in this list in part because the best of their extant plays are so often collected together in one volume; and because the plays of these two, and the tragedies of Seneca, constitute practically all that is left to us of Roman dramatic literature. Both Plautus and Terence wrote comedies which are excellent reading even today. And while they themselves took many of their own plots, situations, and characters from earlier Greek plays, their own works then became and have remained source material for dozens of playwrights up to the present time. Plautus' *Menaechmi*, in particular, a comedy about the inevitable and unending mixups which can occur through the confusion of twin brothers, served as a basis for Shakespeare's *The Comedy Of Errors*, and has helped the flagging inventiveness of many a lesser playwright. *Phormio* is probably the best-known and best-liked of Terence's works.

My copies of the plays of these authors are contained in the excellent two-volume edition of *The Complete Roman Drama*, edited by George E. Duckworth, and published by Random House, New York.

48. CHAUCER: CANTERBURY TALES. The spelling in Chaucer's time makes his English seem much more difficult and different from our own than it really is. So you may prefer, as I do, to read some "modern" edition, in which the spelling or even possibly the wording has been sufficiently retouched.

But Chaucer was the first great writer in our English language. He was, in fact, probably more responsible than any other man for "fixing" our language, and making it what it is. This, it is true, would furnish sufficient incentive only to the scholars to read him. Fortunately, however, he is also vigorous, inventive, and interesting; otherwise, he would never have had such great influence in the first place.

Canterbury Tales is really a collection of stories, of which the *Prologue, Knight's Tale, Clerk's Tale,* and *Nun's Priest's Tale* are the best-known, and the easiest reading. The *Clerk's Tale*, in particular, about Patient Griselda, has become a part of our English tradition.

My copy is the De Luxe Edition, rendered into modern English by J.U. Nicolson and illustrated by Rockwell Kent, put out by the Garden City Publishing Company, Inc., Garden City, New York.

49. CHRISTOPHER MARLOWE: PLAYS. If Newark, New Jersey, were in Kansas, instead of being overshadowed by New York City, it would stand out in popular thinking and conversation as one of America's large cities. Christopher Marlowe has had the misfortune to be overshadowed by Shakespeare in much the same way. They were both born in the same year, though Marlowe died when only twenty-nine years old; Shakespeare, when fifty-two. The younger man left four great plays; *Tamburlaine, Doctor Faustus, The Jew Of Malta,* and

Edward II. They are still excellent reading today. As to the first two, I am looking forward to my third reading of each. (But the professors say that *Edward II* is the best of the lot.)

My copy is Volume No. 383 of Everyman's Library, published by E.P. Dutton & Co.

50. SHAKESPEARE: PLAYS. On Marlowe's shoulders we climb to Shakespeare. And what shall I say, after the thousands of paeans of praise that have already been sung — except that I agree. Forget that you toiled through *The Merchant Of Venice* in high school under some uninspired teacher, or diagnosed the character of Hamlet in college until you wished the king had poisoned him along with his father, and start with a fresh expectation of pleasure.

It is inevitable that in his thirty-seven plays this greatest of all dramatists wrote some which were inferior to others. But I merely add my vote to the universal verdict that the best have never been surpassed. Among the best — still thinking only about the pleasure of the reader — are the comedies, *The Comedy Of Errors, A Midsummer Night's Dream, As You Like It, Twelfth Night*, and *Henry IV, Part I;* and the tragedies, *Richard II, Hamlet, Othello, King Lear, Macbeth*, and *Antony And Cleopatra*. There are many of the others which will well repay a second reading, or a tenth.

As to Shakespeare's narrative poems, *Venus And Adonis* and *The Rape of Lucrece*, I have never waded through them, and with one or two exceptions, his sonnets leave me cold. I'd rather read *Macbeth* for the dozenth time than *Lucrece* for the first.

My copy of Shakespeare's works, a one-volume edition, was put out in 1933, by The World Syndicate Publishing Company, Cleveland.

51. JOHN MILTON: POEMS. There are a few spots in this idiosyncratic survey of literature where my enthusiasm, if left unbridled, would run away. This is one, for I do like Milton.

Last winter I read *Paradise Lost* once again. To me the plot itself is almost as interest-holding as that of any novel; and I always wonder what Milton might have been able to do with such an epic character as the Satan of his imagination, had he been able to treat Satan frankly as the hero of his work.

In fact, many of Milton's shorter poems make us aware that here was a cavalier spirit, caught in the grip of a Puritan conscience, and confined by unyielding loyalties to the beliefs and traditions which he inherited and supported.

But above this interest in the characters he creates and in Milton himself, stirred by the clash of Puritan restraint and pagan dreams, is the appeal of majestic poetry that rolls like a mighty and rhythmic waterfall.

It is to the tremendous advantage of English poetry that it can range from the guttural sonorousness of German epic lines to the feminine delicacy of the lightest French verse. This is, of course, because English combines both Teutonic and Roman roots. But it is strange that a poet so versed in the Latin tongue that he actually wrote frequently in that language should also have been that poet who, when he wrote in English, gave forth the stateliest cadences, built most continuously on the strongest vowel sounds, of any great writer who has used the language. Perhaps this also was a part of his inner pagan revolt against the formalistic mental strait-jacket which his religion and classical learning must have seemed to fasten around him.

At any rate, if you like vigorous poetry that marches

with almost faultless step, singing — usually a deep baritone — as it goes, then read not only *Paradise Lost*, but *Lycidas*, and *L'Allegro*, and *Il Penseroso*, and above all some of his best sonnets. Of the latter, my favorites are the two beginning, "When I consider how my light is spent," and "Avenge, O Lord, Thy slaughtered saints, whose bones...." My liking for the first of these, so widely known as Milton's sonnet *On His Blindness*, as poetry, is not marred by the fact that I disagree entirely with its philosophy, and especially with that beautiful and famous last line, "They also serve who only stand and wait."

My copy is The Cambridge Edition, published by Houghton Mifflin Company.

52. PIERRE CORNEILLE: THE CID. It is not quite as much of a jump from Milton to Corneille, as it would be to Molière, because Corneille himself had the "epic" approach. But it is a long stride, nevertheless. The smooth couplets of Corneille's best French would taste like weak tea after the bourbon highball of Milton's powerful blank verse, but this passing thought, prompted by the fact that they were contemporaries, is hardly fair to Corneille.

Corneille was the first great French playwright, and the founder of French classical drama. *The Cid*, which means "the conqueror," is based on an earlier Spanish play about this hero who conquered the Moors, and is Corneille's greatest work. Although it would not last three nights on any American stage today, it is still a pleasure to read; and the poetry, for all that has been said above, is musical and pleasing.

My copy, a volume which also contains Racine's *Athalie*, was published in 1872 by Henry Holt & Company.

53. MOLIÈRE: SELECTED PLAYS. Even the merest dilettante in French literature will notice at once that I have skipped Racine, and in this instance it is not for the usual reason, as I do happen to have read most of his plays. But although I do not regret the reading, I could have skipped them entirely without the regret that missing so many other books would have caused me.

Moliére, however, whose real name was Jean Baptiste Poquelin, couldn't be missed by anybody who enjoys dramatic comedy at its very best. And unlike the works of Corneille, those of Molière not only could hold their place on the stage today, but frequently do. In fact, within the last two years Bobby Clark has been reasonably successful in a revival of Molière's *The Would-Be Gentleman*, with not too many changes to bring out better the Bobby Clark brand of lunacy. In fact, had there been no changes at all, the play might have been both better and more successful.

The Miser, The Misanthrope, The School For Wives, The Doctor In Spite Of himself, The Abashed Husband, The Hypocrite (Tartuffe), The Learned Ladies, and *The Hypochondriac* are probably the most enjoyable of Molière's comedies. And I do mean enjoyable, as I believe you will agree, if you have already read them, or when you read them in the future.

It so happens that I have a complete set of Molière, in seven volumes, published by Garnier Frères, Paris; and hence cannot refer you to any one-volume collection, in either French or English. But I am sure there is such a collection, of his best-known plays, in one or more good reprint editions of classics.

54. OLIVER GOLDSMITH: SHE STOOPS TO CONQUER. This famous play is well worth reading for many reasons, the chief of which is still the enjoyment you will

get out of it. *The Good-Natured Man*, by the same author, is undoubtedly equally worth while, but I am sorry to say that I have never read it.

My copy of *She Stoops To Conquer* is edited by Thomas H. Dickinson, as part of The Riverside Literature Series, published by Houghton Mifflin Company.

55. RICHARD BRINSLEY SHERIDAN: SELECTED PLAYS. Despite his exciting life, great learning, and important political activities, Sheridan is chiefly remembered for his three great comedies, *The Rivals, The School For Scandal*, and *The Critic*. The remembrance is well deserved, for these plays are as fresh and lively as the best of Molière. One of Sheridan's characters in particular, Mrs. Malaprop — who always aims at one word just beyond her reach and hits another — has become a very part of our language.

If you do wish to pay any attention to my too frequent advice, then read at least *The Rivals* and *The School For Scandal* at the first opportunity. If you don't like them, then you had better not listen to this same free advice any more.

My copy of Sheridan's *Dramatic Works* was published in 1854 by Henry G. Bohn, London.

56. JOHANN WOLFGANG VON GOETHE: FAUST, PARTS I AND II. Dr. Faustus was a mediaeval necromancer who, according to the legend, sold his soul to the devil in exchange for supernatural power while he should live upon earth. How he used and enjoyed — or tried to enjoy — his magical powers, and how he faced at last the horror of having to fulfill his contract; this story has been treated by dozens of writers, and undoubtedly will be retold by dozens more in the future.

The best-known rendition of the legend is this great poem in dramatic form, by Goethe. He began thinking about Part I when he was twenty years old, worked on it off and on for forty years before it appeared as a finished play, and then gave twenty years of intermittent attention to the completion of Part II. Obviously, therefore, *Faust* was not really written by one author, but by half a dozen Goethes who merged from one into the other during that long period. And inevitably it is the poetry, and the philosophic penetration into the questions of living, rather than any stageworthiness of the play, which make it one of the world's masterpieces.

My own first reading of *Faust* was many years ago, when I had acquired an ability to read German which I have largely lost since. And to my mind, the poetry loses a great deal by translation — any translation. But even Part I is not too easy a medium in which to follow the author's mind, unless your knowledge of German is a great deal superior to my little smattering; and there are some places in Part II where you and I, and the best scholars as well, get lost in any language. So read Part I, and study it leisurely, in German if you can; read Part II, if at all, and if you wish to do so, without any encouragement from me.

My copy is the translation by Latham, in the Everyman Edition published by E.P. Dutton & Company.

57. JOHANN CHRISTOPH FRIEDRICH VON SCHILLER: THE ROBBERS. Schiller's name is usually coupled with Goethe's, as the two greatest in German literature. With this, even in my rash ignorance, I agree. But Goethe is always automatically given star billing in this team; and so far, at least, as reading pleasure is concerned, I do not agree. Goethe is primarily a poet, and I no longer know enough German to get the full benefit of the beauty of his

lines, whereas Schiller is primarily a dramatist, whose action and suspense come through even in translation.

The Robbers was Schiller's first play, written when he was about twenty years old. It had a striking effect on the lives of young Germans of that day — just before the French Revolution — including Schiller's own! The play follows the Robin Hood pattern, glorifying the free life in the forest of those who were daring enough to make their own laws. Its popularity was so great that scores of German young men dashed off to the forests to become gallant highwaymen. Schiller himself, through being a deserter from the army in order to see the first performance of his play, was obliged as a result to spend about ten years in exile out of Germany.

From this background you might suspect that the play itself is exciting and romantic drama. Well — it *was*! Today, we must confess, it seems about as mature as a high-school fraternity, and about as convincing as Dick Tracy. But it still serves us, just as it served the German youth of the 1770's, as the best introduction to both Schiller himself and to the whole "Storm And Stress" period of German literature.

My copy of *The Robbers*, a very poor one, is a haphazard translation published in 1853 by Samuel French of New York.

58. PIERRE DE BEAUMARCHAIS: PLAYS. The only two plays of lasting importance which this versatile Frenchman wrote were *The Barber Of Seville*, and *The Marriage Of Figaro*. But they would have been sufficient to give him lasting fame, even if they had not become the bases of operas by Rossini and Mozart. They are full of keen wit, incisive satire, and deft characterization. They created the character, Figaro, the valet who was practically

a one-man secretarial corps, whose brilliance shone against the background of his "dumb" betters; and they are a lot of fun to read.

My copy of *Le Barbier De Seville* is published by Henry Holt & Company; of *Le Mariage De Figaro* by Oxford University Press, New York. Both are schoolbook editions. But once again the liberty is taken of grouping the two plays together in the list, because I am sure an English version of the two together is available in one volume.

59. OSCAR WILDE: SELECTED PLAYS. The best of these are *Lady Windermere's Fan, A Woman Of No Importance*, and *The Importance Of Being Earnest*. Written fifty years ago, they still bear acting today — and reading, all the more. They are light, clever, sparkling, and sometimes thought-provoking.

My copy of *The Works Of Oscar Wilde*, published by Collins, London, contains these three and other plays, as well as all of Wilde's stories, poems, and essays.

60. EDMOND ROSTAND: PLAYS. Most great literary successes burst unheralded on the scene, or appear with almost no immediate recognition of their greatness and build up fame over succeeding decades. But *Cyrano De Bergerac*, by Rostand, was one of the rare exceptions. Months before its first showing on the stage, rumors that something exceptional was on the way had become so widespread in Paris that the whole city was waiting to see if this prenatal fame was justified. It was; to the mind of the Parisians, of the playgoers of almost every country of the world since that time, and certainly to my own. Rostand's work loses more in translation, it seems to me, than that of almost any other French author, because he is a supreme artist in the choice of words. But you can

deduct whatever is lost and still have romantic drama at its best.

Cyrano is the story of a self-sacrificing noble swashbuckler, condemned to eat his heart out in vicarious love because of consciousness of his own physical homeliness. *L'Aiglon* is the story of the pathetic life and death of Napoleon's son by Marie Louise of Austria, who began his days as the "King of Rome," and ended them in consciously futile oblivion as the "The Duke of Reichstadt." *Chanticler*, made doubly famous by Sarah Bernhardt in the title role, I'm sorry to say I have never read, nor seen. But an earlier and less-known play of Rostand, *The Far-Away Princess*, I do like very much.

I have taken the liberty of grouping these plays together as one number in my series, because they are available in English, I believe, in one-volume collections. My only copies, in French, are separate volumes; *La Princesse Lointaine*, a schoolbook edition published by D.C. Heath & Co., and the other three published by Charpentier *et* Fasquelle of Paris.

61. SIR JAMES M. BARRIE: THE ADMIRABLE CRICHTON. Crichton was a butler or upper servant in the household of an Englishman who was master of the appropriate castle-like home in the midst of its broad acres. He exercised all the brains of the whole establishment, but nobody knew it. The master with his family, including daughters, and the servant, were all shipwrecked on a cruise, were saved by Crichton, and wound up as the only inhabitants on an uncharted "desert" island. They all had to start absolutely from scratch, in meeting the elemental necessities and building up the comforts of their new life. Within two or three years Crichton was the master of the island; the others were all dependent and

worshipful servants; and the daughters of his former master were jealously fighting among themselves for the favor of his attention. Then the whole party was unexpectedly rescued by a passing ship, and returned to England. Immediately, both master and daughters expected everything to return to the original status quo, and could not conceive of the admirable Crichton in any possible light except as a deferential servitor once more.

It is one of those plays of supposedly deep social significance, over which I do not usually enthuse, but the satire is so neat, the theme so originally presented, and the drama so effective as entertainment, that there are many hundreds of other books I had rather have missed.

My copy is published by Charles Scribner's Sons.

62. FRANCIS TURNER PALGRAVE: THE GOLDEN TREASURY OF ENGLISH LYRIC POETRY. This thin volume, probably still the most famous of all anthologies of poetry, served as my own first introduction to English lyrics which I read as pleasure instead of studying as school assignments. Although Palgrave has now been swallowed up in a great many more inclusive and useful anthologies, he supplied the yeast which has caused so much bread to rise.

Palgrave's selection was made purely according to his own taste, and that of two or three personal friends, including Tennyson. This taste was, as passing time has shown, almost unsurpassed. There are very few selections in *The Golden Treasury* which are ever omitted from any collection of the best English verse, and which have not become continuously more famous — and more commonplace in our literary background — since Palgrave's day. You can read the individual poems in any collection you wish, but no library, however small,

should be without a copy of *The Golden Treasury.*
My copy is the Everyman Edition, published by E.P. Dutton & Company.

63. BURTON EGBERT STEVENSON: THE HOME BOOK OF VERSE. If Palgrave's is the most famous anthology of poetry, certainly Stevenson's *Home Book Of Verse* is the greatest so far compiled, in the all-inclusive meaning of that much tossed-about adjective. Originally printed in one volume, on India paper, running to nearly four thousand pages, it includes almost every worth-while "short" poem in the English language, written up to about 1912. Subsequent revision, additions, and the comments of owners have caused the most recent editions to appear in two volumes.

This is truly a monumental work, in both size and character. Here you will find the best of the old English ballads, and the best-known of the nineteenth-century pseudo ballads; the rhymes of Mother Goose, and the religious hymns which look to a life across the Jordan; the nonsense of Edward Lear, and the most profound sonnets of Keats; the love poetry of Herrick, and the memorial grief of Milton's *Lycidas*; the four-line poems of Walter Savage Landor, and the complete four hundred lines of Fitzgerald's translation of the *Rubáiyát*; the unorthodox lines of Walt Whitman and the chiseled stanzas of Thomas Gray; the sheer music of Coleridge and the philosophizing song of Tennyson's *Locksley Hall*; compacted rations for scholars, like Emerson's *Brahma*, and old favorites like *The Yarn Of The Nancy Bell*. The arrangement of these thousands of poems is superb; the editing was done with a care and conscientiousness which make the text trustworthy beyond all expectation.

My copy is a one-volume edition, published in 1915; so

well-thumbed that the first cover long ago disappeared, and a new binding is now almost worn out in its turn. Henry Holt & Company is the publisher; and the two-volume edition is available today in almost any book store in America.

64. BURTON EGBERT STEVENSON: THE HOME BOOK OF MODERN VERSE. This is in the nature of a sequel, or continuation, to include poems which have been published since 1912. It is of the same character, and done with the same care, as *The Home Book Of Verse*. Since, to my mind, some of our greatest poems of the last generation have been by authors who wrote only two or three things really worth while, rather than by those who turned out volumes of verse, many of these very best poems are not readily available except in some such "contemporary" anthology, of which Stevenson's is by far the best.

The Home Book Of Modern Verse also has particular merit for those who like the best contemporary humorous poetry. Here you will find such gems as B.L.T.'s *Ataraxia*, Keith Preston's *Warm Babies*, Don Marquis' *King Cophetua And The Beggar Maid*, and James J. Montague's "*And When They Fall.*"

This is also published by Henry Holt & Company. My copy appeared in 1925, but there are probably later editions which would include poems since that time.

65. CURTIS HIDDEN PAGE: THE CHIEF AMERICAN POETS. This book is organized on a different pattern from the usual collection of poetry. It contains works by nine poets only, and nothing else. It contains practically all of the poetical works of these nine men. They are Longfellow, Poe, Emerson, Lowell, Whittier, Holmes, Whitman,

Bryant, and Lanier. It is, just as the title says, not a book of the chief American poems, but of the chief American poets.

I have a particular fondness for Page, because it was through this book that I first became acquainted with Lowell's *Biglow Papers* and *A Fable For Critics*; with Bryant's *The Flood Of Years*, and Lanier's *The Marshes Of Glynn*. Here I read for the first time Longfellow's *Evangeline*, the best attempt yet made in English to use the dactylic hexameter of classical epic verse; here for the first time I became familiar with Holmes's quiet humor, interspersed at unexpected intervals with sublime pathos; here I became familiar with much of the best, and also some of the worst, that America had produced during the nineteenth century. It is a book well worth owning — and reading.

My copy is published by Houghton Mifflin Co.

66. SIR WALTER SCOTT: POEMS. Perhaps it was because I was just at the right age when I first read *The Lady Of The Lake*; perhaps it was because I had just begun to acquire a liking for rhythm and rhyme, without having yet achieved any refinement of taste; perhaps it is simply that I am an incurable romantic. Whatever the reason, *The Lady Of The Lake* has always been one of my favorite narrative poems; and my liking for it has been sufficient to carry over to *Marmion* and *The Lay Of The Last Minstrel*. I am well aware that if these stories in rhyme were written today they would never even find a publisher. But I am glad they were publishable in Scott's time, and I would not have missed them for a great deal. When James Fitz-James, having mingled and fought so nobly in disguise with his misguided but chivalrous enemies, finally reveals his identity to Ellen, the beautiful heroine; when the verse

finally proclaims "And Snowdoun's Knight is Scotland's King!" — well, I almost burst a blood vessel in excitement and vicarious pride. And when in the beginning of the last canto of *The Lay*, the old minstrel orates

> Breathes there the man, with soul so dead,
> Who never to himself hath said,
> This is my own, my native land! —

I was ready to run out, don a uniform, and start beating a drum with one hand and waving a flag with the other.

My copy is *The Poetical Works Of Sir Walter Scott*, edited by Francis Turner Palgrave, and published in 1881 by MacMillan & Company of London.

67. JEAN DE LA FONTAINE: FABLES. The reader will, I hope, pardon me for including this one book which *has* to be read in the original French to be worth the bother. Plain honesty required its inclusion, because certainly there are many books within this list of a hundred that I had rather have missed than La Fontaine.

These paraphrases of Aesop's fables were originally published, I believe, in about twelve volumes. But the usual publication today is of a selection of the best of them, in one volume. For skillful rhyming, for arrangement of verse forms adapted to increase the effectiveness of what is said, for sly wit and subtle satire, they have seldom been equalled by the humorous verse of any language, and it is safe to say that Aesop himself owes much of his lasting fame to the fact that La Fontaine did his fables all over again, in the seventeenth century, in such exquisite French verse. To say that it would be worth while learning the French language just to read La Fontaine's fables would admittedly be a slight exaggeration — but the idea is not a bad one.

My copy, a one-volume collection, was published in 1856 by Didot Frères of Paris.

68. GILBERT AND SULLIVAN: COLLECTED LIBRETTOS. Once upon a time I used to play chess with an elderly gentleman who was as fond of Gilbert and Sullivan as I am. He would make some wild sacrifice in the Muzio Gambit and then sit quoting line after line of *Pinafore* while I studied the mess. Finding what I thought was a satisfactory defense and retort, probably boldly accepting the rook or the queen, I would then come back at him with line after line from *The Mikado*, while he was deciding what piece to sacrifice next. Fortunately these games were always either won by him, or resigned as lost by me, thus bringing an end to the antiphonal quotations, just before somebody carried us both off to the "booby hatch." But did we have fun!

You do not have to have the music, and the stage settings, and the actors, to enjoy the marvelously smart versification and brilliantly satirical wit which W.S. Gilbert poured into these librettos. If you doubt it, just sit down and read any of them through.

My copy is published by Crown Publishers, New York.

69. MRS. WALDO RICHARDS: HIGH TIDE. This is definitely a collection of poems, rather than a collection of poetry. Its two hundred pages contain just about that many separate lyrics, by almost as many of our contemporary poets. To say that this is one of my favorite volumes is merely to proclaim that Mrs. Richards' taste and my own are quite similar.

But while I have since learned that many of these songs are available in Stevenson, or in some other anthology which I possess, it was in *High Tide* that I first became acquainted with T.A. Daly's *The Song Of The Thrush*, Josephine Preston Peabody's *The Golden Shoes,* Alfred Noyes's *In The Cool Of The Evening*, Thomas S. Jones's *Sometimes*, Angela Morgan's *Kinship*, and others that I like as well. And I still think that our taste — Mrs. Richards' and mine — is pretty good.

This book — my copy is out of the nineteenth printing, incidentally — is published by Houghton Mifflin Company.

70. NEWMAN LEVY: OPERA GUYED. This thin volume, far too little known, deserves much greater recognition as a masterpiece of its kind, among all lovers of light verse. Originally contributed, one piece at a time, I believe, to F.P.A.'s Conning Tower, it is a collection of synopses in rhyme of the arguments of all the best-known operas. And what Mr. Levy does to them has to be read to be believed.

His version of *Thaïs* is my favorite; and the flavor of the travesty can be surmised from the opening lines:

> One time, in Alexandria, in wicked Alexandria,
> Where nights were wild with revelry and life was
>   but a game,
> There lived, so the report is, an adventuress and
>   courtesan,
> The pride of Alexandria, and Thaïs was her name.
>
> Nearby, in peace and piety, avoiding all society,
> There dwelt a band of holy men who'd built
>   a refuge there;
> And in the desert's solitude they spurned all
>   earthly folly to
> Devote their days to holy works, to fasting and
>   to prayer.

Or others prefer his *Hamlet*, of which the final lines perhaps best suggest the derisive treatment:

> An' he says "Well, let's call it a day."
> Then the Queen dies, the King dies, an' Ham dies,
> I calls it a heleva play.

The whole book is a delight from the beginning to end, and becomes more so with every reading.

My copy is published by Alfred A. Knopf.

HISTORY AND TRAVEL

71. THE BIBLE: We have put this most famous and sacred of all books at the beginning of the history section, because it is primarily a history; of the migrations and tribal kingdoms and wars of the Jews, of the life and teachings of Christ, and of the spreading of the Christian gospel by His apostles. To what extent the Bible can be read purely for pleasure depends, of course, on the religion or scholarship of the reader. But one of its appeals, above the instruction of its parables, the validity of much of its history, the ethics of its sermons, and the profundity of its moral precepts, is the beauty of its language in the English of the King James version. The scholars who made this translation have probably had an influence greater than that of Shakespeare, in making our tongue the wonderful tool of communication which English has become.

My copy, a gift from my mother, was published by A.J. Holman Company, Philadelphia.

72. WILL DURANT: THE STORY OF PHILOSOPHY. It is quite proper to question the classification of this book in the history section, but it is to be noted that, just as Will

Durant's books on history are one-third philosophy, his books on philosophy are at least one-third history. And certainly Durant himself thought of his work as a history of philosophers, even though it frequently develops into an exposition of philosophies.

Of all the many dozens of books written in this century, popularizing various branches of science and scholarly knowledge for the lay reader, *The Story Of Philosophy* remains, to my mind, so far the best that there isn't even any good second. Few people have ever been able to take so difficult and forbidding a subject, and make it so clear, colorful, and full of interest. As an introduction to the study of philosophy it is like a strong flashlight swept across the floor and turned into the corners of a dark cellar. As a book to read purely for pleasure it has few equals in nonfictional literature.

My copy was published in 1926 by Simon & Schuster, New York.

73. WILL DURANT: OUR ORIENTAL HERITAGE. This is the story of the known and surmised beginnings of our civilization; in Chaldea and Egypt and Babylonia, and India and China. It is founded on erudition which is wide and deep, but never oppressive; it is told in a style that is unbelievably aphoristic, and which yet manages somehow, by the genius of infinite pains, to be unstilted, always clear, and soothing in its simplicity. If all historians, of all ages, had had both the honesty and the ability of Will Durant, the human race might by this time have learned enough about its own past to have profited somewhat by its repeated mistakes.

My copy is published by Simon & Schuster.

74. WILL DURANT: THE LIFE OF GREECE. This is the

second volume in this author's projected five-volume series, *The Story Of Civilization*, of which *Our Oriental Heritage* was the first.

This volume tells us not only about the wars, with other nations and among themselves, in which the Greeks perennially participated; but tells us even more about their customs, their language, their political and social organizations, their sculpture, their mathematics, and their philosophies. And always Durant is thinking of the Greek culture, its science and language and traditions and political forms, as the grandfather of our own current civilization.

My copy is published by Simon & Schuster.

75. WILL DURANT: CAESAR AND CHRIST. This is the third volume of the series. It does for Roman civilization what the second volume did for the Greek period; with particular emphasis, in this instance, on the rise of Christianity as a new all-pervasive force, connecting men's minds and activities, at the very time that the Roman power was disintegrating from the decay of its own rottenness and the repeated attacks of vigorous barbarians. Durant's sense of analogy makes the points of parallel between the Roman state and our own, in both specific details and broad generalities, stand out in unmistakable fashion. It is possible to get a much clearer idea of what is happening to America, and of what is likely to happen in the future, through reading this one book, than through any other dozen histories with which I am familiar.

The volumes in this series have been appearing approximately at five-year intervals. The next two are due to be finished and published, therefore, by about 1950 — the fourth volume being possibly, and for all I know, already on the press. I am sure that if this little reading guide of mine were being written ten years from now, and still held to the limit of one hundred books, two of those which now appear would have to be replaced by the remaining two volumes of Durant. I recommend, with all of the insistence that the kind reader will allow me, that you read all five volumes of *The Story Of Civilization.*

My copy of *Caesar and Christ* is published by Simon & Shuster.

76. THEODOR MOMMSEN: THE HISTORY OF ROME. In assigning one number to this work, and considering it as one book in our list, we are stretching a point — which we shall stretch even further, when we come to Ridpath. For certainly Mommsen's prodigious output is too bulky to appear in one volume and has never done so to the best of my knowledge. But we cannot pay too much attention to that foolish consistency which Emerson says is the hobgoblin of little minds, and Mommsen's history is one work, and for all intents and purposes one book, nevertheless.

I have already referred at some length to the use which Mommsen makes of philology, in determining facts of early history, in the chapters on language in this book. But philology was only one of the divisions of his massive learning. This is history in the best of the older style. Mommsen never writes so entertainingly as Durant; he would be horrified at the superficial sweep of Wells; he conceived of himself as writing factual history, rather than sociological propaganda, in the manner of some of the moderns; and his plodding scholarship frequently makes his pages tedious reading. But there can never be a doubt that Mommsen knew what he was talking about, so far as the state of learning made it possible to know, in every sense. And his *History Of Rome*, remaining one of the outstanding products of sound and painstaking German scholarship, also remains as the starting point for most other historians who wish to write about Rome.

My set of Mommsen's *The History Of Rome* is the four-volume Everyman Edition, published by E.P. Dutton & Company.

77. H. G. WELLS: THE OUTLINE OF HISTORY. Lowell said of Poe that he was three-fifths genius and two-fifths sheer fudge. It seems to me that in the famous *Outline* H.G. Wells is about two-thirds historian, and one-third a writer of propaganda for the Wellsian ideals of socialism. At least I suppose that's what the last third of the book is; I have never been able to stick it out. But I have read the first two-thirds, with considerable pleasure, at least three times; and I recommend it to anybody who wants a quick, easily traversed survey of the high spots in the development of human civilization from the pre-saurian beginnings to its present questionable level.

My copy was published by The Macmillan Company, in 1922.

78. JOHN CLARK RIDPATH: HISTORY OF THE WORLD. Since this work was always published in nine volumes, and rather huge ones at that, the same plea as to the consistency of my inconsistency must be made as in the case of Mommsen's work, above. For certainly Ridpath's famous production is one book, for the purposes of this list; and I should not be called upon to assign nine numbers to it, to keep from leaving it out.

If nine numbers were necessary, however, nine numbers Ridpath should have — and let the critics swoon by the dozens. For it was this nine-volume *History Of The World*, with its hundreds of portraits and realistic illustrations, its romantic approach to the events and characters portrayed, its easy sweeping style, and its presentation of the most ancient chronology with an assurance that knew no doubts; it was this history in the old style, replacing both the pedantry and the meticulous accuracy of Mommsen with the clear simplicity of a born story teller, that served as my first introduction to the peoples and nations and cultures which had preceded me as a boy on a North Carolina farm. The archaeologists have made many corrections in the dates so blithely given by Ridpath for his Egyptian and Chaldean monarchs; scholars have learned a great deal more than was known in his time of the details of Roman life, or the sequences of conqueror and conquered among the Asiatic despots; sociologists with pet axes to grind have come to use history as a medium for their philosophizing, and to hold up to scorn those who are content to write history as the simple chronicle of events which it used to be. But in his day John Clark Ridpath exerted a mighty influence, towards inspiring in hundreds and thousands of Americans, young and old, an interest in history and a desire to learn more about other nations and other times. I am very glad to have been within the reach of that influence, in my own youth; and would not have missed Ridpath's *History Of The World* for all of some fifty other volumes I could even now select from this very list.

My own present set was issued by The James Brothers Publishing Company, of Cincinnati, in 1923.

79. H. R. HALL: ANCIENT HISTORY OF THE NEAR EAST. Professor Hall, as I remember, turned out to be much better at recording the results of other men's archaeological expeditions, than in conducting such expeditions himself. His history, never inspired, and saved from dryness purely by inevitable interest in the very facts and

records which he presents, still gives about the most concise and apparently the most accurate story of the rise and fall of the ancient Egyptian, Sumerian, Babylonian, Assyrian, and neighboring empires. The book covers a geographical spread roughly from the Red Sea and the Persian Gulf on the south to the Black Sea and the Caspian Sea on the north, and a time stretch of about four thousand years preceding the rise of the Persian Empire under Cyrus and Darius. During far more centuries than have passed since, Asia Minor and the lands immediately to the south of Asia Minor were the seat of civilizations which waxed and waned just as those of Europe and America have been doing for the past twenty-five hundred years. This ancient "Near East" is to me a fascinating time and place; and Professor Hall is not a bad guide to take you through it on a conducted tour.

My copy was published by Methuen & Company, Ltd., of London.

80. HERODOTUS: HISTORY. It is to be hoped that the reader has entirely forgotten anything which was said about discussing authors within a section in chronological order. It is obvious that any such thought has been completely discarded, in this section, for other considerations. For Herodotus lived and wrote in the fifth century B.C., and is justly known as the father of historians.

After traveling over most of the then-known world, gathering facts and myths and knowledge and superstition from all the lands he visited, Herodotus wrote his history of the Greco-Persian wars. It is true that he never was able to distinguish the facts from the myths, or the knowledge from the superstitions. But he conscientiously and faithfully recorded most of the miscellany, bearing on his subject, which he had been able to assemble from any and all sources. And even some of his chronology is still useful today, at least as a check against which to compare later and more accurate scholarship.

It is to be remembered that the early Greeks wrote poetry long before it occurred to them to write in prose; and that prose composition was almost a new medium of expression right up to the time of Herodotus. Papyrus, as a material on which to write, although long used in Egypt, was just beginning to replace the parchment and skins of the Greeks and the clay tablets of the Babylonian cities. When this background to this first true history, in the meaning which we give to the word today, is considered, the job which Herodotus turned out seems remarkable indeed. And there have been a great many histories written since which are not as readable or as interesting today.

My copy, a translation by George Rawlinson, was issued by The Tudor Publishing Company, New York.

81. MARCUS TULLIUS CICERO: ORATIONS. Although I had to study this as a task, all during my third year in high school, and was certainly thinking then of the Latin to be translated rather than of the orations as either literature or history, they have stayed in my mind sufficiently in after years to give me an impression of Cicero which would make me very sorry not to have made his acquaintance. Scholar, politician, and philosopher, he stands out as a remarkable and revealing Roman of his time.

The orations against the conspirator Catiline were successful in bringing about the collapse of his conspiracy and the execution of its leading members. The fourteen *Philippics,* against Mark Anthony, were even more famous in their time. But it is the indirect rather than the direct history, the picture of politicians and parliamentary government in a nation remarkably similar to our own, and the interest in the wily, ambitious, but still statesmanlike Cicero himself, which make these orations worth a place in my hundred books. They earn that place more clearly because of their part in stimulating a further reading of and about Cicero, as a part of his life and times.

My copy, a translation by C.D. Yonge, was published in 1862 by Harper & Brothers.

82. MARCO POLO: TRAVELS. These memoirs were dictated by Marco Polo during a year which he spent in jail at Genoa, after the travels were over. They were originally known as *The Book Of Marco Polo.*

As a young man he had accompanied his father and uncle, from Venice, on a trip through the unknown states of western and central Asia, to the even more unknown and mighty empire of Kublai Khan. The young man met with high favor from the Mongolian Emperor, remained in his diplomatic service for seventeen years, and thus saw much of eastern Asia, before returning to Venice in 1295.

Marco's whole book is full of awe and amazement at the things he has seen, and of fear that nobody will believe this account of the kingdoms he has visited and the wonders he has witnessed. But while the Europeans of his time had to accept this strange narrative on his word, modern scholarship has given Marco Polo a pretty good bill of health as an accurate observer and a truthful reporter, who certainly had no need to exaggerate in order to astound his countrymen.

The book had a huge influence on the inquiring minds of Renaissance Europe, has been widely read for six hundred years, and is still delightful reading in 1946.

My copy is published by Modern Library.

83. JOHN SPENCER BASSETT: A SHORT HISTORY OF THE UNITED STATES. The allotment of one number out of the one hundred at this point is not really intended to apply specifically to one particular history of the United States. It is intended to indicate, rather, that some good history of the United States, out of scores available, should be included; because certainly I should not have wanted to have left out such a history of our country for the sake of other books which make up this arbitrary number.

The actual choice of *the* history of the United States to be referred to, therefore, is not too important; nor am I qualified to express an opinion on which is the best out of many dozens that might be considered. But Bassett's history, despite some statements in his chapters on Roosevelt and the New Deal which now seem ridiculous because of his having been too close to the picture, seems to me to be about as well-rounded and satisfactory an account of the birth and growth of our country, from 1492 to 1938, as the general reader would wish.

My copy was published by The Macmillan Company, New York.

84. CYRIL E. ROBINSON: ENGLAND. Here again it is *a* history of England, rather than any specific history of England, which requires a number in our list. But the volume indicated, written by an Englishman, will serve to represent satisfactorily the whole field.

My copy was published by Thomas Y. Crowell Company, New York.

85. CARLTON J. H. HAYES: A POLITICAL AND SOCIAL HISTORY OF MODERN EUROPE. I should not

have wanted to miss all histories of modern Europe, and this one has many good points in its favor.

My copy is published in two volumes by The Macmillan Company.

86. NICCOLO MACHIAVELLI: THE PRINCE. This is put into the history section simply because I associate the book in my own mind with the study of history rather than the study of literature. It is, of course, a discourse on statecraft, written in the early sixteenth century, by an Italian statesman who was chiefly thinking about and writing for the independent, warring, intriguing city states of which Italy was composed in his time.

Somebody has remarked that this author's first name had come to be synonymous with the devil (Old Nick), and his surname had been formed into an adjective (Machiavellian) meaning satanic. His work is startling for its complete disregard of morality, as we think of it, in the advice which Machiavelli gives to princes and rulers who would be honored and successful. Murder and treachery are just as much the tools of statecraft, in Machiavelli's mind, as armed forces or tax collections.

The influence of the book, both direct, on politicians and tyrants who would gladly follow the course Machiavelli charted for success, and indirect, on and through all literature since his time, has been tremendous. Nor, if we can believe our eyes and ears as to what seems to be happening in so much of Europe today, do his counsels seem even yet to have lost any of their appeal.

The book is not very long, its style is not at all difficult, and it is very much worth reading because of this influence it has exerted, if for no other reason.

My copy, a translation by W.K. Marriott, is published in the Everyman edition, by E.P. Dutton & Company, Inc.

87. FREDERICK LEWIS ALLEN: ONLY YESTERDAY. This is a very informal account of the events, movements, and personalities which made newspaper headlines in America in the decade from 1920 through 1929. When the book first appeared, in about 1930, the American public got from it much the same reaction that an individual does in looking through a lot of photographs of himself and clippings concerning himself collected and stowed away only a few years before. It is not only excellent history, of a most unusual kind, however, but is very enjoyable reading today. It is especially desirable reading for a younger generation of Americans who would like to know more about the American scene in the years which preceded the great depression and the New Deal.

My copy was published by Blue Ribbon Books, Inc.

MORE OR LESS SCIENTIFIC

88. THOMAS HENRY HUXLEY: ESSAYS. Historically and scientifically, it seems to me, this is the best approach for the layman to the Darwinian theory. Darwin's own exposition of that theory, in *On The Origin Of Species*, and *The Descent Of Man*, is not easy going for the reader untrained in the biological sciences. Huxley, on the other hand, reads very easily — and convincingly. A great scientist in his own right, Huxley also had the gift of facile expression. Through proclaiming himself Darwin's bulldog, and living up to the duties of this role, he made this gift of expression more important in its actual influence than any of the scientific work which he himself accomplished.

These essays are not needed today, in any part of the literate world, for the purpose of carrying conviction about the theory of organic evolution. But the story was far different less than three generations ago, when Bishop Wilberforce was loosing his fulminations against this new heresy. Darwin may have made a close relative of a monkey out of man, but Huxley made an actual monkey out of Bishop Wilberforce.

My copy was published in 1907 by Cassell & Company, Ltd., of London.

89. HERBERT SPENCER: FIRST PRINCIPLES. In 1860 Herbert Spencer, one of the last men to attempt — in Francis Bacon's phrase — to take all knowledge for his province, announced a *System Of Synthetic Philosophy*. He spent something more than the next thirty years in preparing the various books in this series, of which *First Principles* was the introductory volume. In my humble and old-fashioned opinion, few products of the human brain have reached as high a level.

The caliber of Spencer's thinking can be indicated by the fact that he surmised the theory of evolution, and applied it as a speculation to the whole field of sociology, before Darwin and his allies had advanced any scientific delineations of this theory, or evidence to support it. And the cogency and clearness of his reasoning from known facts should be a model for all those thinkers who wish to enter into the treacherous realms of either physical or social philosophy. Spencer's great thesis is that all evolution is an organizing principle, changing matter from a state of indefinite incoherent homogeneity to one of definite coherent heterogeneity. If this sounds like a big mouthful now, *First Principles* will enable you to chew it, digest it, and enjoy it as well, before you are through.

In passing, it is worth noting that Spencer was almost a violent believer in extreme individualism, as against bureaucracy and the extension of governmental powers over the lives and actions of its citizens. He summarized his opposition to paternalistic statism in a brilliant epigram (which does not appear in *First Principles*) to the effect that the ultimate result of protecting fools from their own folly is to fill the world full of fools. It is this writer's prejudiced opinion that we have been doing just what Spencer warned against, and with the results which he feared.

My copy of *First Principles* was published by A.L. Burt Company, New York.

90. ERNST HAECKEL: THE RIDDLE OF THE UNIVERSE. Haeckel was the first German scholar to muster that nation's scientific thinking in support of the development of the theory of organic evolution. He himself contributed the then amazing and now extremely useful discovery that every individual recapitulates in its own growth the evolutionary stages through which its species has passed.

In *The Riddle Of The Universe*, his last book, he anticipated some of the "popularizing" of science of our day, by venturing to take a general speculative look at the whole cosmos, and man's relationship to that cosmos, in the light of the scientific knowledge which was then available. I have not read the book in almost thirty years, but it was a thrilling experience when I did read it, which I would not have missed for a great many books that I have read since.

My copy, a translation by Joseph McCabe, was published in 1900 by Harper and Brothers.

91. SIR JAMES JEANS: THE UNIVERSE AROUND US.
92. SIR JAMES JEANS: THE STARS IN THEIR COURSES. These are two popular presentations, by one of the greatest mathematical physicists of our times, of what

is known and guessed of the physical universe in which we live by the scientists who study the smallest atoms and the most distant stars with the same objective interest. They have a tremendous advantage over many somewhat similar books, in that Jeans is not only a scientist of the very first rank, but a broad and general thinker on all the aspects of human life as a part of this physical universe; and also in that he is a writer with a style of charming ease and the ability to make masterful use of illustrations.

For anyone who wishes to broaden his horizons, by taking a proper look at his own little life in the perspective of time and space provided by contemporary science, I recommend these two books as tops in their field.

My copies, of *The Universe Around Us* and of *The Stars In Their Courses*, were published by The Macmillan Company, New York.

93. SIR ARTHUR STANLEY EDDINGTON: THE NATURE OF THE PHYSICAL WORLD. In the conversational style of the original lectures at the University of Edinburgh, of which this book is the outgrowth, Eddington here discusses "some of the results of modern study of the physical world which give most food for philosophic thought." It was in order to include this book in my list that Jeans' *The Mysterious Universe* was omitted; for they both plunge into rather deep philosophic waters from the same scientific diving board.

Such recondite conceptions as the Fitzgerald contraction, entropy, and the quantum theory, are expounded in these pages with at least as much lucidity as we poor outsiders are likely to find anywhere else concerning these subjects. I don't claim to have understood one third of the book, but I enjoyed all of it.

My copy was published by The Macmillan Company.

94. ADAM SMITH: THE WEALTH OF NATIONS. This author — and this book — founded the modern science of economics. He is in considerable disfavor today with the practitioners of some of the pseudo science which passes as economics, because he didn't believe that two and two would ever add up to five, no matter how fast and how cleverly you did the adding. He also believed, and pretty well proved, that true wealth was the result of work and production, and not the result of lending yourself money or other bookkeeping legerdemain. But regardless of present economic theories which seem as far from the thinking of Adam Smith as astrology is from navigation, it was on his shoulders that political economy stood for a long time. *The Wealth Of Nations* is worth reading, and should be required reading, for anybody who ever uses the word economics.

My copy is an Everyman edition, published by E.P. Dutton & Company.

95. THORSTEIN VEBLEN: THE THEORY OF THE LEISURE CLASS. This book, like Bellamy's *Looking Backward*, was a product of indigenous American liberal thought, rather than an offshoot of the more extreme Marxian ideology of Europe. It seems to me, in fact, to have been only after Bellamy and Veblen and Markham and many other native sons, talking the American's own language, had softened up the rock of American conservatism, or at least roughened and grated its surface, that the sledgehammer blows of communistic thought ceased to bounce off that rock entirely and without any effect.

The argument of *The Theory Of The Leisure Class* is that money is spent, by those who have it to waste, only in part with an eye to the returns in pleasure or merchandise to be obtained, but even more with an eye to having neighbors or members of the same social set observe the spending — and thus observe the ability of its possessor to do such spending. Veblen calls this "conspicuous consumption," and of course castigates the folly of such waste and shallowness and lack of social conscience. The book was extremely shocking to what a supercilious radical of the time might have called the American upper bourgeoisie; but it was also sufficiently well-founded on observable tendencies to make a place for itself in serious economic theory.

My copy is published by The Modern Library, New York.

96. LUTHER C. SNIDER: EARTH HISTORY. Practicing what I preach, in my own pursuit of a little wider education, I have made occasional attempts at self instruction in such sciences as biology, chemistry, geology, and astronomy. In some of these, if the truth must be told, I found the going too difficult. Chemistry, in particular, I am convinced, is practically impossible to get started in satisfactorily without a laboratory or some preliminary instruction, or both. At least it was too much for me. But geology does not present any such insuperable difficulties. I certainly don't claim to know any; but that is because of so much dispersion of my own interests, and because there have been so few geology books written like Snider's *Earth History*.

This book is a survey of the life of our planet earth, the physical changes of and near its surface, throughout all geologic ages from the Azoic to the last Ice Age only a comparatively few thousand years ago; with particular reference to the forms of vegetable and animal life which have existed on the planet during these various ages. Its author is, I believe, an industrial geologist for one of the large oil companies, to the considerable loss of the teaching profession. I have read many other books on geology, but none which I think can compete at all with this one for the interest of the layman who is delving into the subject purely for his own pleasure.

My copy was published by The Century Company, New York.

97. SIR CHARLES LEONARD WOOLLEY: UR OF THE CHALDEES. This book is the story of an archaeological expedition, conducted by the author, which excavated the ancient Chaldean city of Ur, near the junction of the Tigris and Euphrates rivers, at the head of the Persian Gulf. Among the exciting discoveries was a temple schoolroom, such as used by Bel-Shalti-Nannar, the sister of Belshazzar and daughter of Nabonidus, last king of Babylon, in about 550 B.C. But what made this so exciting was the knowledge that Nabonidus himself was the first great archaeologist; that Ur was then already as old to his Babylon as that city is to ours; and that one reason his daughter was in Ur was the king's interest in the ruins and records of an earlier civilization which then dated back more than two thousand years. And in Woolley's excavation many remnants of this earlier civilization were themselves uncovered, and much contribution added to our knowledge of this distant Sumerian culture, all of which is recorded in this book.

Woolley tells the story of his excavation in a straightforward narrative style, with a suppressed excitement that still shines through the pages; and the result is the most interesting book in the field of archaeology that I happen ever to have read.

My copy is a paperbound edition published by Penguin Books Limited, of Harmondsworth, England.

98. E.T. BELL: MEN OF MATHEMATICS. In this book Professor Bell does for mathematics and mathematicians what Will Durant does for philosophy and philosophers in *The Story of Philosophy*. It is a survey, with biographical sketches of mathematicians, and descriptions of their work through which the gradual development of mathematics appears, from Pythagoras to Bertrand Russell.

Occasionally there are paragraphs or pages which a man who has not gone beyond high school algebra might find difficult to follow. But they can be skipped without any serious loss, and it will surprise the ordinary reader, without extensive training in mathematics, how clear Professor Bell can make most of his exposition, and how interesting.

My copy is published by Simon & Schuster.

99. KASNER AND NEWMAN: MATHEMATICS AND THE IMAGINATION. One chapter of this book is composed of puzzles and games which have a mathematical foundation. One chapter is headed "Paradox Lost and Paradox Regained." All of the book is just what its title implies; a delightful rambling through the byways of both pure and applied mathematics, for the fun of its appeal to the imagination. I enjoyed the book too much not to include it in this list. And even if you found my own chapters on mathematics tiresome, you still might enjoy Kasner and Newman.

My copy is published by Simon & Schuster.

100. OSWALD SPENGLER: THE DECLINE OF THE WEST. Justice Holmes once called this "a marvelous humbug of a book." It probably parades more erudition, more ostentatiously, than has ever been put between two covers, before or since. But the erudition does seem to be

real, and the ostentation can be forgiven. What detracts most from the book's serious value, aside from its unreadability, is the frequency with which most of us fail to be convinced that Spengler's analogies are really true, or prove the generalizations for which he adduces them.

Spengler's theory is that our western civilization is dying of sheer old age, the same as any other organic plant; and the same as died, before it, the civilizations of Egypt or ancient China or of Greece. The seed of his theory was planted by Herbert Spencer; and the conception of sociological organisms having an adolescence, middle age, and decay, the same as any other form of animal life, is easily accepted today. But many of us would quarrel with the dogmatic exactness with which Spengler establishes the minutiae of his parallels. And just one point at which many of us would question his conclusions, is as to whether America is part of the dying civilization of western Europe, or an entirely new plant with its growth and fullness of life still far ahead of it.

My copy, a translation by Charles Francis Atkinson (who deserves the highest praise for a superb job), was published by Alfred A. Knopf.

CHAPTER XII

The Last Word

Because there are so many other books in which I have found either entertainment or enlargement of thought that has made me glad to have read them, the temptation was strong to compile a list of another hundred for "Honorable Mention." But then there would still come to mind enough other titles, which at least deserved honorable mention, so that I should have to include a further list of "A Hundred Alternates." This in turn would lead to "And Not To Be Forgotten"; and so on until my memory failed to dig up any more specimens. For most of the books that I have read I have liked well enough to read again if I had the time.

But as Horace Greeley once said that "the way to resumption (of specie payments) was to resume"; and as somebody else has said that the way to write is to begin writing; so obviously the way to end this listing of books is simply to end it. Also, obviously, the way to bring this book itself to a close is to call some chapter the last one, and stop right there. So the last chapter this shall be. And the paragraphs of summation may be boring, but they will not be long.

One sheep, by jumping across a fence, may suggest the same idea to other sheep. A horse, by starting to run away, may inspire his companion horse on the other side of the shaft also to run away. But beyond such simple inducements to immediate emulation, no animal other than man is capable of transmitting thought to another animal. Except for those instinctive traits which the necessities of environment have taught a species by natural selection, no animal is capable of passing on to any other animal the things it has learned in its lifetime. A smart dog may be taught to perform miracles for a patient instructor, but has no way of transmitting his acquired knowledge to the puppies that come after him. Only man is able, not only to transmit hard-earned knowledge, but to accumulate it in written storehouses that keep its perpetuation from being dependent on the memories and interests of his immediate posterity. It is this capacity to draw on the past, consciously and selectively, which creates such a sharp delineation between the lives of human beings and those of all lower animals. And hence, it seems to me, the source of some of our greatest pleasure is this exploration of the thoughts and records and unsolved problems of those who have gone before us.

It is inevitable that most of these written meditations and chronicles and sermons should be concerned with man himself, or with other phenomena chiefly from the point of view of their effect on man. For to our own species we are naturally the most important thing that ever happened. In reading mediaeval history we laugh at the homocentric nonsense which put man and his earth at the center of the universe, and made the sun and the stars revolve around him for his benefit. But we find the same ridiculous narrowness in the assertion of our own generation that man stands about in the middle, for size, between the largest nebulae his telescopes can reveal and the smallest molecules to which his microscopes give tangible reality. For what has happened, of course, is that man has been able to push his scientific frontiers in both directions, toward the ever greater and the ever smaller, in approximately the same geometric ratio. Starting with himself and the objects immediately around him, his scientific powers have expanded until they can scrutinize objects larger than himself by about the same multiple as can be used for a divisor in telling how far his microscopes have reached the other way. Neither size has the slightest bearing on either how large or how small the phenomena of the universe really might be — by an absolute standard, if there were any such absolute standard — but only on how far down the two paths of exploration man has traveled until today. For all we can guess, the smallest electron we know about may contain millions of solar systems, and our whole Milky Way may be part of one electron revolving about some proton in a cosmic atom.

But this tendency of man to think and explore outward and subjectively from himself as a center doesn't make his thoughts and his discoveries any less interesting for other men. In fact, the more directly he confines his imagination and his reasoning to the impact on man himself of both the universe and other men, as is the case with most novels and histories and all but the works of abstract science, the more interesting are the words he writes likely to be for most of us. And for those who do wish to forget man entirely — or almost entirely — there are the mathematicians and the monistic thinkers and the higher physicists. In the printed pages of any good college or large-city library there is accumulated lore on anything in heaven or earth that might be dreamed of in our philosophies.

Not only individuals such as you and I, but mankind as a whole, can and must find pleasure in gaining an increasing knowledge of our past development, our problems, our powers, and our environment. Whether we wish it or not, the future destiny of our race is ultimately in the hands of the ignorant and teeming millions of Hindu outcasts, Russian peasants, and Japanese laborers; of the provincial farmers and artisans of South America, China, and Central Europe; of the self-centered and excitable rabbles of Paris, New York, and Shanghai. However infinitely far off seems the prospect, and difficult the job, of having a majority of the earth's population achieve an educated outlook on the adventure of living, there is no other possible course to keep that adventure from a tragic end.

Let's dip, for just a page or two, below the present nationalistic jealousies and social inequalities which feed power to dictators and make honest statesmen tremble. There are long-range problems, more fundamental even than these. Civilization, for instance, has always moved in a generally westward direction, leaving stagnation behind it. Is this process bound to continue? Will Europe inevitably sink into the petty chaos of exhaustion, as did the Tigris-Euphrates valley and the Syrian coast of the Mediterranean two thousand years before? Will America have its centuries in the sun, and then yield the leadership to maturing powers on the other side of the Pacific? *Or* — has the world now grown so small, and the interplay of all enlightenment east and west so prompt and so complete, that this principle will have lost its force? Has the line which once had ends and a direction now at last become a closed circle, without either?

The nearest approach to universal peace which the civilized world has ever enjoyed was the Pax Romana; a peace enforced on all other nations by the conquest of one all-powerful nation which then ruled the others as provinces in its imperial system. The parallel between the

Roman state and our own nation is striking in the extreme, even as to details of origin, internal political development, spiritual philosophy, comparative material power, and relationships to the rest of the known world. We are now approaching the Julius Caesar era in our own ontogeny. Will history repeat itself with a Pax Americana? Is the domination of the rest of the planet by America desirable, for the sake of a peace from international wars that is not otherwise obtainable? Desirable or not, is it inevitable, or is there now some other path to peace in the voluntary integration of political entities which have grown in nearness to each other, and possibly even in wisdom, since the Roman days?

The Malthusian doctrine that population will always increase as far as available sustenance will permit, and a little beyond, is incontrovertible by all past experience. Will this principle continue to prevail, as an unavoidable law of nature, until the prairies of America and the pampas of Argentina are as full of human animals always on the near edge of starvation as India and China have already become? Even though means of growing food are improved by science until the planet can easily feed twenty billion men, and every arable plot and shelf on its surface is as faithfully tended as the tiny farms of Holland, will the population then inevitably climb to twenty-one billion, with recurrent famine as the only limitation to this total? Or will birth control and eugenics and other seizures by man of his own destiny enable him to make a conscious adjustment between sustenance and population so that he rises forever above hunger as a force in political emotion? Or is this law so immutable that it will drive super-intelligent human beings off into interstellar space, just as it has driven tiny ants into every corner of our present globe?

Is the exploration of interstellar space, and the settlement of pioneering men on the planets of other stars, but a poetic fancy, or a possibility which we are already approaching with Promethean powers? Is man almost done, about ready to recede as a species through overspecialization of the intellect, as countless species have fallen through some form of over-specialization before? Or, before that happens, is he about to waste a billion years of evolutionary progress on this earth by exploding the whole thing into a gaseous mass, through letting loose forces as far beyond his understanding as dynamite is beyond the understanding of a dog or a chimpanzee? Or is man, having climbed this far out of unconsciousness, and into *conscious* knowledge of his own potentialities and a few of nature's laws, just now ready to begin his real career? Can he, becoming one family and one brotherhood on this little earth, go on from here to explore and populate the Milky Way as surely as his ancestors once moved onto the virgin islands of the Ionian Sea? Will his reach, in knowledge and in space, go as far beyond its present level as this present level is beyond that of the amoebae which sprouted in the primordial slime?

More fundamental than any of these, because its answer must be woven into, as a part of, all the other answers, is the problem of a basis of ethics. That basis, for the last few thousand years, has always hung on a supernatural thread; on the attempt to connect human lives with cosmological purpose. But the conviction that there is any cosmological purpose recurrently fades away, and one thread after another wears thin and loses its strength. Religion is a marvelous thing, for those of us whom it consoles and inspires. But for some minds even during the period when its influence waxes, and for many minds during the interludes when that influence wanes, it lacks compelling reality as an anchor for ethical principles. Can man, from a study of himself and his own needs, arrive at a pragmatic system of ethics which will beget universal loyalty; which will make even the violator feel that he is a traitor to his own cause? Can the feeling of decency in human relations, and consideration for others, be expanded into an unwritten code of laws and customs that needs the weight of no other authority than the universality of its observance?

Five thousand questions similar to these stand across the path of our progress. They will in time be answered by events; events shaped, quite possibly, by ignorance and unconcern. For while none of us know the answers, there are too many hundreds of millions of us who do not even know the questions. Certainly, to rob two poets with one snatch, "a little learning is a dangerous thing," and "knowledge comes but wisdom lingers." It is also true, however, that we must crawl before we can walk; that we can never acquire much learning without getting the little first; and that while wisdom may linger far behind knowledge, it can never come at all without knowledge as a prerequisite. And so it seems to me that the path to a happier life, on the part of the human beings who inhabit this planet, must lead through continued and increasing education of *all* these human beings, however rocky the path may become in the intermediate stages. If this be so, it behooves all of us to delve with more determined curiosity and attentive delight into the storehouse of knowledge that the art of printing has put so readily at our convenience.

One of the greatest advantages and joys of college years is the "bull session," the talk-fest which begins informally and lasts for hours, while half a dozen boys toss arguments and ideas back and forth on every subject from sex to systems of government. The irresistible appeal of these meetings, of this savoring of new thoughts and penetrating into new puzzles of physics or philosophy, lies in the fact that the students' minds are growing; that there is a development and expansion of their mental processes, and of the knowledge on which these processes work, of which they become more pleasantly conscious at such jousts than at any other time. There is a pleasure in mental growth which is one of the divine gifts of the inscrutable fate that has made us what we are. There is no reason, biological or otherwise, why this growth should ever stop at any age, short of downright senility. If the growth is real, the accompanying pleasure has no component of conceit or ostentation; it derives from the innate human delight in the increase of human potentialities and from a feeling of quiet kinship with the strength of other minds. As individuals, and as a race, we live in the midst of turmoil and struggles, of longing and doubts and fears. But over them all study and reflection can sometimes lead us to a serene contentment, to a feeling that somehow we are "in the calm and proud possession of eternal things."

Epilogue

Well, here we are back again. Your guide and commentator will once more be his age. And if the last chapter did not turn you off completely, it will not be "the last word" after all. In fact, we shall have a few uncomplimentary remarks to make about that chapter ourselves. But it will be easier for us to write these honest-to-goodness last words, and for you to read them, if we follow some kind of logical order.

So we begin with a confession. It is that we abandoned the idea of separate footnotes quite early. They were going to provide too much of a temptation for unnecessary comments, and be too distracting from the main line of thought in any particular passage. We soon decided instead to confine our corrections, explanations, admissions, and "improvements" to points that could be covered in a far less formal manner.

One such item is that this book, while not "finished" until almost five years later, was actually started early in 1942 — immediately after Pearl Harbor. (There was a very real connection with Pearl Harbor, which is irrelevant here.) And most of it was written, in whatever spare time your aspiring author could snatch for that purpose, usually on Sundays and holidays, during 1942 and 1943. This accounts for the reference in some passage to his never having been to England. But our first trip to that country (as mentioned in the prologue) was made in February,

1946, for the help it would be in an already rising resolution. We were determined to do all we could in opposing the advance of socialist doctrine and legislation in our own country, similar to what was so visibly taking place just across the Atlantic.

In fact this writer's speech on A Businessman Looks At England had been given probably fifty times — to service clubs, small chambers of commerce, and similar groups — even before that trip was made. It was our increasing preoccupation with the socialist threat, and a corresponding decrease of interest in The Romance Of Education, which caused that manuscript to be more and more neglected during 1945, until it was finally "finished," shelved, and forgotten in 1946.

The above explanation, suggested in the prologue as a possibility, has now come back to us so clearly on our reading of the manuscript that it seemed to be worth repeating in more detail and with more assurance. And if you ask, "Well, who cares?", we answer frankly, "Probably nobody, except ourselves." But we have decided, almost of necessity, while working on the proofsheets supplied us by the typesetters, to let this manuscript go into print exactly as it was. So we do ask for your permission and patience, while we clear up any seeming anachronisms or other inconsistencies.

Please forgive us, therefore, for appearing to convert this epilogue into an embryonic autobiography. We shall continue to follow so embarrassing a formula only where it may be required for putting some thoughts that have been expressed, or incidents related, in their proper perspective. Because, after the last thirty years of a truly busy life, some of the things we have just read in this overgrown and once discarded essay now surprise even the man who wrote them.

Epilogue

As we come to specifics that might need attention, we are able to refrain from any commentary until we reach the fervent praise of Dr. Will Durant on Page 161 and again on Pages 243-245. Even as late as 1957 we used the back cover of our small magazine, One Man's Opinion *(which has long since become* American Opinion*), for a salute to Dr. Durant, and further praise of his books. And today we still think that those first three volumes of his* The Story Of Civilization, *entitled respectively* Our Oriental Heritage, The Life Of Greece, *and* Caesar And Christ, *are probably the best history books ever written.*

But for the sake of accuracy let us add some further observations: (1) The Story Of Civilization, *by the time it was finished in 1967, had run to ten huge volumes, instead of the five originally projected (or announced) as stated in our text; (2) his scholarship remained (with one exception) comprehensive and meticulous, and his writing (without exception) of unsurpassed brilliance, throughout all ten volumes; but (3) his last two volumes in particular put unbalanced emphasis on the ideological motivations or pretenses, and too little on the countless conspiratorial forces — finally merging into one vast conspiracy — which have inflicted on humanity the long revolution that is now coming to a crisis; and (4) the one place we have ever found where he falsified — or at least deliberately distorted — the record, and even contradicted what he had said in an earlier passage, was in his disparagement of the importance of the* Illuminati.

This he did, to an extreme extent, both by what he said and by what he failed to say, despite the fact that Dr. Durant was bound to have known about Weishaupt's group what was already so well known to (and properly evaluated by) the Elector of Bavaria as early as 1784. Such a blind spot about the origin and early development of what has now become the central fact in the history of the last two hundred years is hard to explain. It is especially so when you consider the extreme improbability of Dr. Durant's being entirely unfamiliar with the writings of Professor Robison, l'Abbé Barruel, and Joseph de Maistre.

What conclusions are to be drawn from these observations we do not know. We have merely wanted to make clear that if we were writing this same book today we should want to study Durant far more closely before being quite so uncritical about his lifetime work and purposes. And with great sadness, growing out of nearly fifty years of our admiration for Dr. Durant, and occasional correspondence with him, we confess that this doubt concerning those purposes was considerably increased by one revealing episode. This was his seemingly gratuitous undermining and castigation, a few years ago, of a man whom we had come to know personally and well. This victim of incredibly cruel Communist persecution, to which Dr. Durant in effect contributed, was in our opinion a far more noble and courageous human being, in love and labor and sacrifice for his own country and his fellow countrymen, than Dr. Durant has ever aspired to become. His name was Dr. Syngman Rhee.

A minor addition which should be made to our text is in connection with the quotation on Page 162 from Bishop Berkeley: "Westward the course of empire takes its way." As we did not know, when that passage was written, Vilhjalmur Stefansson has proved convincingly that the course of empire and the crest of civilization have moved steadily northwestward *since the days of the Sumerians with whom the historical record begins. Whether this is because a certain level of cooler climate promotes the energy, ambition, and aggressiveness, of the pioneer spirit*

Epilogue

which builds a civilization, or conquers those to the south of it, we do not know. Or, even if this is true, whether or not the gradual warming up of the planet since the culmination of the last ice age has moved the line of suitable environment steadily into more northern latitudes, we still do not know. But the facts of the past, and the present outlook for the future, certainly support the Stefansson thesis.

Incidentally, we have no hesitation even today about giving full credit to a Communist or pro-Communist for any important and worthwhile achievement which was not carried out primarily to help the Communist cause. This writer once spent most of a whole day in talking with Stefansson, who by that time had already been a member of 104 Communist fronts. But in our opinion this man was a famous explorer who had been enticed into Communism, and not originally a Communist who had done his exploring to serve Communist purposes. And the distinction is important when we come to the names of Albert Einstein and Bertrand Russell on page 164.

For there our ignorance in 1946 about the whole Master Conspiracy was clearly showing. And we should certainly want to revise that passage if we were writing this book today. In fact, as we made clear in One Dozen Trumpets several years ago, we know now that Einstein was above all else a Communist, working for the Communists, all of his life. And we believe — let those scoff who may — that he was a complete phony as a mathematician. That opinion was obviously shared by a truly brilliant mathematical physicist, Dr. J. Robert Oppenheimer, despite Dr. Oppenheimer's visible reluctance to express any criticism of his fellow Communist, Albert Einstein. As to Bertrand Russell our revision of opinion, in the light of later knowledge, would be equally pronounced.

For the next changes of opinion in some hypothetical rewrite of this tome, we can move all the way to Page 220. Having become, during this last quarter of a century, a confirmed skeptic with regard to anybody who receives constant praise in the Liberal press, we might now want to say something different about Pearl Buck. But we have no idea what it would be. We have also become aware that Sinclair Lewis knew what he was doing to help the Conspiracy when he so bitterly ridiculed the "main streets" of America; and that Communist promotion accounted for a large part of his fame and his sales. But we still recommend that you read his best books — with a few grains of salt, and with a realization that pioneering Americans had first to create a country of abundance, so that people like Lewis would have the necessary food and clothes and leisure while they were tearing that country down.

With regard to Kenneth Roberts we do not know yet whether or not he wrote Oliver Wiswell *for the deliberate purpose of weakening American patriotism, by showing the other face of the American Revolution. Nor shall we try to settle that question here. All we do want to settle is that the views expressed in this product of our brain wave generator thirty years ago are not necessarily those of its present management. Especially when those views are about anything to do with the Conspiracy, of which we knew so little then, and not enough today. So, with this general disclaimer, we shall spare you any further comments about the ideological loyalties — or possibly worse — of such authors whom we mention as Beaumarchais, Theodor Mommsen, John Clark Ridpath, Thorstein Veblen, H.G. Wells, John Spencer Bassett, and Frederick Lewis Allen. There is no doubt that our brief reviews of their books, if written today, would convey some different*

Epilogue

— or at least additional — impressions and overtones. But we have no slightest intention of converting The Romance Of Education *into a contemporary tract on* The Realities Of Conspiracy.

When we came, just a few days ago, to read the final chapter of our own book — and this actually was the first time in twenty-six years — we were even more amazed to see what we had written there in the 1940's. And to discover to what extent the subtle propaganda of a huge Master Conspiracy, flowing in on the human mind from almost every source and through so many different channels, had crept into some of our own thinking before we even began to study this Conspiracy or to be fully aware of its existence.

Obviously we ourselves were beginning to swallow, as honest ideological arguments, and as praiseworthy aspirations, some of the very perversions of both that were being ground out by the Communist propaganda machine. It is true that we had recognized Wendell Willkie, even in 1940, as an arch hypocrite who had been rammed down the throats of the Republican Party as their nominee for the Presidency, with criminal audacity at the Philadelphia Convention, by the very forces which he and that Party were supposed to be opposing. But we did not realize that this was all a part of a far greater and deeper conspiratorial operation through which the Communists and their bosses — whom we now call the Insiders *— were already destroying the freedom and determining the future of the American people. Or that Wendell Willkie himself was a part of the plot in which he was being used.*

We knew that a small-time Missouri politician, named Harry Truman, who had been sent to the United States

Senate by an extremely crooked political machine called the Pendergast Gang, was then selected by an actual Communist named Sidney Hillman to become the successor to a dying Franklin D. Roosevelt as President of the United States. But we did not know the incredible extent to which control over everything that was happening in and to our country was already in the hands of Communistic traitors, as manifested by this maneuver.

We recognized that it was folly of the worst order for the United States to get in the same bed with Soviet Russia, even when that bed was called the United Nations. But we had not yet fully recognized that Tennyson's great dream of a "Parliament of man" was being prostituted to the service of an incredibly evil Conspiracy. Or that the pretense of creating this "Federation of the world" was being utilized as one major step towards establishing a brutal Communist tyranny over the whole human race. Or that the United States Government, as a result of Communist influences within and without, was to become the most powerful single force in the whole world for bringing this tragedy to pass.

It is easy to find in that last chapter many other examples of an appalling ignorance about the very realities of today's worldwide struggle. Basically, of course, that struggle is against a power-seeking Conspiracy, rather than against its ideological fronts and sociological pretenses. As we have now been trying to convince our fellow countrymen for many years. But we first had to learn this sad fact ourselves. And there are so many other manifestations of our own shortcomings in knowledge and understanding compressed into those few pages, unfortunately, that we even felt tempted simply to omit that chapter altogether from this present publication. But so far, thank the Lord, we have never consciously yielded to expediency at the

Epilogue

expense of truth. And this would be a most unsuitable time and place in which to start.

That same consideration applies to at least one other matter which we need to mention. Throughout this whole book there has been a recurrent acceptance of the theory of both organic and inorganic evolution. That acceptance was made more positive, and more important to our discussion, in the final chapter. Yet the principle of evolution is a tenet on which a great many of our best friends and strongest supporters disagree with us. And we are giving the whole of our lives in defense of their right to do so. All we ask in return is that they allow us the same religious freedom which we seek for them.

This writer's spiritual roots in Christianity are so deep that we named The John Birch Society for a truly great fundamentalist Baptist missionary. But he had tremendous tolerance for other people's religious beliefs even while he was trying to convert them to his own. There was a time when Christians were burned at the stake by other Christians for believing that the earth was round. Galileo was tried and convicted by the Inquisition for supporting the Copernican doctrine that the earth moves around the sun. Yet there are few Christians today who believe there is any conflict between their Bibles and the Copernican system of astronomy. Nor do we think that there is anything contradictory to even the Book of Genesis in our belief as to how God created man.

But this is not the place for us to enter into any of these theological or teleological discussions. We have ventured to touch on their borders at all only because The Romance Of Education *would lead almost inevitably to the rise of many long thoughts in the mind of any reader. As would any similar introduction to the fundamentals of a classical education. It is the education itself, however, the growing knowledge and understanding of our inheritance from the past — and not the philosophies or the actions to which that education may lead — with which this adventure in learning has been concerned.*

So we end, as we began, by inviting you to explore further the various fields of accumulated knowledge, primarily for the pleasure of the exploration. And because you will enjoy a constant wonder at the deeper fields which stretch so invitingly and amazingly ahead. The wonder and pleasure that we have tried to suggest, throughout these few hundred pages, have already been recognized by many, we are sure, as the theme of that tremendous sonnet by John Keats, of which we paraphrased the final clause at the end of our prologue. We have also lifted some of its lines elsewhere. And the very name of the publishing company which offers you this book was thus supplied by Keats. So let us end this epilogue, and this book, by quoting that sonnet in full.

On First Looking Into Chapman's Homer

Much have I travelled in the realms of gold,
  And many goodly states and kingdoms seen;
  Round many western islands have I been
Which bards in fealty to Apollo hold.
Oft of one wide expanse had I been told
  That deep-browed Homer ruled as his demesne:
  Yet did I never breathe its pure serene
Till I heard Chapman speak out loud and bold:
Then felt I like some watcher of the skies
  When a new planet swims into his ken;
Or like stout Cortez, when with eagle eyes
  He stared at the Pacific — and all his men
Looked at each other with a wild surmise —
  Silent, upon a peak in Darien.

Index

Abashed Husband, The (Molière), 229
Abu Bekr, 65, 87
Actium, 61, 63
Admirable Crichton, The (Barrie), 234-235
Adventures Of Sherlock Holmes (Doyle), 213-214
Aeneid, The (Vergil), 24, 223
Aeschylus, 222
Aesop, 52, 239
Alexander the Great, 56, 61
Alexandria, 59, 61, 62
Alexei, 69
Alexius, 88, 90
Ali, 65
Alice In Wonderland (Carroll), 218-219
Allen, Frederick Lewis, 253, 276
Amenhotep (see Iknaton)
America, 15, 179, 244, 248, 251, 253, 257, 258, 261, 266, 276, 278
American Opinion, 273
Anaximander, 58, 99, 164
Ancient History Of The Near East (Hall), 247-248
"*And When They Fall*" (Montague), 237

Antony And Cleopatra (Shakespeare), 226
Arabia, 63, 65, 66, 76, 80, 81
Archimedes, 58-60
Ardys, King of Lydia, 80
Aristophanes, 222
Ashurbanipal, 79-81
Asia Minor, 248
Assyria, 41, 78-80
As You Like It (Shakespeare), 226
Ataraxia (B.L.T.), 237
Athalie (Racine), 228
Augustus, 87

B.L.T. (pseud. of Bert Leston Taylor), 237
Babbitt (Lewis), 221
Babylon, 41, 64, 78, 80, 81, 83, 259
Bacon, Francis, 98, 160, 254
Baldwin I, King of Jerusalem, 91
Barber Of Seville, The (Beaumarchais), 232-233
Baron Munchausen (Raspe), 202-203
Barrel Organ, The (Noyes), 170
Barrie, Sir James M., 234-235
Barruel, l'Abbé, 274

Bassett, John Spencer, 251, 276
Bates, Katherine Lee, 176
Battle Of The Books, The (Swift), 200
Beaumarchais, Pierre de, 232, 276
Behistun rock, 41, 42
Bell, E.T., 113, 260
Bellamy, Edward, 82, 98, 212, 257
Belshazzar, 64, 259
Bentham, Jeremy, 98
Berkeley, Bishop George, 162, 274
Bible, Holy, 165, 242
Biglow Papers, The (Lowell), 101, 238
Bishop Murder Case, The (Van Dine), 220
Black, J.M., 163
Brahma (Emerson), 209, 236
Bridge Of Sighs, The (Hood), 178
Bright Angel Trail, 14
Brothers Karamazov, The (Dostoevski), 215-216
Bryant, William Cullen, 238
Buck, Pearl, 220-221, 276
Burr, Amelia Josephine, 192
Business Man Looks At England, A (speech), 272
Byron, George Gordon, Lord, 183
Byzantine Empire, 87

Caesar, Julius, 24, 35, 56, 62, 63, 267
Caesar And Christ (Durant), 244-245, 273
Calvin, John, 98

Campanella, Tommaso, 98
Candide (Voltaire), 201
Canterbury Tales (Chaucer), 225
Carcassonne (Nadaud), 52
Carlyle, Thomas, 50-52, 101
Carroll, Lewis (pseud. of Charles Lutwidge Dodgson), 193, 218-219
Carryl, Guy Wetmore, 52, 193
Carthage, 12, 78
Cataract Of Lodore, The (Southey), 168
Catherine I, 67-70
Catiline, Lucius Sergius, 249
Cervantes-Saavedra, Miguel de, 199
Chaldea, 243, 259
Chambered Nautilus, The (Holmes), 174
Champollion, 42, 43
Chanticler (Rostand), 234
Charlemagne, 86, 88
Chaucer, 13, 225
Cheops (Khufu), 15, 75-77, 114
Chief American Poets, The (Page), 237-238
China, 89, 164, 243, 261
Choti Tinchaurya (Hope), 188
Christianity, 72, 86, 87, 91, 162, 205, 242, 244
Cicero, Marcus Tullius, 24, 249-250
Cid, The (Corneille), 228
City Of The Sun, The (Campanella), 98
Cleghorn, Sarah N., 179
Cleopatra, 60-63
Clerk's Tale, The (Chaucer), 225
Cobb, Irving S., 201

Index

Coleridge, Samuel Taylor, 57, 167, 236
Collected Librettos (Gilbert and Sullivan), 240
Collected Stories (Poe), 207
Collins, Wilkie, 213
Colorado River, 14
Comedy Of Errors, The (Shakespeare), 224, 226
Compensation (Emerson), 209
Comptons, 164
Connecticut Yankee At King Arthur's Court, A (Twain), 217
Connelly, Marc, 12
Constantine, 87
Constantinople, 87-90
Coolidge, Calvin, 16, 95
Cooper, James Fenimore, 202, 221
Cooper, Lane, 222
Corneille, Pierre, 228
Cosimo, Tony, 4-5
Count Of Monte Cristo, The (Dumas), 204
Crane, Nathalia, 164
Crime And Punishment (Dostoevski), 215-216
Critic, The (Sheridan), 230
Crusade, First, 85-91
Curies, 164
Cyrano de Bergerac (Rostand), 52, 233-234

Daly, T.A., 241
Darius, 41, 248
Darwin, Charles, 73, 99, 164, 253-254
Daudet, Alphonse, 208
David Copperfield (Dickens), 203

David Harum (Wescott), 215
Davies, Mary Carolyn, 185
Dead End, 13
Debts (Rittenhouse), 190
Decline And Fall Of The Roman Empire, The (Gibbon), 100
Decline Of The West, The (Spengler), 260-261
Deerslayer, The (Cooper), 202
DeFoe, Daniel, 199
Descartes, René, 123, 125, 129, 132, 155, 160, 200
Descent Of Man, The (Darwin), 253
Dickens, Charles, 100, 203-204
Doctor Faustus (Marlowe), 225
Doctor In Spite Of Himself, The (Molière), 229
Dr. Jekyll And Mr. Hyde (Stevenson), 211-212
Don Quixote (Cervantes), 199
Door, The (Davies), 185
Dostoevski, Fëdor M., 215-216, 220
Dowson, Ernest, 191
Doyle, Sir Arthur Conan, 213-214, 220
Drifting (Read), 171
Dumas, Alexandre, 204-205
Durant, Will, ix, 58, 77, 161, 242-245, 260, 273, 274

Earth History (Snider), 258-259
Eddington, Sir Arthur Stanley, 256
Edward II (Marlowe), 226
Egypt, 15, 36, 42, 61, 62, 75, 76, 80, 81, 89, 112, 114, 243, 261
Einstein, Albert, 164, 275

Eldorado (Poe), 174
Elegy In A Country Churchyard (Gray), 171
Eliot, George, 211
Emerson, Ralph Waldo, 37, 209, 236, 237
Emperor Jones, The (O'Neill), 13
Engels, Friedrich, 212
England, ix, 181, 222, 271
England (Robinson), 251
Essays (Emerson), 209
Essays (Huxley), 253-254
Essays (Montaigne), 200
Esarhaddon, 78-79
Evangeline (Longfellow), 238
Euclid, 59, 155
Euripides, 222-223
Excelsior (Longfellow), 174

Fable For Critics, A (Lowell), 238
Fables (LaFontaine), 239
Far-Away Princess, The (Rostand), 234
Faust (Goethe), 230
Fermat, Pierre de, 129, 155
Fifteen Greek Plays, 222
First Principles (Spencer), 254-255
Fitzgerald, Edward, 165, 186, 236
Flood Of Years, The (Bryant), 238
Frederick the Great, 8
French Revolution, 101, 203, 232
Friendship (Emerson), 209
Four Million, The (O. Henry), 218

Fox And The Crow, The (La Fontaine), 52
Frogs, The (Aristophanes), 222

Gaboriau, Émile, 214, 220
Gallic Wars (Caesar), 24
Garden Of Kama, The (Hope), 188
Gibbon, Edward, 100
Gift Of The Magi, The (O. Henry), 218
Gilbert and Sullivan, 240
Gilbert, W.S., 193, 240
Glück, Ernest, 67-68
God And The Strong Ones (Widdemer), 178
Goethe, Johann Wolfgang von, 11, 230
Goldbach, 156
Gold Bug, The (Poe), 207
Golden Shoes, The (Peabody), 241
Golden Treasury Of English Lyric Poetry, The (Palgrave), 235-236
Goldsmith, Oliver, 229-230
Good Earth, The (Buck), 220-221
Good-Natured Man, The (Molière), 230
Grand Canyon, 14
Graustark (McCutcheon), 214
Gray, Thomas, 171, 236
Great Salt Lake, 14
Greece, 44-45, 58, 243, 261
Greeley, Horace, 263
Greene, Robert, 182
Green Pastures, The (Connelly), 12
Gregory I, 86

Index

Gregory VII, 88
Gulliver's Travels (Swift), 199-200

Haeckel, Ernest, 255
Hall, H.R., 247-248
Hamlet (Levy), 242
Hamlet (Shakespeare), 226
Hannibal, 12
Hawthorne, Nathaniel, 210
Hayes, Carlton J.H., 251
Hegira (The), 66
Henley, William Ernest, 166
Henry IV (Shakespeare), 12, 226
Henry, O. (pseud. of William Sydney Porter), 217-218
Hero of Alexandria, 164
Herodotus, 111, 112, 248-249
Heroes And Hero Worship (Carlyle), 50
Herrick, Robert, 235
Hieron II of Syracuse, 58-60
Hillman, Sidney, 278
High Tide (Richards), 240-241
Hipparchus, 120
Hippocrates, 143
History (Herodotus), 248-249
History Of Rome, The (Mommsen), 245
History Of The World (Ridpath), 246-247, 276
Holmes, Oliver Wendell, 174, 237, 238
Holmes, Justice Oliver Wendell, 260
Home Book Of Verse, The (Stevenson), 236-237
Home Book Of Modern Verse, The (Stevenson), 237
Hood, Thomas, 178
Hope, Laurence, 188
Hugo, Victor, 206
Huxley, Thomas Henry, 19, 99, 253-254
Hypatia (Kingsley), 100, 205
Hypochondriac, The (Molière), 229
Hypocrite, The (Molière), 229

Iknaton, 56-58
Illuminati, 273
Il Penseroso (Milton), 228
Imhotep, 75
Impenitentia Ultima (Dowson), 191
Importance Of Being Earnest, The (Wilde), 233
India, 89, 164, 243
Ingelow, Jean, 185
Innocents Abroad (Twain), 217
Insiders, 277
In The Cool Of The Evening (Noyes), 170, 241
Irving, Washington, 203
Ivanhoe (Scott), 201

Jeans, Sir James, 136, 255-256
Jersey, 35
Jerusalem, 88-89, 91
Jesus Christ, 87, 89, 242
Jew Of Malta, The (Marlowe), 225
Jones, Thomas S., Jr., 172, 241

Kadija, 65
Kasner, Professor Edward, 116, 159, 260
Keats, John, 236, 280
Kim (Kipling), 216
Khufu (see Cheops)

King Cophetua And The Beggar Maid (Marquis), 237
King Lear (Shakespeare), 13, 226
Kingsley, Charles, 100, 205-206
Kinship (Morgan), 241
Kipling, Rudyard, 216
Knight's Tale, The (Chaucer), 225
Koran, 66
Kublai Khan, 250
Kubla Khan (Coleridge), 167

Lady Of The Lake, The (Scott), 238
Lady Windermere's Fan (Wilde), 233
La Fontaine, Jean de, 52, 239
L'Aiglon (Rostand), 234
L'Allegro (Milton), 228
Landor, Walter Savage, xi, 166, 236
Lanier, Sidney, 57, 166, 167, 174, 238
Lay Of The Last Minstrel, The (Scott), 238-239
Lazzerini, 151
Lear, Edward, 193, 236
Learned Ladies, The (Molière), 229
Legend Of Sleepy Hollow, The (Irving), 203
Leibnitz, Gottfried, 134, 141, 143, 159, 201
Lenin, Nikolai, 178
Lepidus, 62-63
Letters From My Mill (Daudet), 208
Levy, Norman, 241
Lewis, Sinclair, 161, 221, 276
Life Of Greece, The (Durant), 243-244, 273

Lindbergh, Charles A., 91-96, 164
Livingstone, David, 71-72
Locksley Hall (Tennyson), 236
Longfellow, Henry Wadsworth, 167, 174, 237, 238
Look Homeward, Angel (Wolfe), 219
Looking Backward (Bellamy), 82, 98, 212, 257
Los Angeles, 45
Louis XIV, 79
Love In A Cottage (Willis), 182
Lowell, James Russell, 101, 214, 237, 238, 246
Lycidas (Milton), 228, 236

MacArthur, General Douglas, 49
Macaulay, Thomas Babington, 162
McCutcheon, George Barr, 214
Macbeth (Shakespeare), 52, 226
Machiavelli, Niccolo, 252
Magoun, Professor Alexander, 91
Main Street (Lewis), 161, 221
Maistre, Joseph de, 274
Mamba's Daughters, 13
Mammon And The Archer (O. Henry), 218
Man With The Hoe, The (Markham), 178
Marcellus, 60
Marco Polo, 250
Marcus Aurelius, 87
Mark Anthony, 61-63, 249
Markham, Edwin, 178, 257
Marlowe, Christopher, 12, 13, 67, 165, 181, 182, 225-226
Marmion (Scott), 238

Index

Marquis, Don, 237
Marriage Of Figaro, The (Beaumarchais), 232
Marseillaise, The, 178
Marshes Of Glynn, The (Lanier), 238
Marta Of Muscovy (Stong), 67
Marx, Karl, 178, 212
Master Conspiracy, 278
Mathematics And The Imagination (Kasner and Newman), 260
Mecca, 64-66
Medina, 65
Memphis, 75
Menaechmi (Plautus), 224
Men Of Mathematics (Bell), 260
Menshikov, Prince, 68-70
Merchant Of Venice, The (Shakespeare), 226
Michael VII, 88
Midsummer Night's Dream, A (Shakespeare), 226
Mikado, The (Gilbert and Sullivan), 240
Mill, James, 98
Mill, John Stuart, 99
Milton, John, 171, 176, 183, 227, 228, 236
Misanthrope, The (Molière), 229
Miser, The (Molière), 229
Misérables, Les (Hugo), 206
Mitchell, Ruth Comfort, 177
Mohammed, 63-66
Mohammedanism, 64, 66, 87, 162
Molière (pseud. of Jean Baptiste Poquelin), 228, 229-230
Mommsen, Theodor, 39, 40-41, 43, 245-247, 276

Monday Tales (Daudet), 208
Montague, James J., 237
Montaigne, Michel Eyquem de, 200
Montesquieu, Charles de Secondat, Baron de, 200
Moonstone, The (Collins), 213
More, Sir Thomas, 98
Morgan, Angela, 195, 241
Municipal Report, The (O. Henry), 218
Murders In The Rue Morgue, The (Poe), 207
Mysterious Universe, The (Jeans), 256

Nabonidus, 64, 259
Nabopolassar, 81
Nadaud, Gustave, 52
Napoleon, 42, 56
Nero, 100
Nature Of The Physical World, The (Eddington), 256
New Atlantis, The (Bacon), 98
Newton, Isaac, 134, 141, 143
Nineveh, 78-82
Nofretete, 57
Noyes, Alfred, 170, 241
Nun's Priest's Tale, The (Chaucer), 225
Nymph's Reply To The Passionate Shepherd, The (Raleigh), 182

Octavian, 61-63
Oedipus, King Of Thebes (Sophocles), 222-223
Of Time And The River (Wolfe), 219
Oliver Wiswell (Roberts), 221, 276

O'Neill, Eugene, 13
One Man's Opinion, 273
On First Looking Into Chapman's Homer (Keats), 280
On His Blindness (Milton), 228
Only Yesterday (Allen), 253
On The Late Massacre In Piedmont (Milton), 171
On The Origin Of Species (Darwin), 253
Opera Guyed (Levy), 241-242
Oppenheimer, Dr. J. Robert, 275
Orations (Cicero), 24, 249-250
O'Shaughnessy, Arthur, 167, 178
Othello (Shakespeare), 226
Our Oriental Heritage (Durant), 243-244, 273
Outline Of History, The (Wells), 246
Over-Soul, The (Emerson), 209
Owl And The Pussy-Cat, The (Lear), 193
Ozymandias Of Egypt (Shelley), 173

Page, Curtis Hidden, 237-238
Palgrave, Sir Francis, 235-236
Paradise Lost (Milton), 227-228
Pascal, Blaise, 169
Passionate Shepherd To His Love, The (Marlowe), 181
Pax Romana, 266
Peabody, Josephine Preston, 241
Pearl Harbor, 271
Pendergast Gang, 278
Persian Letters, The (Montesquieu), 200
Peter the Great, 68-70

Peter the Hermit, 90
Philadelphia Convention, 277
Philippics (Cicero), 249
Phormio (Terence), 224
Pinafore (Gilbert and Sullivan), 240
Plato, 98, 159
Plautus, Titus Maccius, 224
Plays (Rostand), 233-234
Poe, Edgar Allan, 168, 174, 183-185, 207, 214, 217, 220, 237, 246
Poems (Milton), 227
Poems (Scott), 238-239
Poland, 8
Political And Social History Of Modern Europe, A (Hayes), 251
Pompeii, 82-85
Pompey, 61-62
Pothinus, 61
Preston, Keith, 237
Prince, The (Machiavelli), 252
Prince And The Pauper, The (Twain), 217
Prologue (Chaucer), 225
Prothalamion (Young), 186
Psammetichos, 80-81
Ptolemy XII, 61
Purloined Letter, The (Poe), 207
Pygmalion (Shaw), 10
Pyramid, Great, 75-78, 114
Pythagoras, 71, 114, 159, 260

Racine, Jean, 228
Raleigh, Sir Walter, 182
Rape Of Lucrece, The (Shakespeare), 226
Raspe, Rudolph Erich, 202
Rawlinson, Sir Henry, 41-43

Index 289

Read, Thomas Buchanan, 171
Republic, The (Plato), 98
Republican Party, 277
Rhee, Dr. Syngman, 274
Richard II (Shakespeare), 226
Richards, Mrs. Waldo, 240-241
Riddle Of The Universe, The (Haeckel), 255
Ridpath, John C., 245-247, 276
Rip Van Winkle (Irving), 203
Rittenhouse, Jessie B., 190
Rivals, The (Sheridan), 230
Road To Rome, The (Sherwood), 12
Robbers, The (Schiller), 231-232
Roberts, Kenneth, 221-222, 276
Robinson, Cyril E., 251
Robinson Crusoe (DeFoe), 199
Robison, John, 274
Rome, 12, 33, 39, 41, 62, 63, 78, 83, 84, 87, 100, 244, 245, 266
Romola (Eliot), 211
Roosevelt, Franklin D., 251, 278
Rosetta stone, 42
Rostand, Edmond, 52, 233-234
Rousseau, Jean Jacques, 98, 178, 200
Rubáiyát Of Omar Khayyám, The (Fitzgerald), 165, 186, 236
Russell, Bertrand, 164, 260, 275
Russia, 67-70, 98, 278

Sakkara, 75-76
Sandwich, Earl of, 35
Sarah Threeneedles (Bates), 176
Sargon, 79
Scarlet Letter, The (Hawthorne), 210

Schiller, Johann Christoph Friedrich von, 37, 231-232
School For Scandal, The (Sheridan), 230
School For Wives, The (Molière), 229
Scott, Sir Walter, 201, 238-239
Selected Plays (Sheridan), 230
Selected Plays (Wilde), 233
Self-Reliance (Emerson), 209
Seljuk Turks, 87-89, 91
Seneca, 224
Sennacherib, 78-79
Shakespeare, William, 11, 12, 13, 51, 52, 70, 101, 165, 224-226, 242
Shaw, George Bernard, 10, 11
Shelley, Percy Bysshe, 168, 173
Sheremetiev, Marshal, 68-70
Sheridan, Richard Brinsley, 50, 230
Sherwood, Robert, 12
She Stoops To Conquer (Goldsmith), 229-230
Short History Of The United States, A (Bassett), 251
Sidney, Sir Philip, 182
Sinshumlishir, 81
Skavronskaya, Marta, 67-69
Sketch Book, The (Irving), 203
Sketches By Boz (Dickens), 203
Smith, Adam, 17, 257
Snider, Luther C., 258
Sobieski, John, 8
Social Contract, The (Rousseau), 98, 200
Song Of The Chattahoochee, The (Lanier), 167, 174
Song Of The Shirt, The (Hood), 178

Song Of The Thrush, The (Daly), 241
Sophocles, 222-223
Southey, Robert, 168
Sparta, 98
Spencer, Herbert, 99, 254-255, 261
Spengler, Oswald, 99, 260-261
Spirit Of Laws, The (Montesquieu), 200
Stars In Their Courses, The (Jeans), 255
Stefansson, Vilhjalmur, 274-275
Stevenson, Burton Egbert, 194, 236-237, 240
Stevenson, Robert Louis, 211-212
Stong, Phil, 67
Story Of Civilization, The (Durant), 244-245, 273
Story Of Philosophy, The (Durant), 242-243, 260
Stowe, Harriet Beecher, 206-207
Strictly Business (O. Henry), 217-218
Sue, Eugène, 201
Sulla, 61
Sumerians, 105, 248, 259, 274
Swift, Jonathan, 199-200
Syracuse, 58-60
System Of Synthetic Philosophy (Spencer), 254

Tale Of Two Cities, A (Dickens), 100, 203
Tale Of A Tub, A (Swift), 200
Talleyrand-Périgord, Abbé, 30
Tamburlaine (Marlowe), 13, 225
Tartarin In The Alps (Daudet), 208

Tartarin Of Tarascon (Daudet), 208
Tennyson, Alfred, Lord, 161, 278
Terence (Terentius Publius Afer), 224
Thackeray, William Makepeace, 209-210
Thaïs (Levy), 241
Thales of Miletus, 58, 114
Theory Of The Leisure Class, The (Veblen), 257-258
Thompson, John R., 52
Three Musketeers, The (Dumas), 204
Through The Looking Glass (Carroll), 219
Tiglath-Pileser III, 79
Time Machine, The (Wells), 82
Titus, 83
To A Skylark (Shelley), 168
To Helen (Poe), 184
To Her – Unspoken (Burr), 192
To Lucy (Wordsworth), 173
Tom Sawyer (Twain), 216-217
To One In Paradise (Poe), 168, 183
Trajan, 83
Travel Bureau, The (Mitchell), 177
Travels (Marco Polo), 250
Treasure Island (Stevenson), 211, 216
Truman, Harry, 277
Twain, Mark (pseud. of Samuel Clemens), 216-217, 220
Twelfth Night (Shakespeare), 226
Twenty Thousand Leagues Under The Sea (Verne), 212-213

Index

Uncle Tom's Cabin (Stowe), 206-207
United Nations, 278
Universe Around Us, The (Jeans), 255-256
Urban II, 88-91
Ur Of The Chaldees (Woolley), 259
Utopia (More), 98

Valley Of Vain Verses, The (Van Dyke), 175
Van Dine, S.S. (pseud. of Willard Huntington Wright), 220
Van Dyke, Henry, 175
Vanity Fair (Thackeray), 209-210
Veblen, Thorstein, 257-258, 276
Venus And Adonis (Shakespeare), 226
Vergil, 24, 223-224
Verne, Jules, 212-213
Vespasian, 83
Vesuvius, Mt., 84-85
Voice Of The Turtle, The, 11
Voltaire, 30, 201

Walrus And The Carpenter, The (Carroll), 193
Wandering Jew, The (Sue), 201
Warm Babies (Preston), 237
Wars of the Roses, 12
Watt, James, 164
Wealth Of Nations, The (Smith), 257
Web And The Rock, The (Wolfe), 219
Weishaupt, Adam, 273
Wells, H.G., 82, 161, 245-246, 276
Wescott, Edward Noyes, 215
Wheeler, Professor, 22
Whitman, Walt, 236, 237
Whittier, John Greenleaf, 237
Widdemer, Margaret, 178
Wilberforce, Bishop, 254
Wilde, Oscar, 233
Willis, Nathaniel Parker, 16, 182
Willkie, Wendell, 277
Wolfe, Thomas, 219
Woman Of No Importance, A (Wilde), 233
Woolley, Sir Charles Leonard, 259
Wordsworth, William, 173, 179
Would-Be Gentleman, The (Molière), 229

Yarn Of The Nancy Bell, 236
Young, Francis Brett, 186
Zeid, 65
Zoser, King of Egypt, 75-76